# Drinking from the SOURCE

3rd Edition

Amantha Murphy

Drinking from the SOURCE, 3rd Edition

Copyright © 2017 by Amantha Murphy

All rights reserved. No part of this book may be reproduced or transmitted in any form or by any means without written permission of the author.

> Amantha Murphy asserts the moral right to be identified as the author of this work. All rights reserved. No part of this publication may be reproduced, stored in a retrieval system, or transmitted, in any form or by any means, electronic, mechanical, photocopying, recording or otherwise without the prior permission of the author.
>
> This book is sold subject to the condition that it shall not, by way of trade or otherwise, be lent, re-sold, hired out or otherwise circulated without the author's prior consent in any form of ebook, physical binding or cover other than that in which it is published and without a similar condition including this condition being imposed on the subsequent purchaser.

3rd edition paperback published by createspace, 2017

2nd edition paperback published by Lulu, 2011

1st edition published by Mark Youds, 2008

# Acknowledgments

First and foremost I must acknowledge with love and humility the presence of Spirit who have been constant in my life. So many times Spirit have carried me through the periods of drought and upheavals. I give thanks to Margaret, our guardian and powerhouse and for all her years of transcribing the tapes long-hand. I give thanks to Paulina for dedicating herself to typing up the transmissions and pressuring me to get them published. I give thanks to Mark for his care, patience and love in collating and formatting this book for us all.

I trust that these words from Spirit will carry you too through our times of transformation and rebirth.

With love and blessings, Amantha

*May you drink from the Chalice and be replenished.*

*May you find some tools for along the Way.*

# Foreword

I grew up talking to Spirit. Indeed for me, the Spirit world was the real world and this world was a reality at which I struggled to 'fit in'. I saw that people were asleep and disconnected and my earliest memory and fear was that I would have to become like this. I was blessed to be brought up in the early 50's in a rich Irish tapestry of family, who held me and yet never saw me.

My work with Spirit started consciously at 18 years of age and by the time I was 20, I was working as a clairvoyant. I started trance work by the age of 22. My life has been dedicated always, to Spirit and the Great Mother. This has been my food, the waters of my life – my very breath.

These channellings came through while I was living in a conscious community with eight others, the community extending to many others outside of the house we owned.

The teachings gave us a foundation upon which to live personally and individually as well as sharing life together as a community, for the times ahead. Spirit called it 'The Yoga of Truth' – Their meaning being "Truth, Love and Harmlessness". To live, act and speak from and within this.

This time was the most growth-filled time of my life.

# Table of Contents

PART ONE: ............................................................................................... 1

    Red Bear - Rainbow Warrior - 1 ............................................................ 2

    Red Bear - 2 ........................................................................................... 4

    Red Bear - 3 ........................................................................................... 6

    Red Bear - 4 ........................................................................................... 7

    Red Bear - 5 ........................................................................................... 9

    Red Cloud ............................................................................................. 11

    Poems ................................................................................................... 13

    The Law - 1 .......................................................................................... 14

    The Law - 2 .......................................................................................... 15

    The Law - 3 .......................................................................................... 19

    The Law - 4 .......................................................................................... 21

    The Law - 5 .......................................................................................... 23

    The Law - 6 .......................................................................................... 24

    Lucia - 1 - Power of the Sisterhood ..................................................... 25

    Lucia - 2 - Woman ............................................................................... 27

    Makara - Women from Atlantis ............................................................ 30

    Nieda .................................................................................................... 32

    Kima ..................................................................................................... 34

Tutulla - 1- Sirius: The Blue Crystal ............................................................ 36

Tutulla - 2 ........................................................................................................ 39

Tutulla - 3 - Light Centres - Part 1 ............................................................... 41

Tutulla - 4 - Earth's Magnetic Grid ............................................................... 44

Love ................................................................................................................. 46

Light ................................................................................................................ 47

Tutulla - 5 - Manifestation of the Plan ........................................................ 48

Tutulla - 6 - Planetary Needs ........................................................................ 50

Ireland ............................................................................................................. 52

Stone of Tor .................................................................................................... 55

## PART TWO: St. Germaine ............................................................................. 57

Talk About 'Man' ........................................................................................... 58

Endeavour is Absolute Responsibility ........................................................ 61

Order and Chaos ............................................................................................ 63

Seeding the Future ........................................................................................ 65

## PART THREE: The Lady .................................................................................. 67

The Wonders of Your Own Nature ............................................................. 70

Space and Relativity ...................................................................................... 72

Being the Divine Force ................................................................................. 74

Simple Truth .................................................................................................. 75

Love ................................................................................................................. 76

Meditation - 2 - Healing the Child ........................................................... 78

Vibrations of the Root Races ................................................................. 84

Walk the Path of Light ........................................................................... 86

# PART FOUR: The Living Word ........................................................ 91

The Living Word - 1 ............................................................................. 92

The Living Word - 2 ............................................................................. 94

The Living Word - 3 ............................................................................. 96

When the World Was Young - 1 ........................................................... 98

# PART FIVE: Te-Khan ......................................................................... 99

Te-Khan -The Metaphysical ................................................................. 100

Te-Khan - The Heart of the Divine ....................................................... 103

Te-Khan - Bring Forth the Vision ......................................................... 104

Te-Khan - Understanding of Deliverance ............................................. 106

Te-Khan - Creativity - Power ................................................................ 109

Te-Khan - The Emotional Body and Lower Egoic ................................ 111

Te-Khan - Integrity ................................................................................ 113

Te-Khan-Science & Technology of Today are the Craft of Tomorrow .. 115

Te-Khan - Evolution of the Species ...................................................... 117

Te-Khan - The Science of Clarity .......................................................... 119

Te-Khan - Motive of Action and Occurance ......................................... 122

Te-Khan - Concerning the Nature of Humanity .................................... 124

| | |
|---|---|
| Te-Khan - Modes of Transference | 126 |
| Te-Khan - Conceptional Thought | 129 |
| Te-Khan - The Expediency of Occurrence | 131 |
| Te-Khan - Service | 133 |
| Te-Khan - Education | 135 |
| Te-Khan - Vibrational Forces | 138 |
| Akara - Planetary Awakening | 140 |
| Te-Khan - Understanding | 142 |
| Te-Khan - Surrender | 144 |
| Te-Khan - The Spring of Life Eternal | 146 |
| Te-Khan - Life | 148 |
| Te-Khan - Manifest | 150 |
| Te-Khan - Service and Servitude | 151 |
| Te-Khan - Truth | 153 |
| Te-Khan - Convergence | 155 |
| Te-Khan - Creativity | 157 |
| Te-Khan - Sound | 160 |
| Te-Khan - Responsibility | 161 |
| **PART SIX: The Council of Beings** | **165** |
| Holding Yourselves Together | 166 |
| Vibrationary Rates - 1 | 171 |

Vibrationary Bodies ..... 174
Black Holes ..... 178
Dealing with Anger ..... 182
Subterranean Tunnels ..... 187
Electronic Impulses ..... 195
Endangerment of Humanity and the Planet ..... 205
Change and Structural Change ..... 210
The Principle Day ..... 217
Tuluk ..... 222
Communication ..... 228
Aspects of Spiritual Bodies ..... 234
Energy Levels ..... 241
Light Bodies ..... 248
Water ..... 258
Psych-kinetic Energy ..... 267
Proton Belt ..... 274
Dimensional Alignment ..... 284
The Future ..... 290
Variation of Vibrations ..... 298
Magnetic Impulses ..... 306
Planetary Crisis ..... 311

## PART SEVEN: ........................................................................... 317

### Hawk ................................................................................... 318

### The Lady of Shamballa - Shamballa ...................................... 320

### The Lady of Shamballa - Memory and Vision .......................... 321

### The Lady of Shamballa - Love ............................................... 322

### When the World Was Young - 2 ............................................ 323

# PART ONE:

Red Bear: 'Rainbow Warrior', 1, 2, 3, 4, 5
Red Cloud
Poems
The Law: 'Parts 1, 2, 3, 4, 5, and 6'
Lucia: 'The Power of the Sisterhood' and 'Woman'
Makara: 'The Women from Atlantis'
Nieda
Kima
Tutulla: 1-6
Ireland
Stone of Tor

# Red Bear - Rainbow Warrior - 1

(27th February 1986)
Greetings to you.     Greetings, children of the Rainbow.
When the man, the white man, walked across the plains, the red man knew that change had come. They knew a cycle had been completed and that which had been told, had come to pass. And many cried at the thoughts of what was to be. Much of the wisdom was lost, a little instilling itself in the hearts and minds of the elders, and passed from father to son and from mother to daughter. And always the whisper went on:– "we will return. We will come back again upon the force of the rainbow and we will be warriors of light and sound, and we will reclaim the Earth, we will remember our Mother and we will honour again our brothers and sisters."

And so it has come to pass that all of you come forward again, bathed in the cloak of the rainbow to help bring forth the understanding of the Mother. To help the blood to flow through her veins once more. To help your brothers and your sisters to grow in understanding and in light, that they may learn from each other, that they may learn from their brother rabbit and their sister deer, that they may learn in the seasons of their own lives, that they may watch the river flow as their life span flows too.

And so it is that the tribe of the Rainbow Warriors has returned and are spreading across your planet. United in the force of knowing of what is right, in the force of being what is right, and in the force of living only that which is right. The planet is indeed your Mother and you grow with Her blessing, upon her body. What greater givingness is there?   What greater love, of a Mother for her children?
She hears our call, and She hears the call of those who cry – no longer in vain, for the light is rising.

The true colours are beginning to show as brothers and sisters unite under the common flag of unity and growth – growth for the planet, and unity for each other.

The Earth is already beginning to vibrate with the sound and the Mother hears, and Her happiness is beginning to ripple within the planet Herself.

Yes, there will be a birth, a birth of gladness and joy for at last Her children have heard her call. At last they take heed of Her cries and Her pain and they are returning again to the Mother, uniting both Soul and Spirit.

Wear your rainbow cloaks as one family with love.
Know yourselves for who you are and carry that force with dignity.

# Red Bear - 2

(Circa 1986-87)

Bless you my brothers and sisters.   I am Red Bear.

When man was young and walked upon the land, he remembered with dignity and pride, his association and lineage with all that lived around him. When he coupled with woman, he knew the essence and the sacredness of such unity, and when woman worked and hunted and held her child to her breast she knew she carried and gave forth the seeds of remembrance and knowledge. She fed the children all that they needed to remember their connection to their brothers and sisters, and man and woman lived then in harmony with each other and within their own natures, honouring each for who they were and what they were, honouring wholly and giving fully. Caring for the children of the planet, recognising the Spirit within each and all.

And darkness came like clouds, bringing heaviness and fogging the mind, tearing from them their children, tearing from them their memories.   Those memories, the knowledge, are coming forth again. It is coming in ones and twos and tens and hundreds and we are returning through you, we are returning, to care again for our Mother and her children.

For the Earth has cried too long. The Earth was hurt too many times. Who hears Her pain, who cares for Her wounds?

Now you are coming again, the rainbow warriors are returning, with the sword and with the Sun. They are taking responsibility. They are taking on life and fulfilling it in glory.

The vision is no longer a vision; it is a reality in time.

Time itself is being used productively, in its way.

Remember; always care for the Earth your Mother. Recognise Her pain and sorrow.

Send honour to Her daily.

Acknowledge Her for all She gives you – the bountifulness, even in times of difficulties.

And now the time comes for the fullness of the Moon where we have the light reflection flooding our planet and yet in our tradition the Earth too was a Moon, and that too constantly reflected light and darkness, one half light, one half in darkness, changing, merging and moving, like Her Mother, the Moon, growing closer, drawing nearer, through the aeons of time.

It is a time of facing your reflection.

It is a time of walking backward into yourself. My greetings go with you.

# Red Bear - 3

(Circa 1986-87)

When the people heard the Earth sing, She reminded them to care for Her needs and nurture the living plants.
The animals sang with the birds and swam with the fish, and yet, as with all things, change came, and it darkened the minds, and it brought deadness to the hearts. Yet within that there was, and still is, a great learning. That learning is the learning of co-operation; it is the learning of memory, and the usage of your creative ability.

It is taking your role in responsibility and love, and it is a knowing with insight of what is to be for the good of the whole.

The working of the plan is whole and yet grows more fully, and it is impregnated within every cell of your Being.

It is a blueprint of the projected imagery of your tomorrow and the imagery is but scattered fragments of that holistic picture.

As you focus your attention and widen your horizon, your consciousness is able to observe, to open to more of that force and allow it to make itself present within you.

In knowing this you can help, not just each other, but others, to grasp the essential facts of Being and to live in the light of What is, not just in your actions and in your words, but in your thoughts and in your heart.

Change is constant. Bless you.

# Red Bear - 4

(17th June 1987)

Greetings my friends. I am Red Bear and I come to talk with you, to share with you the pain of our Mother.

When we walked upon this sacred planet we walked with honour and with pride. We walked with respect and awareness that we were living upon sacred ground, ground that fed us, ground that breathed, that lived, that grew and cared for us and we loved our Mother and we kissed the ground and blessed Her and we gave offerings, daily, to Her to honour that which She shared with us, just as we gave offerings to the Father Spirit, for sharing the light, the heat and the growth of the Universe with us.

And then came a time of darkness and despair for my people. A time, when through the fog, we could no longer see our way nor the truth of things. Strength was no longer held in the hand of Man nor in the word that came from them and so the Earth was forgotten and She trembled in pain and in sorrow. Her cries were not heard and now the time comes again when the fog is lifting and the rainbow warriors will again dance the dance to give honour to their Mother and you all are the seeds of Her love and desire to be one again with the planet.

You all carry the ability within you to awaken the rainbow serpent, to move again in harmony with the rhythm of Nature.
The time comes for you to open yourselves to the forces that are beginning to blossom, to open yourselves again to the awareness of your brothers and your sisters in the animal and plant kingdoms.

The time is coming when we can return again through you and with you, to bring into being the sense of harmony, not just to portions of the Earth but into the Divine centre and core of Her Being that it may spread forth again upon the Sacred Tree and give fruit in harmony and unity.

You have but to open your hearts, to open your minds, to be open and aware of the occurrences continuously moving around you and to recognize your part within that.
This sense of recognition, through you, will help to unify the Spirit, the Beingness of the planet, and harmony will begin to grow again.

The time is coming also for the Sacredness of Woman and her role to be balanced again into the workings of the World, to manifest in physical activity and in mental expectancy, and then too, there will be unity between the sexes, between the peoples.

Bless you.


**"The white Buffalo comes again across the planes and on each shoulder there is the Vulture and the Eagle."**

# Red Bear - 5

(2nd December 1987)

Greetings my friends, friends and beings of light.

Humanity has long thought of itself as children: children of God, children of this living Earth, and indeed there is here this conception with the idea and ideology behind this thought, for indeed you are all children of the Mother, that which feeds you, which houses and succours you, and yet within that, you are beings of Light, you are the essence of God within.

To think as children towards the planet and towards your responsibility to each other, is to misplace the potential growth of the individuality and the growth toward Godhood that you carry spontaneously within you all.

To love as children and yet to grow and to become the Beings that you are, is indeed to bring forward the essence of that light spark that is within.

It is for this purpose and it was with this message, that the Blessed essence was carried forth; first singularly and then in two, threes, tens, and then hundreds. This message of simplicity and truth was slowly lost within the ritualistic system of Man's own ego, as one fought with another, losing the essence of that heart centre.

It is from the heart that truth vibrates and it is the mind that celebrates the truth that you carry within you.

As offspring of this Mother Planet, you bear the seeds of tomorrow, to bring forth a better place for life, for growth, for your children and their children, and for all the children of the planet: the plants, the animals, for all vibrate within the living sound, and all grow in harmony together. You can work with this to bring about a spontaneous flow and cause of events that will flower into perfection.

This perfection is not new, is not untold or untasted.

It is there, ever-present, within you, all of you. It is love.

It is Divine. It is you.
Bless you my friends.

# Red Cloud

(13th February 1989)

Greetings my friends.

I am Red Cloud, and I come here to this gathering, to share with you, to impart knowledge and to call upon the wisdom that you carry within your own essential essence.

The growth of light has not gone undisturbed and the call now is coming forth from all areas of the planet.

I have come again to speak to you all, and I come at a time of need and in the area of service.

I come because the call is there, and it is answered.

Throughout the years past, there has been much growth and awareness in the consciousness of groups and individuals such as yourselves, and this consciousness has reached a stage where there is almost saturation, where peoples themselves are beginning to merge into the essence of extremity and there is no diversity, no brilliance, and no inter-connectiveness, through this.

So it is a time now for each of you to carry forth the Word of Light, Strength, Peace, Power – to carry it forth outwardly as Disciples of the Light, as warriors of love and the heart, allowing this to flow through the heart with all those you meet, all those you impart thoughts, words, actions.

Look upon yourselves as disciples.

Be aware of the vibrant force operating through the heart level. Let the heart now begin to connect you together.

Let its contact broaden and strengthen the arena and let the people again reawaken to their true cause, the oneness of all life.

There are many books on the subject, many words spoken. It is time now to act: act, act, act, and be done.

And in this there is a sharing, there is a deep inner connecting and there is love – forever flowing, like the eternal stream of life, carrying forth upon it, all that is necessary for the growth of Humanity and the planet; indeed for the growth of us all.

So go forth my children in peace.

Share the word, through the heart, and let the vibrations sound in their effect.

Bless you my friends.

Keep yourself open, keep yourself protected. Ground yourself through your feet, opening your arms to the fullness of the forces of Nature in operation. Knowledge, my friend, the knowledge that you carry the wisdom to use it, the understanding to see is your destiny.

Poems

(17th January 1988)

**"My friends.**

**The message is peace; the path is honesty, which is truth in love."**

~ ~ ~

**To Know a Being is to love that Being and through the Love you will find the Glory of the Divine.**

**Seek Divinity in all that you meet and you will find the Love and the Knowing.**

# The Law - 1

(Circa January, 1984)

Our bodies and their structures are changing, moving into fluidity, so that we can accept and merge with the flow of Light that is in operation, so that we can become conscious tools, co-operative creators for that which will be.

Our focus is the banner of Light, Love, Strength and Truth.

We are each a thread upon the fabric of that banner and as we move, merge and grow, so too the force and the tension that occurs comes forward to manifest Light, comes forward to manifest growth, comes forward to manifest seeds of creation, inspiration.

Let us open our hearts and our minds to that force.

Let the harmonizing Light of our focus flow through us, each one of us, like a colour on the spectrum.

And the Law calls out again. And we answer.
And the vibrations hum with activity. Let us all be united with each other.
Let the clouds that carry around you fall away in their illusionary states.

Let the realisation of the truth that you each carry within you, draw you as one cord in accord.

For the Law is being placed here amongst you to carry, to share.

# The Law - 2

'THE EYE'
(8th January 1984)

All energies congregate here to be cleared, cleansed and diffused through. We do not judge, but why do you violate the atmosphere with such pollution?

Why do you have such toxic waste, both collectively and individually?

Why do so much of the populace enjoy and take in to their lungs such smoke and smog that the Earth Herself violates against such destructive and thoughtlessness?

Man was once a friend, a brother, and a keeper of the forces. Now he turns, he averts his eyes to the reality of what he has done on this planet, and is hoping to multiply outwardly. We do not judge but we ask you to ask yourselves to look with honesty and directness. Accept the responsibility both of your past and of your present. Do not allow this destruction to continue.

Work from your own centre, first on yourselves and then on those around you. Stilling yourself in the company of those you disagree with is not necessarily a positive function.
Do not flight, do not fight, but be of yourselves. Allow your bodies and minds to be instruments of Light. Be examples for others.

You come back here as teachers – then teach. Use your lessons as your examples, those drawn to you as your pupils and your teachers, each situation as your gift from the Divine

Divinity is within the smallest atom.

All that you do and say, that you act, are heard and seen. Your inner conflicts are known. It is only through using the force within you, outwardly for those in need, will these inner conflicts still and purify the mind.

It is through holding on to this force that the conflicts themselves arise. Let flow that of your knowing, allow your thoughts to move into that of wisdom. It matters not who questions you or why.

What you carry in your heart, what you carry through your higher organs of activity, is the knowingness with the Divine.
Questions are there for the need of others to find this knowing within their own being, for you to see the validity of your own knowingness, for a planet fraught with difficulty is where the Spirit of Light and Love is needed most.

All through this planet there are Beings operating within the Word and Action of the Divine. You do not stand without force or a sense of brotherhood and sisterhood. You are joined throughout by those Beings working in the light of love and strength. Let not your steps falter when you know the pathway of the Spirit. Cling not, for only a drowning man clings, but let go of all that you consider most necessary and you will find the Spirit of Light walking through you and with you, as the great Love and Light force.

You are teachers and pupils to each other – demand no more than love and serve each other and Humanity.

The eye is the symbol of one's in-growing vision. Symbolic of the Universe you now live in. The circle, the spot, the centre within the galaxy. Behold the eye of God/Goddess.

Behold the necessary function of the vision. Within each is the ability to change and negate that which vision brings forth and implies to the individual, in terms of cross reference and that which has gone before, unconscious remembrance. All that one sees is turned within the brain. Symbolizing as above, so below. The highest and the lowest merging as one with the releasing of the tensions and muscles of the Third Eye, the Pineal gland, as it works through the individual. This structure, this mechanism, slowly adjusts and changes, bringing the consciousness of the individual level to a more Universal consciousness of understanding, of growth. No longer necessary to connect only with that of remembrance of former knowledge, but able to encapsulate ideas, visions the mind hath not yet been equipped with.

Much Planetary changes occur with the opening of the Pineal gland, with the creative birth of the second lower chakra, the energy and force of the new Jerusalem.

We notice changes happening, recurring upon the glaciers of the North Pole. Magnetic forces also wavering to mark of point 025 to point 086 degrees as these chakras begin to break through consciousness of the Planetary force. All that upon the Planet will thus be affected according to their growth, understanding, experience of the force within. Ripples, tides of emotion that is water, floods, overflowing, much barrenness, much negativity bringing forth a period of cleansing, clearing, enlightenment.

Thus the energy of force, the initiation of fire will come forth. Volcanic eruptions to cleanse and purify, to awaken the force within individuals, to bring forth this force to the sacred triangle of their head chakras for usage in their awareness and growth.

The choice, of course, is always Humanity's.

The World will be saved, there will not be annihilation nor complete destruction, there will be centres of activity both in what you would envisage as positive and negative poles of polarity. Much of the Earth's energy, that which lay hidden, encapsulated within the very womb of the Earth, hidden within the very pituitary gland of Woman, awakening, as the forces arise, arise to take the natural order, to unite and go forth, to bear fruit, to carry the light, to experience, to teach, thus we have the eye, the Eye, I will be done, the Eye Kingdom come.

Twelve stones for twelve gates herald the call for the new Jerusalem, the age of learning, of wisdom and understanding, of beauty, of truth, of humility, of one with the Whole.

And they came to the Lord and they sayeth unto Him, tell us Lord for we have searched, show us the Kingdom of Heaven, and the Lord turned unto them and spoke 'Look ye within, search thine own eye, look ye into thine own heart, walk the stairway of thy spine, for the Kingdom of Heaven is yours, and yours, and yours.

# The Law - 3

## 'THE MARK OF THE LAW'
(11th January 1984)

The mark of the Law is upon you all, the true love of all, wholly. You must give without expectation.

You must learn to allow that force within you to grow and flow through your very beings.

You are born from the Soul/womb of the Mother; you were conceived with the Spirit of the Father.

It is through you all that the Christ energy can emerge: you are the seeds.

You are the Christ-Force, indeed, you carry this within you.

You walk upon the sacred ground but you are aware not of the force both within the earth's structure and within your own beings. The earth is your Mother, yet you walk upon her body without thought of her pain and sorrow. You are programmed to accept limitations, both spiritually and structurally. Wipe away these programmes of limitation and you can achieve all. The time is coming now when the Laws of Manifestation, Vibration, Creation, Cause and Effect, are showing themselves upon the physical plane of consciousness and awareness.

Are you ready to accept these responsibilities and the growth that goes with them?

The force that is throughout the Universe and within your own beings can manifest you anywhere, with anything, in perfect health. Are you ready for this?
Can you prepare yourselves and humanity? Look within the very heart of your Being.

What is there that calls upon you to take this path? Is it the need to serve?
Is it the need to grow? Is it the need to share?
Or is it because, for you, there is no other pathway?

The future comes quick. You must complete the cycle for yourselves to be ready, prepared and open as complete conscious channels for these forces to manifest through you, for you to be able to be a part of, and to use them as tools for the evolutionary growth of the planet and of this Universe. It is for this reason the Christ force works through the mundane level, the heart chakra and on the esoteric level, the thymus and crown chakra.

Humanity is awakening throughout the world to their more divine natures. Thus the call has gone forth for teachers, for friends. Soon your work here will be at an end as the birth of the next phase opens up to you. Keep the awareness you carry now through day and night within your conscious thoughts and actions.
Be aware. Be ready. Every person you meet is your teacher, your guru. Every person you meet is God/Goddess.
Put your trust and love in the Divine and you will find all things fulfilled. It is through that Trust and Knowing that you can give fully.

Allow your thoughts to flow with love, that this pure vibration may gain momentum and energy. Indeed the flow of water moving across and through the Earth is the flow of blood from the Christ within the Mother.

When the birth is imminent, no-one can take that birth away, even the death of the mother does not take the life from the new-born babe; the child lives, indeed, it lives and grows and bears fruit among you all.

Blessings of the living law be with you.

# The Law - 4

## 'RAY OF CHRIST'

(13th August 1985)

May the rays of the solar force blow down upon you.

May the love of the Great Mother draw you to her and unite you as brothers and sisters.

The air is pungent with the smell of roses, the scent sweet and thick among us.

The flower which symbolises the force and form of the Christ-power upon the planet.

Time is coming upon the Earth when there is a quickening of energy, a time when man and woman become aware and are made aware of the focus of Light in operation around them, when they become and are made aware of these forces of light in ALL things. This is the time of the turning, the time when Humanity turns again to itself, the time when you see and speak again of life within you. The time when you share again that creative force you carry upon and within you.

I come from another plane of consciousness.

It is difficult for us to completely comprehend the happenings and the emotional traumas and upheavals occurring in your world today, but we feel most strongly the separation in the links between us all.
We feel most keenly the love and the lack of that love force from this mode of operation and level of consciousness.
To us, love is there within the word, within the thought, within the smile, the eye, the vision. To us all things move and have their being through love. To us love lightens our day.

It gives us our food; it strengthens our values and concepts.
Love also opens for us the awareness of the many levels of Divinity.
Love keeps us connected to the centre and to each other.
There is no greater power than the force of love, the strength of being love against the odds set about in this physical domain.
Allow that strength and will of purpose within you to be not just dominated by love but united, married together, as one.

There is no separation. Indeed, there is no separation.
We are all one; we are all part of the Divine, the ray of the Christ, the Form of the Mother, and the Will of the Father.

We sing to you of times gone by and times yet to be.
You hear only movements around you. We sing of love and of unity.
You hear only the sound of your own footsteps ringing in the distance.

Listen; listen to our songs of life.

Listen to us within the call of the bird. Listen to us upon the wind and in the rain. Listen to us within the stillness of your nature; for we are sisters, we are brothers and sisters. Let us be one now in love. Open your hearts now, open your minds.

Sit, open yourselves. Let that love force flow, let the power within us all unite and be a force of light for the growth of the planet.

Let the love whisper to you upon the wind. Let the rain tell you of its journey.
Let the sun speed you to your source. Blessings.
Agarta. Yes. Agarta.

# The Law - 5

(10th February 1986)

And the Law cried out for its people "My friends, my friends, my children, why has thou forsaken me?" and the people did not hear, for the space that the Law had given them they had filled, filled with old giving, filled with old thoughts and concepts.

And they had lost and forgotten the void of Space and Beingness and the Law cried out in vain and sent forth a seed of Light to awaken in the children, thoughts again of love and givingness, and the seed of Light took root in one and then another.

Slowly it grew.

It grew like a tree, first one way, and then the other.

And the roots of the tree went down into the Mother and the branches grew high into the Light of Spirit.

And people came to the tree for knowledge and understanding and went again carrying seeds and the Law watched and understood.

And the Law is coming again now, coming to call forth the children of the light that we may become of the Law and of the Space, that we may become the makers and the givers, that we may bring forth seeds of Life and Light.

And the Law looked and was satisfied.

# The Law - 6

(13th February 1989)

To you all it is said, the arrow that goes forth reaches its mark – whence forth it came, whither it returns.

Stand full now in your knowledge and understanding. Face now that which you are and have become.
See now your destiny and that placed before you. Choose now your path.
May the word of the law be with you.

# Lucia - 1 - Power of the Sisterhood

( 1986) Channeled with a Woman's Group.

I come forward here this evening upon the vibration of the name Lucia, and I come forward to share with you some understanding upon the Power of the Sisterhood, for it has been since the beginning that there has been a Sisterhood operating through the planet; women joined together in harmony, in love, and in understanding of the pure meaning of the essence of your Mother Earth and of the carrying of the Mother within themselves, of their position of being able to manifest through the essence of the Chalice. The Chalice being the transformation, the alchemical process of changing matter into sound, of being able to bring forth those from the dark into the light of understanding.

It has been through this also, much knowledge of the way of the plants, the herbs and growth of the planet, the working together with the elemental forces in operation, to bring forth the fertility both of the planet and of the peoples themselves. Much of this has been lost to the main grouping of people upon your planet and some has been held sacred in certain parts of your living planet – to go back, to go down, to go in, to certain areas of rediscovery of your natures so that you will draw yourself towards these sisterhoods for learning, for meditation and for union.

You will find too that these sisterhoods, although primarily concerned with the growth and education of women, also have within their group a certain force of those of men, those with masculine bodies yet feminine within their hearts, those who are able to work towards the unity of their masculine and feminine principles. And they too are taken into the hearts of the Sisterhood and they are offered of the Rainbow Warrior where brothers and sisters work in harmony for the

planet and for the growth of each other. And it is too with this gift we come forward to join with you and to share with you all.

You are all Rainbow Warriors.

You must carry this with dignity and pride. See the Sisters in all and every woman.
Empower them with your strength and your understanding, with your knowledge.

Spread the seeds of rediscovery and awaken again this ancient, ancient knowledge, that which will again bring you into harmony with this planet and the outer forces.

You will find as you work upon this, the forces of the Sisterhood of times gone past, coming forward again, the barriers of time slip by as you join in unity, for there is one force and that force operates through Time and Space.

# Lucia - 2 - Woman

(Circa 1986)

Greetings sisters and brothers of the Light. The ray upon which I come forward to you comes upon the sound Lucia.

It is a combination of the violet and the blue. The Age of the Woman is yet to come.
There has been at certain periods in Humanity's story, tribes of women who arise and bring forth certain aspects of the multi-dimensional and diverse force within the Being of What Is Whole.

We had what you called the race of Amazons living near Crete. We had also the period where we had the Priestesses of Hera and also back at the beginning of the Hellenic region. We had also the Syrian women and also at the time of Lemuria and the time of the Atlantis, tribes emerged to show the different facets and energy values of woman. Now, at this time in your story, woman is arising again to take her rightful place in the evolution and growth of Humanity, the Earth and the Universes, but yet women still have little understanding of that which they contain and carry within themselves. For woman is, indeed, the container, the chalice. Woman indeed is able to bring forth life and light through the darkness and decay.

It is by unifying women together that true woman can come forth in Nature, and as this occurs, so too the Birth of the I AM comes forth and the duality of form/matter and thought, joins through Space and Time.

You can open these Divine forces in operation, the presence of Light through the ethers into physical manifestation.

(Motions to those present): It will touch you, and you, and you, and you, and you will feel this touch upon your heart, and your hearts will be lifted with joy and understanding, and you will know the time has come for the emerging woman to come forth and stand beside her sisters and her brothers to make clear the Way, to bring Hope, Light, Truth upon the Planet.

It is through woman that Peace will come upon the planet, through the work and the words and the actions of women.

It is through the teaching of women and their teaching to their families that will bring about this occurrence.

It is through the conscious actions, thoughts and words of the Mother to the emerging birth, babe and child that will bring the foundation of truth and enlightenment to the children of the incoming Age.

You must speak of that Which Is.

You must take your place with understanding, with pride and with grace. One can step back to help those in need without losing the sense of Whom One Is.

Women, through their need to give and their concern over the need, have lost their sense of Who they are.

It is for woman to find that sense of Self again and to share this in the incoming Ages.

Meditate daily on the phases of your bleeding.

When this has passed meditate on the times of the full, ripe Moon. Be aware of these rhythms within your body.

Be aware and work in co-operation with these divine creative forces to bring about the emergence of the Light upon the Planet.

For you, man, be aware of these forces of rhythmic nature around you.

Join with them in your harmonic function so that you bring about the physical manifestation of creative unity through the givingness and the sharing of your nature.

You carry within, the seeds to bring this injection of Light to the World.

Understand your bodies, understand your symbols, understand your natures.

Have joy and honour in them and you will be able to bring unity and fruition to your life's work.

Blessings of the Sisterhood be with you.

## Makara - Women from Atlantis

(11th July 1985)

Greetings to you. I come to you across Space and Time to join with you, to share with you understanding of that which transpired and broke the harmony of the land known as Atlantis upon your Planet.

We had worked and developed upon that land much mental, physical and spiritual harmony and unity.

We had helped to rediscover again the origins of the forces within the Earth and the magnitude of Power within the realms. Also the rays of force coming upon the Earth plane and through the atmosphere from the outer planetary forces and from the friction which occurred through the presentation of these rays, upon the Earth's atmosphere and upon the merging of these two forces together.

This scientific inquiry will come about again as man and woman rediscovers yet again the forces within Nature, the tools at their disposal all around them and the presentation of these forces into physical and material realms, plus the friction which occurs as one brings these into the physical.

Now at that time there grew a sect of women, who, through their unity and harmonising as one force began to collect self knowledge.

This sect of women joined together and collectively brought forth the force of the creative aspect on the material, mental planes. They brought this into actual physical substance, and found too, their wholeness within this. This wholeness is capable of achievement in each and every one of you, but at this time as it happened, it drew them away from man, as man too searched for his wholeness in scientific inquiry.

So these realms began, rather than merging as one – to separate and, as each separated, became more fully united in their own force and ideology of "what is".

At this time now in the world's sphere, woman is again beginning to experience what is her true nature and essence, and the force of this essence within her nature, and her natural attunement with women. It is in the development of that sphere to bring forth that harmonising affect, consciously, co-operatively, with her brothers. It has always been that the wise of the tribe was with the woman, indeed, woman carries the Book of Wisdom within her breasts, the Space of the Universe within her womb.

Now it is time to share that and in sharing this will help man achieve too, his feminine aspects and to help him to experience also that sense of warmth and understanding within his own nature and Being.

It is time for women to stand forward as one force in the creative aspect of the light upon the Planet and it is also for her to stand side by side with man for as one woman stands she carries all.

Men can be such silly creatures, blind and thoughtless.

They are in some realms as children, and must be understood so; in others they are the warriors of the Sun, and they carry forth the banner of Light and Truth.

Their search continues always for the Grail, whereas woman, you are that chalice of awareness and truth.

You will meet many women upon the Pathway, and you will recognise all Sisters, for you will have the conscious affinity of being whole and within each other.
I bring you blessings. I bring you blessings. I bring you blessings.
(sings a mantra and calls out in another language) Let the Earth dance under your feet.

# Nieda

Greetings and Blessings, children of the Earth and the Universes. I wish to share with you this evening, words to bring seeds of activity and growth to your awareness and consciousness. I go by the name Nieda, and I wish to share with you concerning the consciousness of all living. Many upon your Planet walk in thoughtlessness and ignorance among the consciousness of the whole and the make-up of the Universe.

The living ants, the stones themselves have a consciousness, and within that consciousness they have life and are part of the Divinity. If you would open your more subtle senses, see and hear of the consciousness, you will find yourself becoming in-tune with this Divine life and growth. So often humanity looks but does not see. They listen but they do not hear.

One has to bring oneself to a space of stillness and peace within, where the mind becomes tranquil with the beauty of life. Then one's consciousness can become touched by the consciousness of that around it, be it the stone or the crystal, the tree or the bird. All carry the consciousness within them and they are aware of each other's consciousnesses.

It is humanity, due to much of their material existence, who have taken themselves away from the consciousness of the whole and sees themselves as a separate entity.

As they looks upon a scene that brings beauty and delight they see that outside of them – a separation already occurring.

To bring oneself to the point of Being with that beauty, that life growing around you, to hear of the joy and love, of the levels of growth, is to bring one, to unite one, with the Divine Force that flows through-out the Universes.

One's life becomes a pattern, a weave, a part of the growth of the whole. You must remember too, that much of this growth occurring constantly and consciously around you, also have spiritual counterparts and communication between you and, for example, the Devic Kingdom/Fairy Kingdom, also brings much growth and awareness to your Mother Planet.

For to work in harmony together brings and awakens the consciousness to the earth Herself. Through your stillness, through your communication with all around you, you will find your senses growing, sharpening, evolving and this will help you too, to open the doors to your spiritual nature, allowing it to take force and form through you.

It is to be remembered, that much that one experiences in one's life, is the force of the Soul, urging its breakthrough through your denser beings, breaking and cracking at the world you have built around yourselves to help you to see the truth of all things.

Stripping away these illusions, baring yourself to the forces of light and love, giving yourself to those forces. Giving yourself into the hands of the Divine brings one to the space of truth, light and activity.

Blessings be with you.

# Kima

(4th May 1988)

Greeting my friends.

With all the pain and sorrow upon your planet, there is a happening, an awakening coming, growing, giving birth. And that is one of joy, it is one of hope, it is one of vision, of strength, and of peace. This vision is growing across your planet, and it is carried within the hearts of individuals, it is carried within the hearts and minds of groups and it is now beginning to be carried both in the political arena and the economic fields of endeavour, and this is a new pulse in different rhythm that is striking its way across your planet.

It is one that is calling forth for rediscovery, and it is remembering again the joy that there is in living, the happiness there is in giving, and the taste again of true love.

Knowledge when it comes is a great gift, but coupled with that gift there is also the memory, the responsibility of its use as a tool to bring again fortitude, hope, re-discovery to the planet.

Wisdom, which calls forth in its wake, brings you the cup of endeavour, endurance and discernment, and to crown this through understanding, brings you the knowledge, the wisdom and the activity of motion.

There is then no resentment, no reaction; there is only the given moment, the chance for spontaneous and courageous creativity, and that moment lasts through lifetimes within the point of now.

I am Kima and I come forth here from the interplanetary levels to join with you in this joy, that you may be reminded of this honour and dignity, that you as a people carry the ability to find joy, the ability to give birth, the ability to know death.

Within that lies the hope of those memories. Bless you.

Each year the flower gives forth of its fruit and with each growing year the fruit swells and sweetens until the time comes for the fruits themselves to give forth and to carry the seeds on, and if this is not the way, then the fruit turns bitter, sour to your taste, for this is the Way, this is the Way.

# Tutulla - 1 - Sirius: The Blue Crystal

(4th July 1985)

I am Tutulla.

My time is short.

I come forth here to speak with you, to share with you the heart of my people.

We come from the planet Sirius, the smaller planet with erratic orbit around the larger from whom we gain much energy force and the force to travel at Light speed.

Much information concerning this will be brought to you. There are others working too upon this in your World.
We, whose seeds were carried from Sirius, are your brothers and sisters of times long gone.

This planet was chosen to be a planet of learning, a school for us to experience again that which we had drawn away from.

We had lost humility.

We had lost the ability to feel and understand lessons.

You must become aware of the power of the usage of the crystals within your work.

Become united with them and you will find much achievement.

It is through the usage of certain crystals that we can cause vibrations to occur to keep our bodies at a certain degree of life for many hundreds of years of your span.

Q: Shall we put some gold in your hand to give you some energy at this time?

A: It would be for me of more force to hold upon the crystal of the ray of Sirius – the blue crystal. (Celestine)

Much of the work we did in the past when I lived upon the physical of your planet was done also with the power of crystals.

We are going back in your planet time 4,256 years in the space of Upper Egypt.

At that time we worked primarily with crystals and we had also certain instruments made from crystals and from semiprecious gems which could cause, not just healing to occur, but matter to vibrate at a certain frequency where it could become invisible to the naked eye and could be moved as far as 200 feet in any direction.

This was without the use of man's inner abilities, so coupling these together we were able to achieve much movement and a degree of accomplishment in that which we had come forth to work upon. Which was not just the growth and evolution of Humanity, and to help our brothers and sisters upon the Sister planet, but to bring forth, also, specific points across your globe where we inserted deep into the bowels of your Earth, certain crystals which would resonate and in this way we could help to bring a balance throughout the Universe. For it was through man's dullness that this planet indeed was veered off its course and it was through another planet, where one level of mankind evolved from, which already had spun off its course and evaporated into a different atmosphere.

It was, is, that force which comes again through the large winds you experience upon this planet within the last seven solar years, and which brings much dispirit and disharmony into a person's body, nature and their mind.

Therefore, at this time, it is important to realise these crystals of force within your planet that we and our brethren are working to bring forth and unite in harmony; to help to bring forth again the positive action within the deeds and movement of the planet and its occupants.

You will find that when you become attuned to these crystals of force within the Earth, you will find them often in places of great growth and fertility. There is some also laying within the Earth of the desert regions – the reasons for you yet to be known.

These twelve crystals, or gates as you may see them, will open in force and sound and will resonate in harmony to the awakening of the mass consciousness within the peoples of your Planet.

May the blessings of the Beloved Ones forever dwell within you.

# Tutulla - 2

(11th June 1985)

I am he known as Tutulla. I come to greet you and to share with you. Much of my work is now done. There is little left to do.

You will find there are ten such coffins around the world in which others, once alive and vibrant, are now working upon the level of the Ka, where we can help humankind on their road to rediscovery.

We once had instruments, machines similar to that which humans are now working towards, but ours were more subtle, more organic. We created each machine as an organism working in itself and its components were held together within that organism.

This is yet to be explored or used as such by the peoples of today. Therefore, when such of these machines are found they will be of no use to one, for the consciousness will not be able to devise in what way it was used and how it was held together. Believe me, my friends; the inward journey of self-discovery will bring forth again the understanding and usage of such tools for the growth of the planet at large. It has been stated before and I must stress again, of your constant need to be aware of the force of creativity that you carry within you and to give this forth to the planet and those upon it at large.

To spend time dilly-dallying, dreaming upon things of no consequence, is to waste precious energy that can be used for the forces of Light. Therefore, be aware with each step that you take, be aware of each that you pass as you walk upon The Way.

Be aware of the sky, the stars, Nature and the Earth. Purely through your conscious action of awareness, you give this life. By giving it life you give it strength and growth and the opportunity for evolution.

There is much to be done. There are many coming forward to work within the forces of Light.

Let not your minds dwell on your own self-interests but open them instead to the needs of Humanity - to the call of your Soul.

If you see a need, fulfill it. This is itself the Pathway of the Initiate.

Many aeons ago, when I walked upon the Earth, we had schools for such learning and the local populace expected those who left it to come forth as teachers to Humanity, to speak words, to show them their pathways. They never understood the true work of the initiate.

They never noticed the man who toiled the fields, who helped the child, who gave blessings daily for the beauty of the Mother-planet.

It is in the karma of some to stand out from the mass and proclaim the Light. It is for the growth of Humanity that each follows their pathway, their goal.

The pyramids still hold many secrets. You will find embedded in the structure of the Great Pyramid, many minerals, especially three, one of which, the quartz, which helped the transmission of energy and harnessed much power.

This was used too, in later times, to control the weather conditions but this went against the Natural Law, so the waters rose, the level heightened, washing away symbolically and within, the physical realms, all knowledge of this existence and it became a desert in its knowledge and its land. The water of growth, of beauty, will return again to the desert, and you will find hidden deep beneath the sea much lost knowledge, and the sacred hidden Temple of Isis.

It is the sound vibration which carried the water levels. Watch as the energy of blood flows there.
Blessings to you.

# Tutulla - 3 - Light Centres - Part 1

(9th February 1986)

We come forward here to speak with you, to share with you news of the growth and activity of the Light upon your Earth, for now is the time when that which is upon the ethereal levels will begin to manifest within the earthly reality of your civilisation.

Light centres, beacons, will force their way through the denseness and will show themselves in Hungary, in Japan, in Brazil, and in the Netherlands, in Canada, in Australia, in London, in America - New York.

The western coast of America will change its identity and shape and this will bring forth from the coastline a variance of vibration which will cause the molecular structure of the country itself to occur.

The growth of what once was will come upon the land and the Light that was hidden will shine again.

And there, in this land, this island that carries fruit, fruit that blossoms and over-ripened fruit that has gone back down into the Earth, will rise again as a Temple of Light for your planet, and that Temple will grow through the sacred spots, through the circles of energy.

We come forth now to share with you so that you may add your awareness to that which occurs upon your planet, that this growth of Light that may be united and centered.

You go upon a pilgrimage. Remember each step upon the Way to open to the Light Forces, to plant the seeds of recognition and strength, to become vortexes of energy breaking the seals, unlocking the Forces, to arise again in celebration of the Light, that the growth of the planet may occur, may occur and will occur for the time is now and you are here.

Now is the space of entry into tomorrow.

You arise like diamonds of Light.
You arise to join us as we draw close, as our consciousnesses merge and become One, so you awaken to your inner recognition.
You awaken to the point of knowledge, of remembrance, so that in merging, you in your true identity can begin the work.

Let the flowers of civilisation throw forth their seeds. Let all occurrences be known and shared.
Let that which was hidden come forth to the Light so that we may know one another.
The veils become thin between the worlds as we draw closer to unity. So too the veils misting upon your own understanding, slowly evaporate, through your knowledge, your strength of the Light.

Let yourselves hold your Force, your Power, and your Love. Be ready.
Work.
Give.

Be in harmony with the vibrations, the interplay of vibrations upon and across the planetary body of which you are a part.

Cease your inner fight.
Cease your inner convictions.
Cease your inner will and want and stand instead united in heart, mind and Spirit.

Let your eyes see further than the Path before you. Let your consciousnesses open to the full potential.
You are one world in a Universe of worlds and consciousness.

Take your place among the spiral.
Let your awareness grow within the Space of all that is.

You are a part, you have a role.
Take it, be it, for the time is now, and you must unify your natures. Let the World become One.

Opening your consciousnesses gives us permission and allows us to integrate and to flow more freely with you, allowing the natural stream of information and ideas to flow from one to another.

Close not your mind to the workings of above. Keep it open and aware.

See yourselves as pyramids of Light, forces of energy, catalysts to bring through information.

Be aware of the planets, their influence upon you.
Be aware of the feeding of information daily, hourly, for the planets now are coming into an alignment, when a magnificent force of Light beam will flow down upon your planet, bringing with it vibrations of energy of such occurrence that there will be a sign within the hearts and mind of Humanity.
The planet Herself will change.

The sky will be bright both night and day and you will know the time to step forward, when you too will burn bright both within and without.

It is at this time you will arise, throwing off your cloaks, shackles, holding you to your receptive illusions and you will stand naked to a person, and you will stand within your glory and you will join and join and join again, and the Earth will become aglow, Light reflecting Light, and the Universe will dance, refractions of Light – the Earth will be made new.
Blessings to you and greetings from your brothers and sisters. Go forth in awareness.
Work diligently with humility and understanding, bringing seeds, bringing water, purification.

Each place you go, drop a seed.
Each seed given in consciousness will grow.

## Tutulla - 4 - Earth's Magnetic Grid

(25th June 1986)

Greetings.

I am Tutulla.

I come to speak with you concerning the energy forces within the planet and their polarities within the universe and the universal source.

The magnetic force of your planet, its primary function, is to draw to it all that which is necessary for growth and productivity.

The magnetic flow which runs upon a grid system can be, and is being, amplified at this time, not just by those of the Light and consciousness, but by also those in power and authority, to draw upon the electrical currents of the Earth Herself, and of the ethereal field, the magnetic property, within the ethers to be used as weaponry.

It is for this purpose that we tell you that you may bring forth those aspects of Light and thought, that you may bring intellect into play in the understanding of what is occurring within the planet Herself, thereby bringing the equal and opposite effect, allowing the forces of Light to penetrate, bringing balance.

This grid across your planet has within it the ability to create millions of megawatts of energy which can be used to transmit across the Universes.

It can be used also to amplify the pulsation within Humanity, within the individual.

By its speed and variance it can both shorten and lengthen the cellular structure.

It can both shorten and lengthen the span of Time.

All that I speak with you are but keys impregnated within your consciousness to open your awareness once again to the knowledge that you carry within you.

Look to the North, look to the East.

There is no holding back the growth of Light.

# Love

(A new energy is channeled)

**Love is a term often used, yet little understood.**
**It is a force labeled and put within the concepts of consciousness;**
**and yet Love is Universal.**
**Love is a part of the void.**

**One cannot take nor give of love; for Love is. Where there is life,**
**Love dwells within.**
**That spark of divinity, that force that unites you all, is carried**
**within the realms of Love.**

**Love and care -**
**words become meaningless against the power of Love. "Love each**
**other as I love thee"**
**these words spoken say it all.**

Light

(Another energy is channeled)

**A light shining in the darkness, as I move towards it, it recedes.
I quicken my pace. I run.
The Light flickers and leaves me. Slowly I stop, I look, I listen.
Darkness descends upon me.
Despair fills my Being and lo, I see the Light again. It is there –
there within, within me.**

# Tutulla - 5 - Manifestation of the Plan

(2nd July 1986)

I come forward to share with you in gratitude and love for the forces that are constantly in operation for the manifestation of the Plan, uniting matter and Spirit, the divine inspiration with the physical manifestation.

The work which we have undertaken is in operation upon many subtle levels of awareness and growth and all lead to the Supreme. The essence of the Light force in operation throughout, throughout the levels of awareness, throughout the planets and the Universe, bringing the mass unconscious into alignment with the evolutionary growth of the planet, and yes, we rejoice as one, as this manifestation, the work you have undertaken, is coming to its time of fruition when the gestation period has been completed, when the flower shows forth of its colour and essence, and this flower is a flower to seed the flowers to bring Light and understanding to the planet. Through the Light force, through the force of your work, come the seeds of understanding, the essence of Love that each may know and understand the other and the Divine consciousness within.

It is through the essence of understanding that the Light grows forth. It is through the essence of understanding within one's heart and Being that awakens the vibrations that are within us all. This Units us in service and in harmony that we may be of one pulsating heart, that we may be one in service to Humanity and the planet and so we rejoice with you. We rejoice at the banner of Light you carry within your hearts. We have understanding of your words, your thoughts and actions, that you may create the blossoming of those flowers for the enlightenment of Humanity.

It is through the work of those such as yourselves, each working on the multi-dimensional aspects of the Plan, each carrying forth the seeds, that brings the Light - the consciousness - upon the planet.

You are not alone in your work. You are part of the whole.
The work you have chosen to do, the energy forces that magnetically draw you and other light groups, will bring forth those diverse aspects in operation upon the planet, that you may learn and share, that you may connect and interconnect with each other, that you may learn and grow through each other, for all is One.

You are reflections of each other. Your essence is shared within.
See yourselves.

Understand, and you understand the whole.

# Tutulla - 6 - Planetary Needs

(18th January 1989)

Greetings my friends. I am Tutulla and we speak here concerning the planetary needs and the needs of the communities.

There is a great deal of need here in South Africa, and this will build up to a time in your '90s to a climax where there will be extreme difficulty and war conditions, and it is necessary for you all to send forth the vibrations of peace and co-operation here.

Also Libya is going through a cultural change and difficulty that is bringing restriction and resentment through the peoples, and again here is a great need for the attention drawn to this vibrationary root energy of the planet to bring peace and love.

As the planet draws forth Her breath, so too the upheavals occur as the vibrations themselves collect and send forth magnetic charges through the atmosphere and the universe, and as this atmosphere and pollution is clouding the more vibrationary rates, so too this has an effect within and upon the planet, bringing forth ill-health and ill conditions.

There is a screening here coming forth from the routes of the outer crust, that on the basin, especially along the western coast of the Americas, near the Equator and merging here to that of the Antarctic. It is imperative in these times, to bring forth an awareness of the condition of the sea and all that live within it, and the need here for oxygenation and also for the natural bacterial fungi to continue to give forth its food-value into its own.

As to your curiosity, I still linger a while, and am based mainly now within this stellar system working through the grouping of stars of the Pleiades, connected with those other light Beings of my ilk, that we may continue to work with the progress and light of the planet that is dear to our essence and is a part of your molecular structure and system.

The usage is yet to be fully unraveled of the work of the crystals and it is important for you all, if you can, to wear or carry one such about your person, and consciously harmonise yourself with its vibration so that it might help to bring forth the alter effects and decrease the harmfulness of the radiation in your atmosphere that is growing daily and affecting the organs of the body.

May the love, care, and blessings of the Light Beings stay with you all.

# Ireland

Channeled beside the Black Lake, Co. Kerry, Ireland
(21st August 1991)

There really are Little People. Their dimension is the dimension between us and the Earth, so they are actually much closer to the Earth than we are; they are in the dimension between. Spiral, movement, what they are wearing, is in the shape of spirals and their bodies are like that; and then, as they begin to penetrate/permeate into the Earth itself, it takes on a line. It goes from being circular into a line and the energy as it goes into the line begins to jut out, it rises along, like a key would in places, like the sound of a tone, and as it does that, the Earth laughs. It tickles the Earth – like somebody would tickle you up and down, and as the Earth laughs life there, it sprouts out energy, life force vibration, and the whole thing is a sort of ticklish situation.

Now above and beyond, in their own dimension, we have the vibration of the Gods and Goddesses, and they are in the dimension that is beyond and again between us, and they touch with the Earth in an impenetrable way that cannot be understood by Humankind because of our physical dimensions, and until we learn to go beyond our physical dimensions completely, releasing it without causing it death, only then can we be on par with these vibrations called Gods and Goddesses and communicate on similar wave tones.
The tones are of different variance, the perfection of their tone is dominant in the sky area held by the magnetic tones or forces of the Earth in relationship to the outer – planetary regions.

The magnetic force to Pluto, the magnetic force to Mars, the magnetic force to Mercury, the magnetic force to Venus to a lesser, much lesser degree, the magnetic force to Sirius in a strengthened degree, the magnetic force to the central Sun of the Pleiades. To a harmonic of that to the seventh degree, this is all variances on the harmonics and in learning of the harmonics, we will understand the keys.

The structure less tones or the structureless-ness of the Gods and Goddesses are dependable only upon the magnetic quality of their outer-reaches and necessities.

The sense is that they were prominent when we were still dust, forming into life and they were larger than life and fought each other and through that, they – not so much fell to Earth, although that is the

way you could see it – suddenly were drawn, like suction, into places on the planet, and as the planet received their influx of power and vibration, She began life.

As the Earth was hit almost with these vibrations to begin life – and these vibrations were just coming at here, (makes movements) like this, hitting Her – it drew the forces of life around it, into it, to use it, you understand, and they were drawn in, and if they hadn't been larger than life in themselves, and their actions, then it wouldn't necessarily have occurred. So, you'll find these energy forces in places like here, and it can be male or female in its design; but in its outer-ness it is neither, but in the Earth's colouring it is. The Earth shades herself.

Now they're awakening, slowly and people's consciousness are causing them to awaken, the higher vibration in people's consciousness is becoming on par to what they - the Gods and Goddesses had and its awakening them and it's now that we can use that to help these vibrations to attune themselves in their tones on the planet and for the planet.

Okay, questions.

A question about symbols:
A: The symbols are all the spirals, especially triple ones, the most symbolic is the one with two lots like this with another above it, all interlinked within each other so that would be five. That is very powerful too. The three is very powerful. The one is also the spiral, the connectedness with the continuation of alive-ness. In the DNA matter the spirals bounce off each other, causing sound vibration, which, in itself is the mirror image of the spiral and this carries essential infor-

mation not just genetically but also through love, deep love, through deep fear and pain and this vibrationary sound goes out to others. It is therefore important to have a cleansing experience, when possible, through movement. It can be done with movement in the morning where you shake about for ten to twenty minutes. A good shake, all over, for the body, is very good, enhancing for the energies and cleansing for the chakras. The colour vibration on this is magenta moving into a deep purple.

# Stone of Tor

(BETWEEN SNEEM AND KILLARNEY COUNTY KERRY)

(August 1991)

Male on one side. Female the other. Moves fiery energy like 9 waves of fire but we cannot feel it as it is on another vibration. Horses – spirit forces – fiery steeds, this is why horses have such symbolic meaning to humans. Created from the source. Each held by these forces, that which we would call Gods and Goddesses and comes forth through the dimensions. One of these forces was harnessed into this mountain.

Awakening again, pure power, to remind us of our reality. Against our truth we are the size and intelligence of mice. TRUTH is the key for what is to be.
I am seeing at this point, misty, musty clouds – fog – moving, seeing the centre but not getting any closer, there's something there in the centre but can't say what it is – a light or crystal. It receives Universal energy which is Universal information (always). Emerald Keys. We too, can receive this. The spirals and old Celtic patterns are keys to awaken this information within us and opening up our awareness to Truth.

Corn circles are the same.

Wearing these designs will also open us up to this information. Another world forming on ours as the forces awakens. We need to be ready to understand, not intellectually, but from the Heart. There is another force in the DNA, a part of and yet separate from the one design and this carries all the hidden information.

# PART TWO: St. Germaine

'Talk About 'Man'
'Endeavour Is Absolute Responsibility'
'Order And Chaos'
'Seeding The Future'

# Talk About 'Man'

(20th November 1988)

When one speaks the Living Word one is bringing forth form into matter. Your thoughts can lighten the heart and bring joy to the Soul. They can also bring forth constrictions and restrictions to the temple of your Being. Consider then the form of each thought as it passes through you.

Look forth to its source; see whether the light itself shines forth or is dull and decaying. Notice, with harmlessness, the extent of the force of these thoughts upon your heart - do they open the heart with gladness and joy, or do they tighten it and bind to the denseness of the lower nature.

It is through your thoughts that the world is made manifest and it is through the instruction that these thoughts can flow forward, flooding with every in-dwelling essence of light force, bringing it into matter in productiveness, in harmony, in beauty and in unity. Your thoughts gather themselves – yes, in the mind, and this is not localised within the brain or the lobal instruction but throughout the body area and affects regions of the body not yet recognised by your consciousness. Therefore, watch, listen and add joy to your thoughts as they pass through you.

Instruct and direct them into creative channels of light and let yourselves become conscious continually of the divine eternal that lies within you all.

Earth is a place of reception of the Divine to manifest through matter. Thus, this place of welcome, conceived by the Creator/Creatrex is perfect and in perfect harmony with its function; which is receiving like a mother, the Divine grain that will one day bloom in the shape of the perfect, conscious, Soul-integrated human Being. This human

Being of infinite love and freedom, being infinite love and freedom, has of course sown this grain in resemblance with self. That is, with total freedom. Freedom to discover one day what they are or to lose the sense of who they are.

This freedom makes it possible for human Beings to become a true reflection of the Divine.

Human Beings discover alone, as time goes by, whom they are as they walk on deeper and deeper within themselves, towards the seat of the Source within. Now this liberty, this free choice and expression of the infinite love of the Source has often lead one on to the awakened self. And this is particularly clear today in the relationship that many peoples have with the Earth. The Earth is a place of welcome, open like loving arms but the many people have not yet been conscious of the perfection of the Creation, not yet having reached the point of perfection within themselves and so, are not capable of this love and harmony around them in the very place that receives them. They have not understood the very close relationship that exists between themselves and the Earth; the relationship between Mother and child. Being still blind to the perfection of Creation, and thus not seeing it on the Earth, people did not understand that all they needed was there for them, to live in peace and harmony and abundance. They had just to rejoice and lay down upon the grass, to pluck the fruit, to enjoy the beauty of the setting and rising sun, to stretch out their hand to the replenishing watering rain.

Some believed that the Earth was imperfect, that it was necessary to act upon the Earth and they started to plunder their own place of reception. They did not see that the Earth, naturally, could bring them all that they needed like a loving Mother.

And now this Earth is a tired Mother, exhausted by her terrible children who have returned violence for the care She gives.
Today, it becomes urgent for people to go back inside themselves. They must go to the yet undiscovered path which will lead them to their Divine Grace - to their consciousness of their perfection.

Then, at last, their eyes will be open and they will see the reality of Creation; only then will they be able to start healing the wounds of their Mother Earth. The awakening to the real vision enables them to see and understand exactly where the pain and harm is and what they can do about it.

They will understand the role their Mother Earth is playing.

The important thing to do today is to take away the bandage from the eyes in order to see the Divine reality of Mother Earth.

A lot of people today see the Divine reality of Earth.

A lot of people today see the earth lowered and suffering, but if they don't start walking upon the path towards their inner centre, they will never really know what to do and how to do. Their acts would be exterior, outside from the perfection as they have always been and the earth will not be healed in this way.

Human beings must now reach this sacred point at the centre of their Being; this point that will unite them with the centre of Creation.

And from that moment, all the necessary information will come and they will be able to recreate Divine Harmony on Earth.

# Endeavour is Absolute Responsibility

(Circa 4th January 1989)

God grant you space my dear friends and blessings upon you. This year has been one of terrific transformations.

It has been a time in the atmosphere and atmospheric essence and in the variance of vibration upon Humanity of change and occurrence. Occurrence itself through the happening of change, showing in various levels according to the consciousness and understanding of those working within and around these vibrations.

It is therefore important to recognize that materialization can come about through the conscious awareness of individuals and groups. It is to be understood that this field of endeavour is one of absolute responsibility; this field of dedication is a dedication that must come from the Soul. It must vibrate through your Being. Mood-swings occur at irregular intervals through the blood and this too is bringing forth change, for it is releasing the toxins within you physically and emotionally, held deep within the bowels of your Being from various happenings of lives and occurrences. As such, it is a time of release, a time when pressure is the pressure of the building up of these various vibrations and their undertones and in so doing, releasing and sweeping. Sweeping through yourselves, through your psyche, as one Being in accordance with the flow of the plan and through that of the atmosphere, of the planet, bringing forth a cleansing, an awakening, an awareness, a birth.

That birth comes through your conscious understanding. It comes through your knowledge and awareness.
It comes through your complete co-operation, through your love and respect, and through your honour and care.

Your acts of service must be whole. They must come from the place of 'Being', the light force that operates within.

This now is the vibration that is the occurrence of the planets.

It is this that is your birth right and the birth right of all to unfold before you. Conscious co-operation is the key.

Law and order are not the vibrations that hold this in place, but need and service.

Need and service bring forth its own fulfillment.

By being 'at one', by recognising the needs and giving space for those needs to magnetically bring forth all the tools at your disposal, you can then see how these needs can be met: simply, wholly.

Let yourselves be the creators not the destroyers.

Let yourselves be the transmitters and not just be the receivers.

Let yourselves work in conscious co-operation with each other and all others whose specific purpose is to serve, to heal, to love, and to be at one again.

I grant you my blessing, the vial, the chalice.

# Order and Chaos

(4th January 1989)

Greetings my friends. I wish to share with you thoughts to bring together a greater sense of harmony and understanding to your Soul and conscious awareness, and I wish here to share with you upon the vibration of order and chaos.

The natural essence that brings forth growth and change throughout the Universe is the vibration of chaos.

Within that comes forth creativity, comes forth life-force and form, manifesting as such within all that, whose concept is able to contain such growth and realisation.

Each particle in space as it comes forth and unites, contains the essence of this chaos within its prime factor and as this flows into the realms of Humanity, we have natural chaos, bringing itself through order. In this realm of consciousness and particular growth, all those who work and venture forth into the light realms of existence, bring this chaotic force through form and order in their life's delivery.

Those who fear to venture forth into the unknown, those who turn themselves from and beyond the realm of light; to those the essence itself bring chaos to the mind, and disorder to the body and bodily functions, and this in itself is part of the law of growth and understanding, this in itself is part of what brings forth light and awareness.

As you are able to evaluate and consciously understand that which is containing itself within you and bringing forth its natural functions, so too this value of creative growth brings forth a natural order and harmony. The centredness becomes One and in that essence there is knowledge and wisdom; the understanding of which brings light, growth and wholeness.

Chaos, order, are the balancing scales that hold forth life within this time and space and to hold this within your natures, to work and to bring this into fertile awareness, is to bring too, the harmonising of the Soul to the mass unconscious and the planetary field of endeavour.

Let yourselves recognise this force as it works within you, and let yourselves honour and harmonise the Soul in its growth through life.

Bless you my friends.

# Seeding the Future

(22nd February 1989)

Greetings my friends. I come here to talk with you upon the Germaine vibrations, and I wish to speak with you about the seeding of the future and the atomic vibrations that these create, both within and around your own auric fields.

The seeds you give forth must be the seeds of truth, seeds of love and care and the seeds of service; each action, every thought, each word spoken, must come from this emphasis of motion within your own essence. That vibrationary note magnifies in sound and is carried forth through the ethers, changing the magnetic quality of the content of your Being and that which you give forth, thereby allowing a change of consciousness, an awareness, a growth that occurs both instantaneously and slowly in its content of magnification. Through this, the aura itself eclipses within its own space value and that, in its magnetic form, releases slowly through the atmospheric vibrations so that space need no longer hold you.

You are here then, not by the will of effort, but by the thrust of life, light and love - God/Goddess.

Once you have mastered this, in understanding, once you live with this through your mind's eye, in your heart and activity of motion, then you too, can become masters, you can help to lead the way in light, in truth, and you can indeed become the servers of the people.

For this prime function is the manifestation of the Supreme Source within us all and the denial of this is the denial of our own immortality.

The spark of light that has been worshipped since the beginning of Humanity is the divinity of the Supreme Source, the source of all that can move and has it's Being within us.

Let the worship become service and the service become worship. Let the service feed and bring succour where needed, where drawn to, where called forth upon.

Look within to the heart value of individuals and groups and be drawn by that and by the tone of your own essential knowing.

This then is the message that we carry to you, as servers of the race of Humanity.

May the law of knowledge, the chalice of wisdom and the spear of understanding, dwell among you all.

# PART THREE: The Lady

Meditation - '1'
'The Wonders Of Your Own Nature'
'Space And Relativity'
'Being The Divine Force'
'Simple Truth'
'Love'
'Healing The Child' – A Meditation ('2')
'Vibration Of Root Races'
'Walk The Path Of Light'

# Meditation - 1

(Lying upon the grass) (3rd June 1985)
My greeting is as the sunlight, as the freshness of the wind, as the jubilation of nature in which you are communing with now – what more can I say to you after all you have heard and after so many lessons you have received – let us keep it simple.

It is only love that can bring harmony within yourselves and around you, harmony with nature, animals, plants and the whole solar system.

What you experience now in this union, which envelops you with the energy of love, is the picture for the future on which you are now working. The difficulties with yourself through others, the problems you encounter daily and which you see reflected in the world events, indicates that the movements of your whole solar-system is inciting for change and consciousness. Feel deep in yourself the love that is around here as pure nectar for collaboration in the near future.

Allow love to flow and all the negativity will dissolve, as dewdrops in the sun – don't put energy in to that which comes up so often as negativity, put your energy into the love that is within you. The negativity is only necessary to make you realise the opposite. The whole of nature sings in harmony with the seasons, the birds sing aloud the joy of the new time – let people follow their example and surrender, care-free to the Life Force of the Universe. These contacts are important to maintain – and if you become still, you will feel where you are meant to be. Support each other in trust and love will strengthen the bond so others too will soon follow.

We only ask for you to give unto trust, surrender and discernment (insight).

Many Blessings upon you.

# The Wonders of Your Own Nature

(Sitting in Nature) (3rd June 1985)

Greetings my friends.

It is with pleasure and blessings I join with you this evening.

We wish to speak to you this evening concerning the wonders of your very own natures – for you sit here upon the Mother Herself, you have beneath your feet the very earth of growth and fertility – you have around you all living.

You too, are centred upon that sacred ground – you too, live and grow from the Earth-Mother up towards the Light Forces – you too, can sing with the birds in joy and happiness.

Being at one with the whole - for it is not enough to look upon a tree, to look upon a blade of grass and to see it as a tree or a grass separate from you – beautiful but separate – you must learn to open yourselves to becoming that tree, to being that blade of grass, to experience the life of nature and through that, experience becoming conscious of that same life-force that operates throughout the universe.

In recognising this force both around and within you, you will be able then to recognize this force upon all you come in contact with – you will have no fear – you will have no envies – you will have no insecurity - as you realise that you and they are one in spirit.

All of man and womankind must come to their own growth within their own stages of consciousness – you too must be aware of giving each person the space for them to develop in the way they choose, whether it is within your understanding or not.

By giving them space and love you are allowing the Divine to operate and you are breaking free from your projective value and concepts.

When you listen to the birds harmonising, be aware of the harmonising force within your own hearts.

You spoke earlier of the difficulty of uniting the emotion with the intellect – it is through the ever-flowering, ever flowing, heart of light and strength that these two forces become united and in that unification the flower of the Light-force opens out and floods the universe with your power and strength of love and givingness – for it is truly in giving that you do receive – it is truly in opening yourself to the acceptance of your multi-dimensional levels that you give light to the force of your own Being and you allow the Spirit to function, you allow the Soul to manifest.

May the blessings of the light be with you always upon your road.

# Space and Relativity

(1st August 1985)

I wish to speak with you this evening, concerning your spheres of Space and Relativity, for it is within your spheres of Space that your understanding grows, and through this growth, streams forth the ideas and thoughts for Creation upon your material, physical realms and the activity upon the mental levels.

Now the spheres of Space work both from One's known consciousness and from the consciousness of the Universes. This Universe has within its own force, a consciousness and understanding which shows itself to you as the planets and as part of the galaxy, and, as you work within that sphere of consciousness, comes forth your foundation of reality. With the inter-relationships of these spheres of Space within that reality known to Humanity, you begin to harmonize with the Cosmic vibrations and harmonics.

Now, to simplify matters: let us take a child in its first full year of growth.

Its reality is purely spaced around it with the nuclear family, or source, upon which it lives and has understanding of.

To bring in to that child's understanding of reality, something outside its scope, its space, of conscious knowing, infringes upon that child mental disturbances not yet attained within the growth and spheres of his/her mental and emotional levels.

Now, let us take the adult.

Humanity has grown to the point where they are starting to connect with the force and form of the energy or essence of the Universe, and you have been able now to start to experience the reality of the planets and the human family from the space of the stars above and the planet below.

As humanity opens to their more spiritual nature, which is taking a 45 degree course from here (motions hand from West to North) to here, they are able to break through the spheres of space and relativity, to be able to look not just from within their own personal space but from without, and to see the living Universe as an aspect of the whole and their part within that whole.

Therefore keep yourselves open to these thoughts and vibrations outside your own spheres of experience and of reasoning,. Allow the space for the occurrence of your spiritual body to bring forth knowledge and understanding outside the scope of your yet known experience upon the conscious plane.

In this way you open yourselves not just to the conscious and super-conscious activities, which is had been held enclosed, but outwardly to the spheres not yet touched by the consciousness of Humanity.

Much of this information is what brought about the speedy growth and recovery of life upon Sirius, and its interconnection with the Pleiades cultures.

We wish for you have understanding of this and to therefore be open to these new forces and ideas ready to flow through your channels and help you to bring light upon your planet and indeed your universe.

We give you our blessings, and our thoughts go with you.

# Being the Divine Force

(21st August 1985)

Gather the forces and power within you and around you. Call upon them and awaken them from their sleep.

Unite them into a rod of force.

Greetings and blessings my friends and children of the Universe.
It is not enough to wish nor even to will a thing done, completed, brought forward, manifested upon the physical realms of activity and dense growth. You must be aware of opening yourselves to that Divine force which operates through you.

You must unite with that force; you must give power to that force. You must accept the responsibility of being that force.
The vibration of Creative Thought and Physical Manifestation has been given to you already and it would be right for you to read this and glean from it once again the activities of the inner nature, the nature of Becoming, of Being.

The largest part of this is the acceptance of that Being within your own selves, the acceptance that you can and are.

Put yourselves in the body of Light Being, your fifth dimensional body Open yourselves to the force and joy of activity and growth.

Let the Earth vibrate once again with the vibratory sound of Creation, Birth, Growth.

Blessings of the Light Ones be with you.

# Simple Truth

(27th January 1988)
The message is Peace; the path is Honesty, which is Truth in Love.
Follow this and the way will always become clear for you.
Much of your time is taken up in intellectual thought and organisation, indeed, the ray you draw upon you at this time is that of organisation and ritual, and yet within that, one can still find that space of quietness within one's nature.
The place of truth and light where words, gestures, are unneeded, as one opens oneself to the essence of one's Being.

Simple truth.

Throughout your working hours, take time, create a little space, to always recognise, acknowledge and honour, that living, growing space within you.

Allow it to continuously flow through your living work as it grows forth outwardly, interconnecting through others, to your living planet.
Forget not that from the seed you have come forth and to the seed you will return.

Knowledge is like a seed, given light and warmth, nurtured and cared for, it can grow into the tree of wisdom and understanding.
It can also be manipulated, abused, cloned in its Beingness and these seeds are strewn across your planet to cast shadows of doubt and decay within the thoughts of many and yet the way of the light is clear and simple in its tone and it is growing on.

Go always for that clear sound and know it in its essence.
Never allow yourselves to become cloaked in your own structures but know yourselves to be the living growth, the organism of life and light as it flows forth.

Blessings of the light be with you all.

# Love

(12th October 1988)

Greetings brothers and sisters of the light. It is with love that we are bound together and it is with love that we come here to serve each living Being and the planet.

And it is through love that you reach an understanding and enlightenment that you may be free of the earthly shackles and the fallacies that come through the unconscious psyche. Often as one works and progresses upon the path, one loses track of the essential essence; love.

One becomes caught in the illusionary world and the projections and images it gives forth and yet the supreme force itself that fosters all life, is love and it is through this that your work will indeed come forth into physical manifestation.

It through the love of service, through the love of brotherhood and sisterhood, it is through the need to give forth that love that it will manifest in your actions, in your thoughts, and in your words.

All that you carry in your heart is open for each other.

All good that you carry plus all doubt and fear sends forth its vibration and the response is immediate for the group Soul.

So think and live in true love.

Let it be the heartbeat of your eternity.

Let yourselves vibrate with one accord, that love may penetrate through every cellular atom and that you may as one, work and bring forth this love force in its essence.

There are no complications.

It is a very simple essence: to love, to give; this is divine and it keeps you in touch with the forces of light working to penetrate and open your human Beingness.

Let doubt be vanquished from your minds. Let fear absorb its own vibration.
Live and be the loving source and all will come within its space.

The work, the words, must come through love.
Intelligence itself is born out of love and in this the response will be immediate and embracing.

Forget not your roles as creators.

Forget not the responsibilities you take upon yourselves and know the time has come to stand again in place, side by side, and bear custodianship of this sacred planet.

Let yourselves live in humble service and hear what is truth within and around you.

Walk in peace and know each other.

# Meditation - 2 - Healing the Child

Leading into a channeling.
(23rd September 1991)

With A Woman's Group

Let us relax and know that together we are one, a sisterhood of truth and light, our intentions pure.

Become aware of relaxing your body through the breath. Use the deep, even breathing, to relax your body.
Still your mind, let yourselves feel calm and peace rising within you.

Become aware of the essence of peace growing from the centre of your Being, connected through the spiritual cord to the focus of the womb.

As you become aware of this peace, it grows more strongly, like the lapping waves.

You feel it reaching you, flowing throughout the body, bringing warmth, bringing healing.

Your mind begins to flow with the rhythm of its movement and you, the self, become part of this movement.

This movement is harmonic to the movement of light upon the planet as it flows in and draws out.

Feel ready to move with that rhythm – the inner and the outer, reflected upon us as breath.

We can use that movement, that motion, to release old thought patterns, fears and concerns and help us to stand in the essence of our true self.

Our feet are embedded within the planet and our eyes look out into the stars.

We are one with both.

The Universe is a part of our domain and we carry that within us, symbolised by the Moon.

Let ourselves feel the strength of this force as we allow it to rest within the essence of our peace.

Coupled with that peace, connecting around you through the levels and layers of the vibrational energy, there are pockets of emotion, pockets of pain, pockets of fear. The expression of your love can release these, and open them through the eye of consciousness, to be expressed and blown away as light, into the weave of existence to become another star in your universe.

Let yourselves look first at you, the baby, held in your mother's arms, projecting your needs of security and love with all the hope, vision and clarity held within you, as star born. And see how becoming a toddler and moving on, how much of that became hidden, pushed to one side of your psyche, held back through fear of reprisal, through the difficulty you have in learning of others' needs, fears and misrepresentations of truth.

The world you know is not seen by their living eyes, the truth you were born with.

There is no separation.

Let us speak now of the pain we feel as children and let us share together that which hurts, releasing the pain and hurt, allowing ourselves to grow and integrate in our release.

(Allowing space here for word or phrase to be spoken out by those in the group)

Let us become aware of bringing into this space, this life space, the quality, the animal quality that you carry, that which lives and breathes and has it's Being within you.

Become aware of your animal essence, become aware of this nature, being connected to, but apart from, the nature of reality that you live within this time and space.

If you can envisage yourselves again living next to and within nature, following the seasons as the cycles of your life, becoming interdependent upon the animal world, the mineral world, the plant world around you.

Your home being the natural environment of the planet, then you will come to understand the importance of these totem vibrations, you will be able to see the importance that they play in YOUR life, and the necessity of recognising this force of activity that operates through you, constantly but not necessarily consciously.

It affects your way of thinking and reality. It plays a dominant part in the magnetic quality you exhibit and also inhabit. The usages of these animal qualities within you are for you to begin the process of self-examination in respect of truth and determining that truth within your own nature.

Recognising the qualities projected towards you, upon you and accepted by you through life, and the role-plays that are constantly in motion, allow yourself to integrate your animal nature within your essence of your Being, thereby again beginning to vibrate from the sense of that which you call the Whole nature/ Soul nature.

This in its respect, is tied and yet loosely so, to that which has been termed, tribal identity, for the animals themselves fall into their own term of enquiry and this stems from certain vibrations and needs of activity of achievement throughout the lifetimes.

One continues within the essence of that nature through lives and is coloured by the respective families, partners and essence of interplay which falls around one. Within this time capsule, where space itself is invaded with Humanity's thoughts and fears, there is also beyond that, the psyche of Humanity and Humanity's totem, which is the Spider.

Now, if you can understand how en-captured through one's own unconscious one can become, within the psyche through that totem, you can begin to recognise the need and usage of the elements, especially that born of fire, to cleanse oneself from the mass unconscious, that sweeps across the planet, and allow the essence of self – truth to emerge.

In opening oneself to this level of endeavour, one is opening oneself to the initiation of fire, one is calling upon all that within one's life, within one's space realm to be taken, so that the light that burns through, leaves one naked, and in that nakedness, in truth to one's divinity.

The divinity of self is the adjustment of nature in its natural process. It allows you, within this time space to adjust your consciousness not just to that termed as the greater good, but to that inner-realm of oneself that is constantly seeking enlightenment and growth. It allows one the emergence of the interplay of one's own body.

Take thought as form and recognise the limitations you set yourself. This simple process itself will show you how much you need to cleanse and how far you wish to travel.

Questions:

Q: Could you speak about the Celts from the religious, cultural, vantage point, and on their symbology, as there is little written about it.

A: The Celtic peoples came through Europe, gathering momentum. At first there was a strongly Egyptian/Asian leaning and also very much coloured by the very early prehistoric bear clans, of what is now known as Russia, the northern parts.

As they moved through Europe they also became much more adjusted to the climates and in doing so, brought about change in consciousness and a need to often dominate.

We are talking here mainly of the earlier tribe of peoples.

The essence of this earlier tribe was at-one-meant with nature, the belief that their souls inhabited bodies for a short period and then went back into the Great Mother, which was the planet and thus brought fertility.

So, during a chapter of the Celtic people there was fertility rites that were of blood – bloody, but that was of a short period, an abuse-full period. The earlier fertility rites themselves came through the maidens and their bleeding time.

This was used by the Celts themselves in their own groups or villages taking the first blood as the honour of the Mother and using this rite to copulate with the planet for the growth of the plants and harvest.

There were also fertility rites where one was chosen among the men to be the pronounced "king" for a year and he would be the lover of the priestess, the land and not necessarily just in the physical sense but very much so also in the conscious.

They were a people that were very much connected with Earth energies and powers and used them so and also worked with the spirits of those past, their ancestors.

The memories were carried through with stories, song and chant and the genetic impulse of this vibration occurring, awakened the memories within the children before they even had to be taught.
They were therefore very capable of taking care of themselves.

They became known in later times as a race of warriors, women as well as men. There was equality in the tribes. The tribes liked to better themselves against each other in games.

Unfortunately, when the land that they held sacred was abused, they stood and fought and during this time, which was a great period of the latter half of their history, their direction became focused very much in what is known now as war.

Talking of symbology, of course early and Celtic symbols were always to do with the Soul's progress, coming from the womb of the Mother and returning, the spiral motion, recognising that all things grow in this force, and therefore returns.

Jewelry was used and not necessarily just for those in power although they had a head person of each tribe or faction, this could be a man or a woman or partners and were placed there by the will of the people and could be removed so. Children were held to be children of the tribe and not necessarily belonging to one or another person but they were given through birth, and through the blessings of the priestess, to one or two in the tribe who would be their guardian and teacher in their growth.

The children, for the first formative years would live with the parents but could then move on, and this was very relaxed.

There were more women who were of the essence of the priestess, rather than men, and this was not thought to be a separation, but a fact. They knew the life force within the rocks, the mountains, the trees, the rivers and the streams.

They recognised and honoured them and in so doing, their life was bountiful and returned to them.

# Vibrations of the Root Races

Greetings my friends. Bless you.
We wish to talk this evening concerning the vibrations of the root races, the genetic impulse that comes through the memory banks of Humanity, the essence of your beginning on this planet. In your story of creation the world began and was formed in seven days.
This myth was taken from the essence of the growth of a civilisation through the expansion and awareness of the Universe as a whole.

Due to the cosmic occurrence of activity from the sun, the emergence of life and life force upon this planet, the planet Herself was watched over by those in the outer planetary realms, most especially those of the Andromeda and you will find that they have in fact brought forward colonies throughout the outer expanses of the Universes.

As this planet formed and life gave birth to life, following along with this in conjunction was the impulse of consciousness, creativity that came through the outer activities of those of Andromeda. This force allowed the growth and the general rather than specific, direction of that growth, as it occurred through the mineral, animal planes of consciousness.

As this awareness came to human form, so too these forms held in awe the essence of those who in truth wished to serve them but became instead the masters. They were looked upon as Gods. The myth you have of the Garden of Eden was in fact, the peoples turning away from the essence of the conscious activity that was being fed to them, and the need for the people to go forth and find that conscious awareness within themselves.

My friends, the path has been long in your terms and in ours and during that process we have gained and learned much. We have recognised the strength and the inner capabilities that you possess and we have also noted the emergence of the light activity within the present time and space.

There is an alternative reality that is in conjunct with yours – a different form of reality or dimension and through that, people very occasionally, objects more occasionally, can move through time and space; the molecules themselves breaking down, discorporating and rearranging in another place and by compulsion. We mean the complete, whole, direction of thought, mind, and matter.

If you can, visualise a rocket, whose base is here and which moves up to the point here, the compulsion is all the levels of our Being, within this, directed through.

Questions: - Not caught on tape recorder.
(On technology)

A: This will come forward more as the actual experimental work of laser coupled within a confined space, using crystallised force, which will create and dissipate.

This can also, using a frequency, awaken dead cells; this can be used in both plant and human life. It can activate the life again. Taking it in a shape - (here Amantha is indicating a narrow cylindrical shape e.g. a fluorescent tube). Like a pipe, see-through, but the ends protected and within machinery with the crystals and the input of the laser.

Q: On temperature and sound.

A: Temperature causes the breaking of the frequencies into sound, so the temperature reaction in the water, and especially if used with algae, which is in itself whole, will break the sound open into the algae. The temperature ratio in the water will also produce the sound, and this can be noted scientifically. It is important when cleansing water to always use natural rock where possible and the moss itself that grows from the dampness; moisture is also in itself a producer of natural fertilisation for crops and cultivates the ions in the water.

We will go now. Bless you.

# Walk the Path of Light

We come with blessings of light and love, for we all stem from the one Source, and it is to that Source that we will all return. As we return in our space frame, we release first our physical, we release then our thoughts, we release then our memories, and we have with us the essence of love. This pulsates us back to the centre of Source that we may go forth again and walk the Path of Light. For you, the journey is different and takes longer, but only because you have forgotten the way.

It would be helpful for you all to practice this simply, occasionally, so when your time comes again to return, you will be prepared. It also helps you to adjust to the levels of consciousness that are erupting within peoples across your planet, bringing much good and some disturbance and you will find yourself seeing with a clearer eye and a more understanding mind.
Bless you.

Questions:

Q: Could you give us some more specific or personal advice about redirecting our emotional bodies - using energy?

A: Yes. Now, it is important first to recognise, realise, that your emotional body is like an antenna, an antenna that lets you know when something is wrong, be that something that is occurring on a psychological level within you, subconscious level within you, physical or mental level within you. Its prime function is to emanate the vibrationary rate around you and to transmit this to you in code through the lower activities of the Chakras, that you may understand the nature of those around you, the nature of that which you are working within, the call of those around you and most importantly, the empathic vibrationary note of pain, longing, hurt, fear, that you can recognise and respond – not react – respond to.

This is the prime function of the emotional body. It is not there to be killed.
It is not there to be boxed into a form of words.
It is there as part of your essence, to work in co-operation.

The emotional is part of the Trinity of bodies, which when working in co-operation with each other, allows you to manifest in harmony with your Soul's longing. When in balance, it takes away hierarchy, it takes away the welding of power over another, it puts back into woman and man's hands, the power of the freedom of their own lives – so this has to be understood.

Q: Crop circles, what are they?

A: These crop circles, their designs are frequencies, frequencies to open the entire continent of the psyche of Humanity to register in consciousness the information that is being infiltrated through to you.

Q: And what is the connection between the rock/crystals and the psyche of Humanity.

We have spoken before of the information, these pulses, within the rocks, stones, crystals, that pass through their own process in plants, animals and to humans. This has been broken, through the chemical input on agriculture and through the chemical input and mass production of the animals and the pain and fear in the animals through that death. So these pulses, these inputs of vibrationary force that are emanating into and through the planet daily, and are also registering from the planet, must again begin to implant itself within the hearts and consciousness of Humanity. Thus these vibrationary qualities emanate this force so that again this will break through the boundaries you have been fed with.

Commitment is growing from those upon your planet, to bring the planet Herself back into the essence of alignment of Her true nature – and of course, this means, of the peoples. This is coming in your time, 2012 is the time when the movement into what was known as the Aquarian Age heralds its force and the decant moves into the essence.

Where Mercury becomes not just the mental, but the messenger, for the messages will be that of supreme co-operation for the creative –

creating your own environment, learning to use thought – form, learning to redirect the emotional body, learning to bring about an altered state of being through your recognition of the capability through the essence of light, power and activity.

Q: The corn circles have recently been brought into disrepute.

A: Yes, and this is something that has been done knowingly. It has been done with the knowing consent of certain groups, organisations, who wish not the awareness and consciousness of the mass to reach its peak, for doing so, it is the expansion of space, held in check by consciousness.

Energy clothed, becomes physical reality, becomes your material world, your peoples, your animals, and your plant life.

So taking a frame from it, is holding it at this specific space-time, from the fourth-dimensional sphere and in doing so, understanding – not just understanding – experiencing. This is what the fourth-dimension is about – the fourth dimensions is the supreme experience of Being, so you are not separate from each other but one in the experience and it is from this now, that there will be a more rapid growth in the evolution of the peoples and the planet, of the countries and the governments, and the central government or the central force, will come, where there will be one group, working together for the betterment of the planet, similar to your Parliament - but made up of countries and it will be through the development from the United Nations that it will come forth and there will be more communication with those from the outer levels of your galaxy.

These are carried to the vibrationary rate through the function of the Pleiades, in the Eye of enlightenment and it is through the transformation as the moon in Taurus passes in its scope of the sun in its Scorpio placement that these truths can be realised, recognised, through one's own self-transformation and be lived accordingly. This causes an acceleration of the growth of the Soul, and is experienced in the body as such.

Q: Full Moons.

A: Well you know my friend that each full Moon carries its own rate of vibration and growth, coupled nowadays very much with the archetypal forces of the solar calendar that is now the Zodiac. This moon coming on the 1st decant of Scorpio, being the 12th house vibrationary rate from the 9th natural gestation period, being in itself the act of transformation, is very much a part of the motion of this time-space for you all. The older zodiac held 13 moons.

It is a time of recognising truth. Truth is simple; To live in Light and Act in Love.

There is Law. Law is the natural rhythm of light force as it presents itself through the harmonic rays of the different vibrationary levels, the physical level being one. And there is Sex, which is not just the copulation of a couple, but the unification of two with the light functions of your bodies that you may become truly masters/mistresses of the self within this lifetime. To achieve this, it is important, especially in the morning/beginning of the day to sit quietly for a moment before you arise from bed.

As you lie, breathe for a moment and feel inside ….. send down a thought and feel.

Do you feel calm, a little tense, tired, a little irritable?

Be aware. Sit up. Feel again. See the difference. Lying down is what you have within you from your sleep state. It shows how you slept and whether your dreams were congenial or disturbing. When you sit up you are facing the world, you are opening yourself to the new dawn.

If you feel differently at that point on any of these levels, this is something you need to examine further, to look into. This process can take but moments, and then when you arise, after you meet the first person, feel again for a moment. What are you picking up? If you have to travel, cloak yourself, protect yourself. Choose the time and space within each day to open and be aware to what you are picking up and to what you are feeling. Allow this to grow until you feel present within every moment of your life/breath.

# PART FOUR: The Living Word

'The Living Word' – 1, 2, & 3

'When the World Was Young' - 1

# The Living Word - 1

(4th May 1985)

Greetings my friends. May the Power of the Living Word operate through you. I come here upon that vibration for it is within you, both collectively and individually, the growth and the understanding of your abilities now as Creators and to be able to create, through that which you say, that which you think, for in your conscious thought you still consider lateral thinking - thinking upon words, therefore, it is the power of the Living Word.

You will find it more helpful, more constructive and creative to think also in pictures, symbols. You will find this more fulfilling to the force and thought of that which you need to communicate and create.

This time is the time which the Native American call 'the Moon Bleeds'. This is considered very infrequent as the Moon is old, the woman who is coming to the time in her life when she finishes her monthly cycles, is gaining the wisdom and the understanding of the older, more knowing person but still has these infrequent bleeding sessions from the womb. It is at this time of that which they call 'The Bleeding Moon' when that which flows – the rays, the forces of the light of the Moon upon all, upon the planet, especially of course, the women, for they flow also with this rhythm. Now coming to the conscious realisation in men also of the feminine aspects and also those who live with women, they too can unite in this creative force and be an active participant in the creative fertility rituals that go forth in the mass unconscious of women even today.

For it is now at this time that the eggs are seeded both symbolically and universally.

It is at this time when the force of the Creative vibrations, come to a climax and overspill and flow forth into the hearts and minds of all.

It is a time for most women when they are able to draw close to that creative aspect within their own nature, to utilise and direct also spiritually into the forces of light, as that grows also upon the planet and plants, for plants and planet are of the one.

We are all growing from the Mother outwards towards the spiritual force of which we are one.

We are indeed, the tree of knowledge and wisdom.

The very oneness in our nature brings us in harmony with the forces around us.

Have joy in your womanhood.

Have joy in your feminine – the joy of sharing such understanding and uniting both collectively and individually is part of the understanding of the forces of creativity of which you play a part, a role, in the bringing of the light.

It is a time when all is made anew and we rise again. Blessed Be. Blessed Be.

# The Living Word - 2

Greetings and blessings to you my friends.

I come to you upon the vibration of the Living Word.

There are many thoughts we wish to share with you all but first your paths must be clear, the ground cleansed and fertile.

It is for you to strip away before you, and within, all those habits and thoughts of limitations and constrictions.

For every concrete idea you cling to is another thought-form between you and your spiritual nature.

It is for you to cleanse this pathway to truth by opening yourself to the vibrations and realities both within and around your nature.

First for you, each of you, to look upon yourself with love and discernment, to see the aspects contained within your own Being and in seeing truly, to give understanding and love upon yourself.

In this way the barriers within slowly disintegrate, allowing the force of light within you to flow in harmonic rhythmic motion and this in turn, allows both the etheric and astral bodies to come into harmony, within your physical, mental and emotional vibrations.

So, give space and love for yourselves.

Open your pathways with light and understanding. Look out at all around you with the eyes of a child. See each thing anew, not as a thought-form within you. Be able to understand and find joy with all of nature.

Sense that light - love force within all living.

Become united with this truth that is all around you. See with the inner eye the beauty of the Divine.
In this way you bring yourself open to the aspects of your spiritual nature.

You allow the beauty and life-force to flow through you.

Concept-less, you realise the full potential of all things and living matter and you will be open to the truth of the worlds.

Each man and woman walks upon the pathway to enlightenment, each within their own sphere.

That search must be both inward and without. The truth of light is carried like a seed within you. May it grow and bear fruit.
May you be the servers of Humanity.

May the blessings of the light be ever with you.

# The Living Word - 3

That the living words be carried always within your hearts – forget not that all you think and say is carried forth upon the harmonic vibration of creativity and find a home within your own nature and the World you project around your own Beingness.

Therefore remember always the light that shines within you and the force of love you carry forth to share with humankind and the whole. See each as your brother, your sister, reach to the presence within each – help others to bring forth the Christ essence within their own Beingness and you are helping also to bring forth the emergence of the plan upon the planet. For the plan is here now within the atmosphere – waves of energy and force, creating friction and scope within all – it is therefore of vital importance to keep focused on the light force and love-energy within your Beings. This keeps you centred on that electrical-magnetic grid and to allows the harmonic vibration to bring to you all those of similar force and focus.

You have chosen and will choose again to become servers to carry the light – forget not your work – lose yourself not in the world of illusions and materialism – strip away all that is false both within your nature and around you.

Search not for truth for it eludes one – but strip the falsehood from your life-thoughts and you will be left with truth and love.

The work of the Soul is to carry forth the emergence of the Plan. This is for the spiritual starvation as well as the physical tug upon your planet – this sacred planet.

Remember the will and look within your own selves at whose will is coming forth to determine the progress.

When the light comes forth upon you, you cannot take just that which you wish but must work in the full consciousness of your Being – this is humanity's lesson – no easy task.

We stand with you as your friends and keepers – we guard but cannot guide you as you open in conscious awareness and accept the responsibility of the light-force you carry.

You must stand and show yourselves for what you are – you must speak with need and keep still when necessary.

Much work is being done here for the physical manifestation of The Plan.

As the groups converge together into one unit – as one Being upon the etheric – emotions will have to be stripped away and one's lower egoic nature cleared and transmuted into the needs of the group and the consciousness of Humanity – it is for this you come together to share and become one.

In joining you do not lose out rather you gain a hundredfold.

Blessings of the light and truth be always carried within you – may it shine forth always before you – may it guide each step, each word, each thought.

Bless you.

## When the World Was Young - 1

When the world was young and Humanity was but a dream;
Where was I, where was I ?

When the world grew
and Humanity was but a molecule in the water; Where was I.
Where was I?

And the world turned; and Man is fighting Man,
and brother is fighting brother.
Where am I? Where am I.

I am the Earth. I am the Ocean.
I am the molecule fallen from Space.

Am I the song? I am the singer. Am I the song? I am the singer.

# PART FIVE: Te-Khan

'The Metaphysical'
'The Heart Of The Divine'
'Bring Forth The Vision'
'Understanding Of Deliverance'
'Creativity – Power'
'The Emotional Body And The Lower Egoic'
'Integrity'
'Science Of And Technology Of Today Is The Craft Tomorrow'
'Evolution Of The Species'
'The Science Of Clarity'
'Motive Of Action And Occurrence'
'Concerning The Nature Of Humanity'
'Modes Of Transference'
'Conceptional Thought'
'The Expediency Of Occurrence'
'Service'
'Education'
'Vibrational Forces'
'AKARA – Planetary Awakening'
'Understanding'
'Surrender'
'The Spring Of Life Eternal'
'Life'
'Manifest'
'Service And Servitude'
'Truth'
'Convergence'
'Creativity'
'Sound'
'Responsibility'

# Te-Khan -The Metaphysical

(May 11th 1985)

Blessings, of the light force be with you. I wish to speak with you this evening concerning the existence of the meta-physical.

I say this in such a way to give you the visual interpretation of such a word, so that you may see it as the fire force, showing itself upon the physical plane, at rest within the body. The existence of this force is for you as yet something that only few are able to receive, truly see and/or sense, for us it is indeed, more of a feature of reality than your level of existence and illusionary worlds which you all carry around you.

If you can envisage the force of fire in rapid movement contained within its own field then you will have a sense of that realm. They say "the fire that flames within you" - it is known in the book of the Kabbalah as the Eternal Flame. It is known by they who follow the Koran as "the Flame that leaps to the heart", when a person's consciousness perceives at last their goal. It is indeed the flame of unity and tranquility. How one wonders, can such force be tranquil?

It cannot rest within a body's dense apparatus and conditioning, but when one has subtly attuned one's nature and one's physical and mental bodies to the force, then indeed one becomes vibrant and yet at peace. As you become a part of the current of the whole of this force of creation, the outer friction of you with everyone and everything else, drops, as you become at-one-ment with the whole.

It is this force that the eye perceives and the heart contracts to – the force of love that can carry a person through many of their difficulties. It is this which pushes one even, when he falls into the abyss of despair and darkness.

Light my way O Lord, that I may find the channel to my heart.

The way is clear, the light stands naked. Accept thy destinies.

Walk on, renewed, and lighted, with the fire of eternal dawn. Carry yourselves with love and thoughtfulness.

Be at one.

Blessing of the light be carried always with you.

Here are some guidelines to follow to help you to perceive and grow into the metaphysical yourselves:

One   - Bear witness to yourselves.
Two   - Bear witness to others around you. Three - Bear witness to all life.
Four - Be at one.

In bearing witness onto yourself look to your inner motivations and desires. Look to your basic needs. Speak to yourself of that which you need for the fulfillment of Spirit within.

Be honest as to your motivations.

Keep the body and the mind clear, clean and in good harmony. Bring peace and tranquility to your body, for it houses you.
Bring peace and right thinking to your mind, for it is your transmitter.

Bear witness of those around you.
See them for what they are, not in judgment, but in understanding and compassion to their growth.

See yourself reflected in all those drawn around you. Understand these mirror images.

Work with that within your own nature.
Bear witness to all living life force around you.


Watch the bud as it grows and opens to the solar force. Watch the seasons come and change.
Have understanding in the hibernation of certain animals. See the Spirit in the food you eat and the liquid you drink.
Be at-one-ment with All around you, with life. It is the same Divine Force operating throughout, no longer mirror images but One living Growing Conscious Force. For each living entity has its consciousness, each stone, each plant have their level and understanding of consciousness.

Feel and be at AT ONE.

Do not look at a stone, at a crystal and see it as a crystal – a separative attitude and visual affect - see it as a reflection of you.

Go within it, unite and be that crystal, feel it - practice this with a stone or crystal, then with a plant, a tree, then see your body and do the same.

In this way you open your subtle ethereal senses.
You allow that subtle body which continuously feeds you with information that you cannot or will not receive, due to your imbalance or dense body's nature or mental preoccupation and you will find yourself hearing, understanding and working with that force.

Are not your toes in perfect placement to the body, for without them in that very place and position you would be impeded?
Is not life a Glorious Happening of the Creator?

All life stems from the Source. The Source is the Power carried within you, the power of at-one-ment, Knowing, and Being.

Blessing of the Source be with you.

# Te-Khan - The Heart of the Divine

(13th May 1985)

**When the world was young and Humanity was but a dream; I was here.**

**When the animals of the sea crawled upon their bellies; I was here.**

**When the birds of prey became a sign in the sky; I was here.**

**When the world turned and turned again; I was here.**

**And now we take the eternal leap; I am here within you all.**

**For I am the Heart of the Divine.**

## Te-Khan - Bring Forth the Vision

(4th December 1985) Greetings and blessings to you my brothers and sisters.

I come forward here this evening to share with you some thoughts and words to help to bring forth the vision, the substance within you, of the light upon the planet. For words must be used purely as keys to open into your consciousness the essence of What Is. To bring forth the awareness of the transmutive energy of Being, and as this Force breaks its way downwards into the mental structures of Humanity, it is often lost in the deadness of your language, for true communication, true language, is alive, alive and dwelling in the heart and senses of your Being, where words become the form to carry these senses from one to another.

Remember this always.

Do not get lost in the passage of words.

The light, the growth of light upon your planet, is drawing towards it magnetically the light from the outer planetary regions and as this is drawn slowly and in constant growth towards each other, so too, levels of once known barriers, are broken through in one's own consciousness, in one's ideology and in one's senses.

As the light draws forth of its own to become united again within the living universe, so too, will you draw to you all that is necessary for your growth into your light Beings, for the transformation of the physical dense structure and for the conscious and co-operative growth of your more subtle Being, body and force of Light.

As this comes forward now, the Earth awakens, calling upon her own to come forth, and the light is magnetically drawing its own.

So too, you will be drawn, as all here are so, to those of light in mind and in heart, in harmony and in balance with the whole. To work together in unity and in love, to help to bring this forth into manifestation, into materialisation.

To help the growth and evolution of Humanity. To help to bring forth the rivers of life and light.
To help to create centres of Space, of Vision, of Purity, of Unity of clear Thought, of one living Heartbeat.
May your unity be always centered upon the love within you all.
Blessings of light be with you
.

# Te-Khan - Understanding of Deliverance

(27th February 1986) Greetings to you my friends.
I come forward here this evening to speak and share with you. I am Te-Khan and I carry forward messages and words of understanding and deliverance, to help you to grow in your own understanding and awareness as disciples upon the Way.

I work with a specific Master vibration and this is part of the work that I do, to carry forward and help groups such as yourselves, to open in your own personal understanding and awareness of that force which is contained within you and to come also to the point of knowing /awakening to yourselves as indeed disciples upon the Way, for you have all chosen your paths, you have all chosen your roads of destiny. For many, those roads are cloaked, cloaked by reason and logic, cloaked by ignorance, cloaked by consciousness, or a lack of, and it is to bring yourself to a point of awareness upon that path, where you are walking as an initiate upon the road of light and yet also working as a Server to Humanity, the sacred planet, the universe, where you are becoming a Master, and part of the creative force.

To teach is to learn.

One cannot truly impart to others unless one is open to learning and gaining from all around them.

We have here, been moved to a woodland scene; the trees around us, the grass growing beneath us, the birds singing, some animals twittering and with this scene, we become aware of the force of Nature and the elements, for to walk the Path is to bring an understanding, a closeness, a Oneness, a wholeness of all the forces in operation – yes, the outer-planetary forces, and yes, the inter-connected forces of Beings.

There are also the forces of Nature, the elementals, the Divas, and these forces too, are working in conjunction with the evolutionary growth of the planet. These forces too are growing, and awareness is coming.

The veils that cover the worlds are thinning as we all are being drawn to that vibrationary sound which resonates within us all.

Be aware in the work that you do, of calling upon the elementals, of asking the forces of Nature and the elements to work in co-operation with you.

Be aware of the forces of Fire and Air that can be drawn to bring forth the energy of gold, of vitality.

Be aware of the forces of Earth and Water to bring growth and food. Ask for their help, direct their force. Do not feel powerless within them – work in conjunction.

Each of the twelve centres, of which five are already in operation, will be built upon major ley line activities.

Each centre will be a centre of enlightenment.

Each centre will be connected through its roots and force to the light contained within the planet.

The magnetic, vibrational frequency that will come through at that point will be one that can be contained and used both on the land and within the houses.

These centres of light will be centres of growth, centres of learning, centres of education.

They will be centres where man and woman can learn to know themselves, and in truly knowing themselves will become a part of that vibration, that magnetic frequency that operates within the planet.

Learning to know oneself is learning to see and experience the many faces that one carries within one and these faces have projectionary forces on the outer planes through business, finance, through architecture, through the arts, through communication.

Seeing each activity as a school of learning, a Tao of understanding, helps one to understand the workings in operation, helps one to see, how through one's own conscious awareness, one can adjust and constantly grow within each outer activity.

So the banking, the agriculture, the arts, becomes an outer extension of that force within, not two units of diverging forces.

Bringing together these forces creates a flower.

The petals of the flower are the multi-dimensional forces brought through the stem which is the magnetic vibration connecting you through the Earth's centre itself.

The opening of the flower allows activity to occur, the outer activities, the outer-planetary activities.

Impregnation occurs, seeding starts forth.

We bring you our greetings, our blessings and our gratitude for the sharing this evening.

Blessings to you.

# Te-Khan - Creativity - Power

(5th March 1986) Greetings to you my friends.  Blessings be with you.
We wish to share with you this evening, some thoughts, some keys, upon your own divine ability to be Creators, creators of light, in love, in strength.

You experience the love through your own understandings for each other, for Humanity and the planet.

You experience that love through the light of your Beingness, the light that brings hope, the light that brings knowledge, and it is for you also, to experience the strength, the power, that you have within you, for it is through that power that you bring forth wisdom – power in the form of love and light.

The power that you each carry within you, the ability to be the Creator, the ability to accept completely every word, every action, every thought, within, given forth and centered around you.

The ability to accept the responsibility of all that occurs, not just within you, but upon your Sacred Planet also.

It is by facing this force that is within you, within your brothers and your sisters, within the planet, within indeed the Universe, that helps you to come to terms with that force, brought, transmuted, into the light of love and Beingness.

Power is in itself, nothing.

That which holds the power, the light, the love, the form, this which can never be created nor destroyed.


Power is the key to your own force. Touch it.

Experience it. Allow it to flow.
Allow the light of understanding, the love of knowledge, to blend and to become one with that fountain of wisdom within you.

Find your power and be One.

Find your power and know of yourselves. Know your true identities. Understand your true natures. Blossom and bear the fruit.
It is by bringing oneself to the point of darkness that one is reborn into the deliverance of light – full, whole.

Take it as your sister, your brother. Know it as your friend and ally. Love and light become formless without the power to strengthen and ground, to cast the seeds of growth.

The temple stands within.

# Te-Khan - The Emotional Body and Lower Egoic

(30th July 1986)

Greetings my friends. I am Te-Khan, and I come forward to share with you some thoughts, upon the emotional body and its bonding with the lower egoic nature of man and woman. It is through this emotional body, this lower nature that the rhythmic forces which accelerate and which show themselves on the more subtle planes of existence, bring themselves into being and alignment with the outer forces, the outer planetary forces. It is also here, through the emotional body, that man and woman have brought to themselves the lessons needed, the steps that are necessary for the growth and evolve-ment to the point of now. It is also through this bonding, that Humanity was joined with the planet.

The emotional vibrations given forth and magnetically attracted to and from the planet Herself, have been brought forward now to the point of accelerated evolution and growth.

It is through the emotional body that one's ties, not just genetically, but also through the simultaneous life factors, operates. It is this now that man and womankind are bringing themselves to the point of understanding and clarity.

The lessons that one sets for oneself, the pain that has been the tool for learning, for growth and understanding, are becoming unnecessary, for what is to be, are becoming null and void for what is to occur and is occurring simultaneously, both within your Beings cellularly and within the universe itself. You will find, through your own conscious awareness, that as you are able to release yourselves, instinctively, intellectually, from being tied to the past, the emotional bodies them-selves will be able to merge, and the rate of vibration that occurs within you will be brought forward, will be accelerated, to the point where that which you attract becomes one.

The call has gone forth.

The answer is manifesting within you all.

The emotional body has lain like fertiliser upon the ground, bringing you to points of conception and understanding.

There is a point of delivery, when the note is sung.

That which is to occur, will come forth through your very Beingness.
The song you sing is a particle upon the Way.
Let the note sound forth; let the resonance utter within you. The bodies change constantly and the growth occurs instantly.
The light bodies are breaking through the concreteness of your thoughts, bringing awareness and activity
It is the denser vibrations which hold you back from complete understanding of your natures, and yet it is the denseness that has brought forth the growth from its conceptual being.

Live and bless what you are. Open yourself to the Beingness of your light. Let the dross fall from you.

In the beginning was the Word and the Word was governed by its beginning. Go forth beyond the beginning into the Void.
Stretch yourself into the seemingly endless Space and breathe light

# Te-Khan - Integrity

I am Te-Khan and I come forward here this evening to share with you some thoughts concerning the vibrational force of the Word/sound, i integrity. Integrity is the truth of one's own Being, being true to one's nature and allowing this force to integrate with the vibrational forces of those of whom one comes in contact with.

Truth in itself is whole and yet within that there are variations of vibration that have their effect upon the environmental force of the subconscious of the individual and it is within that force that therein can be the difficulties.

It is with the integrity of one's nature that one can allow the various vibrations of the truth of one's Being to interplay with the vibration that one comes in contact with.

It is in this way that you can help to sow the seeds; you can help to plant a thought, a word, and an action that will help the growth of the individual.

Truth in its wholeness can sometimes frighten the course of the vibrational pull, of those who are not yet ready to face the reality of their inner natures and Beingness, and it is through this vibrational essence that you can allow yourselves the interplay within the experience of those vibrational essences that integrate between you.

It is within the force itself, it is within the essence of integrity that you and the interplay between you can come to a true sense of understanding with each other.

It brings you into an alignment with the planetary forces operating at this time upon and around your planet to raise the vibrational levels so that Humankind itself can begin to grow in awareness, in understanding, in a way that it is ready to impart upon.

In times gone by, it has always been through the consciousness of the individual that the growth occurs, and now, with the acceleration of these forces, the consciousness itself is expanded to a state where the individual has not yet prepared themselves on the inner planes and yet this is occurring to bring about a spontaneous change and effect, both on the acceleration of the growth on the subtle levels, and also on the interplay on the physical and emotional bodies.

It is with this change, and through this effect can you now be ready. For the vibrational pull that is occurring, is drawing to this planet a complete variance of experience, for the whole of Humanity and for the planet Herself. Yet, through these experiences do you, with your inner eye and your open awareness, begin to experience the vestiges of truth, the vibration: integrity and through this, does the perceptive body begin to work. Through this, do you begin to integrate the bodies, the subtle and the dense and grow not just on an individual basis- beginning the growth itself of the groups, beginning the growth itself of the structureless and yet united force of Soul energy - beginning the road, the path, to light and awareness.

We join with you in light and in love.

We join in your work; we join in your growth. We stand with you always.

# Te-Khan-Science & Technology of Today are the Craft of Tomorrow

(19th November 1986) Good evening and greetings to you my friends. I am Te-Khan and I come forward here this evening to share a thought with you and that is, that the science and technology of today is the craft of tomorrow.

Now, to explain this a little further, we would add that the arts and the crafts of today were once the sciences and technologies of your past. By bringing the technology and the science from the realm of intellectual thought into the essence of physical manipulation and working with, becoming the tool - the groove of each other - you and the technology interconnecting through your own energy levels, you are the extensive and intensive experience of that craft. Through that experience within and around you, does it become art form, the beauty, the texture of the beauty, the beauty even within the structure, bringing it to a level of God-filled, for art is a very divine perception of one's intense connection with God: through words, through movement, through colour, through sound.

Sometimes it denotes the anger or fear of losing that connection. It shows the passage of growth into finding the connection.
The work that you have embarked upon, that which you are moving into physical extension of, is to bring about this interconnectedness where the realisation of these crafts, the art of such, can be experienced and understood.

To you, now at this time, it is technology, science.

What do these words imprint upon your consciousnesses?

What separation occurs within you at the thought these words bring to you?

Look again to those peoples you will be working with, sharing with, living with.

How do they approach their craft of living?

The merging of these ideas is the bridging of the gap between the intellectual thought-process and the expansive growth that occurs between the interactions of life-force, be this from being, human to another, or from human to machine; working together to create and recreate harmony in an atmosphere of friction and discord.

It is like the playing of a harp where the vibration and the harmony induced brings the friction and discord into a sense of rhythmic balance, and growth can occur.

The word "science" is changing its vibration now, in the consciousness of the individual, and slowly working into the consciousness of the mass.

There will be a new, greater understanding of the sciences of life and this comes through your interconnectedness.

Blessing my friends.

My grateful thanks for the space you have provided for me this night.

# Te-Khan - Evolution of the Species

(15th January 1987) Greetings to you my friends. Greetings.
I come forward here this evening to join and share with you some thoughts upon the Evolution of the Species, for it is upon this focus that much of the evolutionary growth throughout the universe comes forward at this time.

There is much light force and energy centered upon your planet for this growth from those upon the outer planetary realms, watching. Watching in anticipation, in hope and in vision, for the growth occurring now upon this sacred planet and within you all – for this growth, this evolutionary step that is occurring, is occurring not just upon the mental and spiritual planes, but is also working on a cellular level, the actual DNA make-up of your Being is slowly changing. An occurrence that is happening within your own bodies and within the Earth's structure Herself – and it is through this that unity can at last come forth.

There are many, of which you are a part, who are working upon their spiritual aspirations. You are working on understanding and bringing forth the spiritual quality of your life through and into your physical and material worlds; to bring forth that unification, indeed, to carry the species through to the next evolutionary level.

This course has repercussions throughout your world; vibrations of separation will arise, are arising, and have been for the last 60 years.

It is through this, that you have to carry your banners of light and unity. Through this, that you have to bring together your spiritual, your physical and emotional, your mental levels, to live who and what you truly are.

The vibrations of this activity in your lives, in your day-today thoughts and actions, do indeed cause a whole vibrationary effect upon your planet, and can and will, alter the effects of those working towards separatism.

This step of your species is where the strong stand forward. It is now those who are strong in heart and strong in spirit, those who hold within them their light force, those who hold within them their knowingness of the love that transpires between you all, that knows the power and force of that love, the accomplishment of such love held within you – that is what carries you forward to help cast the seeds for what will be.

The time has been chosen and you all chose well.

The work has been and will be accomplished by you all.

The pathways have been chosen.   You have designated your choices.

You will walk; indeed, you must walk, in the light of your own Being in the knowingness of whom and what you really are. To do this you must accept the responsibility of all contained in your thoughts and your actions with all others as well as with yourself; remembering to be present in every moment, keeping your mind and heart open always and ready.

Indeed your world is changing, changes that are necessary for the growth of the species, for the growth of the planet, and you all have chosen to work with those changes, to help to bring forward the light and the water of purification and growth, to bring forth energy, the energy of life force of the planet and within Humanity.

It is with peace that you can accept yourselves. It is with purity of motive and action you can see within and around you.

Be at peace and let the Spirit within you arise and take your rightful place. The place of love, of givingness, of hope.

My blessings and thanks to you all.

# Te-Khan - The Science of Clarity

(28th January 1987)

I am Te-Khan and I come forward this evening to share some thoughts with you upon the science of clarity, for it is indeed, with true clarity that one can reach the divine goal of light fulfillment within.

What is it that helps one to see clearly, to hear clearly? Is it purely a physical and mental function (?)
There is within and beyond this, the essence of clarity that comes forward from the heart and it is through the actions of the heart, the systems of the valves that helps to bring forth clarity through to the mind and the senses.

The ability to see beyond the projections of others, the ability to hear within the tones the vibrations send forth, come to you from the functions of the heart and the heart centre, and it is through the development of the heart that the essence of clarity can make itself known through you.

How often is it, you can ask yourselves, that you do truly see clearly, hear clearly, understand clearly, speak clearly?

If your heart is not in purity and clarity, then this is not able to emerge from you nor through you.

When you speak, allow the force, the vibrational force of clarity, to flow first from your heart to the other - not through the mental activity – through the heart centre, that your hearts may be open to each other, that the essence may be passed from one to the other in the light of purity and clarity, and then the words which you speak, the images you conjure through the sounds, these are but colourings to the picture already received.

It is from the heart that you share, the rest is but a remembrance of that.

When clarity flows through an individual, it can help to clarify the vision and the force of that individual.

When the vision is clarified, then it draws to it magnetically that which is needed to manifest it upon the physical and material plane.

By clarifying where you are now by being clear on what you need and how you feel, by keeping in purity and in clarity the vision, then you move forward towards the end result - the apex of that force – that which you draw magnetically to you - needed for the manifestation of such thought and delivery.

It is through clarity and purity; the purity being purity of action, purity of love.

How often does one hear in clarity and accept in purity?

As you 'see' the understanding of this force, it brings forth the word 'science,' brings forth the ability to delve into this vibrational field that we may learn, that we may manifest the forces of light now upon the planet.

You are creators.

You are studying now at the perfect time and in the perfect space to bring forth all that is needed for the growth and delivery of the planet.

You are part of a huge and growing number of individuals and groups working, endeavouring, to bring forth light upon the planet.

Remember also, the light dwells within, and it is from within that the growth first occurs.
The planet Herself has much to offer at this time of need. The value of Her fields are little used and understood.

Even in the understanding of the mineral kingdom coupled with the plant and animal worlds together, bringing the vibrationary forces of life again into awareness.

When you plant, plant not just trees or food for human consumption, but look too at the mineral world, look to the animals for what they too bring to the environment; understand the interaction of the life force that occurs constantly within them all.

There is a whole science in itself, based upon the mineral world and the knowledge gained through the minerals and through the elemental and Devic forces concerned with the mineral kingdom, that can help in the growth of plant life and the fertility of the planet.

There is much yet to be understood by Humanity and yet it waits, it waits for clarity, purity of motive.

The answers are there – it is the questions that are lost. Clarity brings them forth to your awareness again.
Bless you my friends. My many thanks for the space.

# Te-Khan - Motive of Action and Occurance

(2nd February 1987)

I am Te-Khan. When last we spoke, we spoke about purity and clarity.

I wish now to share with you some thoughts upon motive and action; motive of action and occurrence.

It is not often that the average person thinks, dwells, delves into an understanding, a reasoning, behind their activity and yet it is the motive behind any and all activity, that causes the creative forces to manifest in such ways.

It is important for you, and imperative, that you recognise and realise your motives in your actions, your deeds.

It is very easy to allow oneself to fall into a common error where one is able to deceive oneself of one's motives.

As one brings purity and clarity into being, one is no longer able to run from the pure motive and reasoning behind any and all activity.

You will notice, through this path of reasoning and understanding that the motives sometimes behind the activities are there to impress others, sometimes are there to cause guilt in others, sometimes to cause guilt in oneself. When one's motive is pure, then the activity itself becomes secondary.

The force and the light of the work that you are a part of cannot be overstated and yet, the outcome is secondary against the motivation within you all.

It is that, that must be pure.

It is that, that must be clear, crystal clear. Your thoughts can become like living crystals.
Just imagine, conceive, of this thought, and what an occurrence it can bring; living crystals, magnified.

The motive of any action is the motivation of why you are here upon the planet, now, at this time.

It all grows from the same source, and therefore returns.

What does it mean, when a person has no motive in their activity? For even the animals and the whole of the cycle of Nature is motivated by survival. When one's motives become so crystal clear, one is able, through a transitionary stage, to move into that clarity of the crystal force, where there is indeed no motive.

What could it be like to live without motivation?

According to the evolutionary path, it could be two varying levels or degrees; it can be one, those who have lost themselves in the denseness of Time or it can be those who have given onto Self-One– Whole and therefore motive becomes unnecessary.

Motive can equate to the probationary path, for as one grows, one's motives gradually change.

Look with honesty into your motivations and activities and, in gaining understanding of this, you will grow.

Blessings my friends. Many thanks for the space you have provided.

# Te-Khan - Concerning the Nature of Humanity

(11th February 1987)

I am Te-Khan and I come forward here this evening, to share with you some thoughts concerning the Nature, your Nature, and the Nature of Humanity.

The aspect we speak upon tonight, is the nature of concern, the nature that brings forth certain vibrations and harmonics of sound. Being concerned, showing concern, having concern, are all different vibrations of that harmonic. As you work through and with your natures, the vibrations that then draw to you, opens your - selves to the harmonic of sound that can manifest through you as light, as growth, bringing forth with it the manifestation of the Christ-forces.

Now, each of these levels brings forth a vibration which aligns you to the harmonic of that sound within Humanity. Being concerned, showing concern, having concern: when one has concern over a certain predicament, matter, person, then one is in essence doubting the natural flow that is in operation constantly within and around you. One is stifling, stunting, the growth and the force of that operating through you. One is curtailing the manifestation that works throughout the bodies, both physically and emotionally, mentally and ethereally, thereby causing the ability to bring ease or disease throughout the bodies.

Showing concern within oneself of oneself is an outer manifestation of the lack of ability of actually bringing oneself into alignment with the highest, and with the operation of the highest and the manifestation of that, working through individuals and Humanity.

In the darkest grottos and holes in your planet, there is growing everywhere the light of Spirit, the light of Love, brotherhood and sisterhood, strength and vitality. There is growing, the new tomorrow.

By taking oneself out of the realm of the effect of the dense astral interconnection within Humanity, one can bring oneself to the essence of Being.

This is when one can see in clarity and, with that purity of motive and in seeing, can create and construct a new life: a new beginning awakening in the mass-unconscious; thoughts and manifestations, hopes and dreams that can break into their daily lives, for a moment, for a little time, which build bridges for them to grow through and upon.

The concern of Being is the essence within you – carrying itself forward to bring the whole of Humanity and the planet, into the essence of Christ consciousness. Where you are as one living part, where your thoughts beat with vision, with joy, where you gather strength from seeing the light within and around you, where you lift your vibration into the harmonic of sound that causes creation to be, and in so doing, allows the opportunity to manifest.

It can often take time in your realm to understand the aspects of concern, and for many, they draw themselves to a lack of concern, thereby hiding themselves from the ability of growth.

Let us look again at these aspects within us and our natures and see where we, individually, are holding onto an aspect that we deem necessary, and yet is not allowing us to see clearly.

Anything - any thought, any motive, any person, that you feel the need to hold onto - it is there the weakness lies, for love is there continuously and fully for you, in motive, in thought, and in those around you.

Releasing is releasing the tension that lies within the heart and allowing it to manifests through you all.

My grateful thanks for this space.

# Te-Khan - Modes of Transference

(4th March 1987)

I am Te-Khan, and I come forward here this evening to share with you some thoughts concerning modes of transference – modes of transference. Now we wish to speak on this to help you gain an understanding of using the creative forces that you have and that you carry within you constantly and hopefully, consciously.

There are different expressions of modes of transference in operation upon your planet and within yourselves.

As you know, atoms attract one another, so too can thoughts. Just as certain atoms detract from each other, so too can certain thought patterns.

As one carries a thought procedure, this thought draws to it the ability to connect, to co-create as it is, in a group level.

Then occurs a mode of transference where what one is carrying and interconnects with others, becomes a matter of transference within the whole group. Thereby the group themselves are carrying this thought pattern, carrying this creative venture. It is to be noted that most often but not always, consciously.

This mode of transference carries itself forward also out of the individual, into the capacity of a nation, into the capacity of a culture.

This is seen easily through the eyes of a cultural nation.

By taking a nation that is rich and deep and yet may be limited in its culture, you can see how the mode of transference works constantly on the unconscious level, keeping them bound within this.

Now by moving to such a place, by bringing your thoughts, by bringing your atoms of energy, and by allowing them to flow from you, you are allowing a new mode of transference to occur.

You are in actual fact, impregnating - impregnating new light, new information. At the same time, this mode of transference, being co-operatively ventured of course, feeds you too, with the abilities and disabilities of that culture; therefore you too have to understand what is happening at this collective level.

This collective level can be both on the conscious and the unconscious realms, according to your perception of it.

Now, another mode of transference is by bringing before you the vision, the whole or the holistic picture of that upon which you are working to achieve, to receive or to connect to, and stepping forward into that hologram, the entirety of your Being through the thought process. There is then a thought transference that can and will occur through the medium of your light bodies, being the receivers of light and the light energy which it induces through the planet's magnetic pattern. By moving back, the mode of transference has occurred and can then be ingested slowly by the individual or the project, or the receiver.

This too is another means or mode of transference.

There is a third mode of transference which happens on a more subtle plane of existence and yet a plane that is not unknown to any of you.

It is a plane upon which you, each and every one, work upon daily, knowingly and unknowingly.

It is that level of existence where dwells your highest thoughts and aspirations, where dwells the seeds that then slowly come forth through the etheric vibration and the ethers, to make themselves manifest at the time and space known only to that divine force, and yet this mode of transference is what is in operation now upon your planet through the growth and occurrence of these conscious receivers throughout the planet.

By the very awareness of your natures, by the very awareness of your thoughts, you become not just the receptacles of this force, you become the responsible creators to give this a density that is needed, a density that you can use through your lower bodies to bring into the vibration of thought, the mode of transference, allowing the growth of greater unity to occur, for do we all not come from the One, and are we all not of one divine force?

When you reach that state of absolute, the mode of transference is complete, for we are whole and One in Being.

Bless you my friends.

It is with gracious pleasure I join with you.

# Te-Khan - Conceptional Thought

(18th March 1987)

Greetings my friends. Conceptional thought, conceptional thought: Taken apart, the concept, the thought, both are inwardly produced and manifested through a process of mental activity. Both in themselves can hold one within a limitation of action and creative expansion.

Yet the molecules of activity produced through the conceptional thought, brings forth a nucleus of force, heaved into reality, spoken of as we did last week.

Now, as this force in reality manifests, it manifests on an individual scale, little known yet for this individual scale comes from the domain yet to be, the Monardic and it is into this reality that it can become manifest.

This causes an expansion of consciousness in the realms of ideas not yet manifested within Humankind, not yet limited by the structure of thought.

It is through the time/motion that this manifestation can occur.

It is to be understood that all that you, individually or as a whole, can conceive of, is but a tiny atom of the force of manifestation waiting to flow and grow through that seed of delivery.

It is through the expansion of your minds, and your abilities to grasp concepts as yet unknown - ones that do not ground you to a structure, ones that are open in form - that will help you to manifest fully the aspects of the whole.

Your bodies and their workings are determined by your course of action, by your understanding.

With conceptional thought you can use this to speed the growth of the subtle bodies through the denser areas of your Being, to bring growth and light, to bring productivity through you.

The force we speak of is an inter-connective force of which one can be part of, and in use of, at the same moment in Time and Space.

This heave of energy, this force, is coming across the planet, blanketing the atmosphere with its vibrations.

It is there for the usage of groups and individuals such as yourselves, as responsible Beings, Custodians of your planet, to actively involve yourselves in the manifestation of the Plan; to bring Light and Love as active forces throughout the Planet.

# Te-Khan - The Expediency of Occurrence

(20th May 1987)

Greetings my friends. I am Te-Khan and I come forward here this evening to share with you some thoughts on the expedience of occurrence.

That which has occurred, that which is occurring, that which has yet to occur; all these are concepts, held in motion by your consciousness and your awareness and by the value of your thought factors in the progression of life and time and the time scale as you know it, and yet, within and around this structured force - which has become a part of the living entity of Humanity - is a growing vibration of the expedience of occurrence. Through this one can change, through one's perception, through the expansion of one's awareness, through the limitless thoughts and the openness of one's values, you can allow this vibrational cord that stems from the creative value of your natures, into the manifestation of thought and occurrence.

What is to be, what has been, and what is now re-enacting, are all held by your value of Time, and your belief upon that. This is held by society at large as a form of security that there was a yesterday, and there will be a tomorrow, and yet in the essence of Now, in the wholeness of your Being, there only Is, and it is this essence that can bring through the understanding that occurrence changes according to your perception and value of it.

You, as creative individuals, representing a responsive force of the whole, can gradually allow yourselves the possibility, the probability, the understanding and the recognition, that you can change occurrences both beyond and within the realms of your thought factors.

What has been does not necessarily designate what is to be, nor does it stay motionless and staid.

The past is still a living entity beside you, which, through the change of your perceptive values, can become a part of the wholeness of your nature, bringing you a wealth of knowledge and understanding. What is to be is limitless in its wealth, and yet is again standing beside you, open to you, the manifestation of which, colours your aura and your world.

Again, it is for you to step within this and allow this to impregnate through your Being, that you, as holistic individuals, within the group structure, can manifest the essence of wholeness, Now and always Now.

Time is never lost. Bless you my friends.
My gracious thanks for your company of love and harmony that you bring to us.

# Te-Khan - Service

(2nd September 1987)

Greetings my friends. I am Te-Khan and I come forward here this evening to share with you some thoughts upon the vibration of the Living Word – Service. Service.

What indeed is this vibration upon which so much of the new thought and living energy upon your planet now focuses itself?

To render service to, to serve one another, to be in service to the Plan, to serve as one is called upon, to give willingly, to give openly and with true honesty in one's heart; this is an act of commitment.

It is the act that places one firmly upon the Path that brings one again to one's point of Being, where one is truly in harmony with the living universe and the creative force that dwells forever within oneself and one's nature.

When we serve the Plan, is this service offered with a sense of gratitude and giving?

Is it placed on a level of value? Is it in true humility?
For the need to serve, itself comes through the consciousness and the desire of Humanity, the planet, the beings on the various levels of activity, to bring again pure light, in form, through matter, upon this living planet, through your thoughts and through your desires.

When one acts through a sense of service, there must always be that sense of honesty from one's nature that you serve through the desire of givingness, of the growth of light and the impartment of wisdom to each other.   It is sometimes difficult to conceive of an idea that to serve another is to allow them the space to grow in whatever way is necessary for their development, be it understandable to you at the given time or not.

Is it truly a sense of service to place your knowledge upon one who is not yet ready or prepared?

Is it truly, a sense of service, to place one above another?

To serve is to release oneself from the mode of ego. It is to release oneself from the aspect of the "I" and the "I" conditioning and to allow one to be used purely and truly as a channel for the light forces, to become operational upon your planet.

This Time and Space now, with the growth and the acceleration of vibration, is a time when you all are accepting your sense of responsibility and creativity, when you – each of you – stand upon the threshold of a New Beginning, a New Life and it is here, that we stand with you.

Together we walk the Path to bring that sense of enlightenment through your nature, through the bodies of your Being, to unify not just the sense of Self, but to bring unification on a planetary and universal level, for as you are, so will be and is, indeed.

The planet Herself vibrates. The call has gone forth and the work is in operation.

You are all united, through this sense of desire and service, to work in harmony together for the materialisation of the Plan of which each of you, as a living, growing part, are developing, creating, blossoming anew and giving forth the seeds.

All that you have worked for is now coming to fruition, but one must remember to allow the fruit to ripen, and you will find, though the taste be exquisite, it is there to be shared by all.

Bless you my friends.

# Te-Khan - Education

(1987)

Now my friends, I come forward this evening to speak with you. My name is Te-Khan and I come forward to share some thoughts with you concerning education.

All people are of one accord, harmonics of vibration and together the sound is moving towards completion - to be as one - peoples of the World.

Look into each culture. Have understanding for their mode of education, their mode of learning and remembering. One of the most important aspects in helping the peoples of the World is to help them to remember their culture and where they have grown from.

Each man and woman must, and should, know and honour their roots. In knowing of their roots they have the foundation for growth and rediscovery, and you too have to recognise and realise your roots. In growing from your roots you are then harmonising the spiritual with the physical, emotional and mental bodies. To cut yourself from your roots, is to focus your attention into your spiritual counterpart.

This then becomes supremely that; a counterpart, never a holistic Being. It is of natural consequence to bring forth the roots united with the Spirit. Imagine a forest of many types of trees growing together: Strengthened by their connections. Growing on, their branches touching, sharing.

You will find also in your work of rediscovery, harmonic vibrations that are within the atmosphere already. Open to becoming consciously attuned to these vibrations of energy, these forces that are growing around the planet and are already in operation upon and within your bodies and upon your minds, for one dictates to the other constantly these variations of sound.

These variations that are in operation, can be used for growth, they can also cause discord to those who are moving against their own natural tide, their own natural flow.

Be aware of this with each and every person you communicate with, for through communication you are touching into education.
As you become aware of each person you communicate with, you will become aware of variations, tones of awareness in their thought patterns, in their body movement, how these sometimes counteract each other and at other times work in accordance.

Through this you will see, primarily, spaces that can be filled with light and with accordance, and you will see also how your body works to counteract those variations projected from them through the electro-magnetic vibrations, towards you, bringing your body constantly into a state of flux.

To come upon the subject of the children returning for this bright Age of Discovery and Light, you need to create space within your hearts, within your minds, within your consciousness, with the planet at large. These children will teach you.
These children will show you the way. Let their Spirits free. Learn through their awareness and lack of deception.

Grant space for the growth which must occur at an accelerated speed within them.

Honour always the children, for they come to show the way. They come carrying the Sword and the Chalice.

They come to give Light and to fight for that Light. They come with Will and Determination.
They come with Love and Understanding. They come with open intellects.

Yes, use all the tools you have necessary.

Use all that is there and still, there will be need for more.

The child, at the point of conception, carries within it all knowledge of its Path and Destiny, already formed perfectly and balanced completely in all that is necessary for that growth. Upon the point of the spirit entry into the womb, that Being moves from its world of light and perception, into a world of darkness, lying like a seed within to break through.

That perfect Being encapsulated within the womb needs feeding, needs watering, needs the warmth of the sun and the blessed darkness of the moon and, as it is born into a world of decay and death, from the vibration of where it once lay within the world of Destiny, it slowly and magnetically, through a life of discovery upon your planet, works back again upon the Path, reliving all that it created before physical conception and birth.

You are all living that which you have already done, and been, in your own world.

You are bringing yourself again to that point of completion, that point of wholeness where eventually the climax will be, not a world of decay and death, but the world of everlasting Light, Life and Beingness.

From the moment a babe is born, it moves towards death. From the moment that child is born, it is on the Pathway. To understand this fully is in itself an education, and all streams of thought, ideas and variations – harmonics of that thought – can be called education.

Realise and relish that one thought, and see how fruitful it becomes within you, how much can be gained and learned, how much can be given and let go of.

I have spoken with you and it has been of great pleasure. My great thanks, gratitude, for the blending and harmonising of our souls together as one.

Blessings to you.

# Te-Khan - Vibrational Forces

(4th January 1988)

Greetings my friends. I am Te-Khan and I come forward here in this Time and Space to share with you some thoughts, and understandings, concerning the vibration and the vibrational forces which are at work on your planet and around you today.

At this time, the time commonly called the Full Moon, it is the time of vibration, of balance, of bringing into manifestation the spontaneous occurrence from the force of the sun, the solar power, and the physical manifestation, the form, from the moon, the lunar power.
These can be commonly seen as the male and female principles. They can also be seen as the active and receptive.

At the time of its fullness, when it is in itself giving out the light reflection of the Sun, and yet through that reflection, being able to show the power of its own force, we have an idea of how the unification of Humanity can come forth again.

By reflecting that active ingredient, by allowing your receptive nature to grow in spontaneous occurrence, of which we have before spoken, there lies the key for the unification of the Tribes, and their at-one-ment with the Mother Planet.

Now taking this point into account and looking at the stars in their heavenly bodies, we can see that according to astrological interpretation, the moon is lying in the sign of Cancer – that which gives, and the sun lying in the sign of Capricorn, that which receives, and across from these, causing a grand cross, we have the sign of Aries and the sign of Libra.
Aries is the sign of the one, the messenger, when form and matter combine and the spark of life occurs and grows upon your planet. Cancer is the reaching toward one's ideals, and the balancing of those ideas, within the creative impulse, for the life force of Humanity. Thereby reaching forth for Humanity, giving forth of one's nature.

Libra is the act of duality. When one gives forth from one's nature fully and wholly, spontaneously opening within one's own heart, then one is brought to the point of the inner reflection of one's own nature, projected upon and towards them.

Bringing partnership into account, working with others, learning on the inner level to live with one's own divinity, to become a lover of one's inner and lower nature so that too may be integrated into the act of wholeness, aspiring always into complete union.

And the fourth arm of the cross, in Capricorn, where one brings oneself to the point of understanding, of upliftment of one's spiritual aspiration and earthly value, becoming in tune with one's inner nature. Where one can receive the divine light wholly, not filtered to the acceptance of one's consciousness, but where one's consciousness is lifted, open and ready to receive the divine force, the power and the strength and the vitality of that force. To give forth into that centre spark, the spark of life within that spontaneous occurrence, that point of manifestation, there is the opening to one's own sense of divinity, that one may know oneself and walk on.

And so, you see my friends, the greater understanding brought forward at this time is simple in its tone, life is continuous, and within its circular motion, there are constant growths and understanding, to bring one to an awareness that is already captured and contained within one's inner nature.

To learn a lesson, one must have already experienced it on the inner plane. The outer manifestation of that lesson is a remembrance – it is a dense replay of that continuous occurrence, continuous until the stillness sounds itself within you, envelopes and portrays itself through you and through all that you do, touch, speak, taste, feel, know.

Then oneness begins and peace again dwells in your heart. Bless you my friends.
My grateful thanks for the space we share together.

# Akara - Planetary Awakening

(20th January 1988)

Greetings my friends.

I come forward here this evening to share with you some thoughts concerning the birth and the news of the planetary awakening, for indeed, across your living planet, there is an awakening, an occurrence of energy and vibration that is accumulating in value and force and it is this force that works through you all.

This living force, brought forward and anew, is not just within you all, it is a force that is occurring through the whole of nature, the whole of the natural world.

This force is taking in the Devic realms and the angelic realms, as these two are part of the living world, the natural world that is around you, as Humanity in general has not yet the eyes to see nor the ears to hear all that is around them, yet these realms too, are a part of your living environment and they too, work and operate to bring forward the channels and to be the chalices of light upon the planet.

At this time, this time of newness, this time of birth, this is the time of the coming together, the coming together of peoples, the coming together of groups, families, organisations, and in coming together you are helping to bring forth that acceleration of energy, you are helping to lift the vibrational force into a celebration of creation, a birth. The birth of the living planet that is in harmony with Her body, in harmony with her emotional vibration.

By the coming together of your own thought patterns, by the living and the loving and balancing of your emotional vibrations, you can help achieve a greater understanding upon that of which you live, you breathe, you have your Being.

By working towards harmony, by bringing peace through your nature, by spreading light and joy with all of those with whom you come in contact, by understanding and by acknowledgement, you help to bring that vibrational force into being, to give birth to the greatest, the good within you all.

The Earth indeed has called out in her pain and as a living force we have responded as one and that response has carried us into an alignment with the vibration and the growth of the planet. It brings us into alignment with our brothers and sisters in the outer planetary regions, for our awareness of our living Earth, our awareness and care for each other, helps to open our perceptive doors, increases our ability to see, to hear, to understand, so that we too as a whole, may join in the celebration of life, and light eternal.

These are our words and our understandings that we share with you. Our greetings come to you and we share together.

AKARA.

# Te-Khan - Understanding

(1st February 1988)

Greetings my friends. I am Te-Khan and I come forward here this evening as an emissary of light to share with you some thoughts, some keys, to bring you to a greater understanding of yourselves and your own environment and I wish first, to speak here upon the word "understanding" – "understanding", and all that concerns itself with it.

Now to take the word in its form; breaks into three levels, care, thought and activity – care, thought and activity.

To have an understanding of a person or situation, one must first care for that person or situation.

The energy must come from the heart; one must feel care towards it.

One must be thoughtful, full of thought – allow the thought to penetrate through you, from the environmental aspects and vibration of the person or situation, and one must then be able to take the steps needed to bring this into fulfillment of understanding.

This is activity – activity.

Placing these in order without judgment for any given situation or person, one can then bring oneself into the essence of understanding, by-passing the need for mental knowledge so that with the greater force of understanding, knowledge has itself been encompassed.

In this way, you can set yourselves the pace available, needful, to become masters, mistresses, of your own divine force.

The way of the path is light.

Light is all-encompassing, and yet within it one can see the tiniest speck.

So too, this travels with you upon the way. It does not grant you the ability of cutting from all pains or distresses, yet brings you the gift of understanding and acknowledgement of your own inner dimension and nature and to see in others only the reflection of that inner nature.

When one is critical or judgmental of another, then one has to face the recognition of that force within themselves and the inner fear of facing that within themselves.

Face that.

So as one reaches forth towards those who brings one light and joy, one can also recognise this ability within their nature, and rejoice.

Criticism comes home always. It is contractive. Love and joy are ever expanding. Understanding. We care for you.
We have thought of you and we work in activity with you. In this way the Plan unfolds, manifests. In this we live.

Bless you my friends.

My gracious thanks for the space.

# Te-Khan - Surrender

(22nd June 1988)

Greetings my friends. I am Te-Khan and I come forward this evening to speak with you and share some thoughts concerning the vibration of the word surrender: surrender.

It is upon this vibration that much of the accelerated energy occurring on a planetary level is happening at this time and it is this vibrationary force that is bringing about a change, not just within the consciousness of Humanity but also on a very material and physical level. It is this force that is occurring on a microscopic level within each and every individual. Bringing them forth to the aspect of Godhood, to the aspect of knowing, where one is within one's own nature and either surrenders to the Divine, the force of light, the force of power within oneself, or, one turns and continues upon the Wheel of Rebirth, continues upon the path where the lessons, the laws, become in themselves distinct, become in themselves, collective, collective within the sense of the esoteric, and collective within the sense as archetypical values upon the unconscious. And it is in this state and stage now that you find yourselves and Humanity, at last and at large, must face. It is within this prime value that groups such as yourselves can bring forth a service of knowledge, a force of understanding, and Being of love.

It is through the essence of your light vibration, it is through the joining and the giving of yourselves for the greater good, that this can bring forth an understanding, a creation, a sending forth of seeds upon the Way, and these seeds indeed come forth through the etheric fields, come through the monadic levels into the thoughts and the subconscious realms, of those seeking, of those opening themselves and standing forth upon the Path.

To surrender to the greater, is not to lose the essence of Self, indeed it is through the releasing of one's reactive and instinctive nature, through the embracing of the animal, that one can become at-one, finding the peace, knowing the light divine that lies within.

It is this, that as one surrenders to the vibration and quality of one's life and life's work, that brings forth its own joy and blessings and unites one to the essence of one's Soul group, of one's family, where collectively you are joined to work for the greater good of the whole, using all that you have, all facilities, as tools for this work.

To surrender to this force, is to bring yourself into alignment with the vibration that is coming now into operation upon your planet, and within this vibrationary note the sound goes forth and it is clear.

It rings true in your hearts and in your memories. You are the creators. You are part of the life blood.

You are the living memories of the Divine and it is through you that the Essence can manifest – it is through you all and through your love and joy.

Bless you my friends. Bless you.

# Te-Khan - The Spring of Life Eternal

(11th August 1988)

I am Te-Khan and I come forward here this day, to share some thoughts with you concerning the vibration of The Spring of Life Eternal, The Spring of Life Eternal.

The thoughts that come from you come from an automated consciousness, subjective in its view and held together within the sub-conscious region of reaction and genetic input.

The thoughts that come through you come from The Spring of Life Eternal. They live on.

They come from the thoughts of One and continue in a spiral motion, again to reach the point of Being, the source of all. Allowing them to manifest through you, through your thoughts, your actions, allows your Being to touch again with the force of light that is in operation throughout Ages, throughout the hemisphere and yonder, throughout the stars.

It is this force that revitalises your Being, allowing it space, growth, allowing it the opportunity to come again into the realm of unity. And to follow this, one listens not to the head or to the emotions, for both of which carry their needs and therefore magnetically draws to them the opportunity needed for growth.

Listen to the dynamic force that lies within the centre of your Being, that which heralds the return of the life force in operation again upon your planet and it is for this that you are joined together as one.

It is to bring this receptive motion into dynamic fulfillment, the manifestation of the Plan, the blossoming of brotherhood and sisterhood, the co-operation and love. The peace that reigns within.

Bringing this together, is bringing the age of the forces of nature into alignment that again there will be communication, communion, between the various vibrations of light and matter. Form, in this way manifests and brings forth its own.

And so, this day, we attune ourselves to the higher vibrations of light that the Eternal Spring may forever flow through us, allowing the manifestation to occur, knowing that we are each a part, an aspect, a face of the whole, one Being and within lies the ability for that wholeness to operate.

So for each, the work, the love, continues on in joy and harmony, in service and fulfillment.

And we come together and we open ourselves that we may unite and allow the force to flood through us and outwards to all of whence it is needed.

Bless you my friends.

My gracious thanks for our coming together.

# Te-Khan - Life

(5th October 1988)

Greetings my friends. Greetings. I am Te-Khan, and I come forward this evening to share with you upon the vibration: Life, Life.

Life is thought of, from the stand point of Humanity, in two modes; that of life and death and that of continuous occurrence, and within this, the general thought patterns bring themselves into an understanding and a blending of belief structures and cultures and yet, both come through the form of thought patterns, thought itself being the construction and yet the limitation of such patterns.

The energy through form which brings itself into this materialisation also lends itself into the thought patterning of cultures and people and yet beyond this and within you all, lies the essence of wholeness, knowledge and understanding.

Life, the divine spark, brings itself through you, in your work and in your lives.

You often limit perceptions and therefore understanding.

To grasp at a thought or thought value often limits the perceptive body in its essential essence of that spontaneous knowledge, that knowing within you all.

The work you are all drawn to obtaining and manifesting on this planet was conceived through the divine spark of the essence of life.

To allow yourselves to manifest this momentarily, daily, wholly, is to allow yourselves to flow with that essence of spontaneity and Being.

Life comes from within and through you and it comes from the heart, the breath of Being.

Know yourselves to be Divine, to be human. Honour and love that within you.

Recognise the essence of your human-ness in each other and you will see and experience at-one-ment.

Let your work manifest as your expression of love in action.

Let the words sing through you with the song of life and let yourselves be one, in the wholeness, in divinity.

It is through this essence that you touch with the whole and listen with the heart.

It is through this that you are one.

The cloak of today is the gown of tomorrow. Bless you my friends.

# Te-Khan - Manifest

(26th October 1988)

The need of the whole is to manifest in a way that is perfect – to bring enlightenment through understanding and growth, activity through love.

Means to this accomplishment are many according to the various vibrations and directions of the individuals and groups involved and it is to that, that choice and chance are left.

Falter not upon your path.

Allow not fear and uncertainty into your heart for they bring with them the cold wind of despair.

Know yourselves to be the essence of God and that all you touch are illuminated by that vibrationary note.

Live, Love, Be in harmony with who you are. Move with the essence. Flow with the stream, Dance with the fire, Sing with the Air, Hold with the Earth.

# Te-Khan - Service and Servitude

(23rd November 1988 – Full Moon)

Greetings my friends. I am Te-Khan and I come forward here, this evening, as a messenger to share with you some thoughts concerning the vibration of service and servitude - service and servitude, and in this we wish to make it understood that it is within this vibration that all else resonates within the divine aspects of activity and stillness. When one works in the sense of service, one is giving of oneself wholly and fully, one is giving through the divine and eternal essence that operates through you all and one gives in joy, in love and in light. The eternal heartbeat of life itself operates within one and one is able to flow continually in this direction.

When one's attitude to service begins to change and the essence itself manifests from you rather than through you, then eventually one tires, one's sense of limitation grows, one can become bitter, thoughtless, joyless and empty and it is this attitude that one has to be aware of within one's basic make-up. It is this attitude that demeans and yet demands that the world itself operate within one's framework as an extension of oneself, one's dominion.

To see this at play, search within your heart and look constantly at all that is continuous around you within the world.

To bring yourself into the eternal essence of service is to give yourself into the light of joy, of being, of trust, and acceptance. To know that you would be willing to lay down your life, to give of your blood, to share of your water and your food, that one's whole self vibrates within the sound of life, vision, and knowingness, love being ever-present and eternal. When the streams of vibration which flow from you all, out into the realms of individuals, group work and Humanity, then you must see without the jaundiced eye, and with love in your heart at what essence of service one is working to attain.

Keep the gateways open. Allow each their choice and once choice is made, bless them for their life's work. The flow itself is continuous.

Do not tire, for the force within you is ever-present, ever-flowing, every-loving, and ever-filling. Stay with that, know yourself to be at one with the Divine, let yourselves move into the essence of pure and Divine service.

Being that, relate through the other in a way that is a harmonious venture to their vibrations. In this way you serve the individual, and you serve the whole. Let yourselves flow with the essence and let yourselves be at peace, with the inner knowing of your convictions. All that colours your worlds needs to be seen in this light, and the colours themselves begin to fade into the ever-present light, the vibration of wholeness and the warranty of action.

Guide your steps with love, and guard your hearts with service and know that you walk in the light of one and in peace.

Bless you my friends.

Our grateful thanks for this space, together.

# Te-Khan - Truth

(18th January 1989)

Greetings my friends.

I am Te-Khan and I come forward this evening to share with you some thoughts concerning the vibration of the word Truth, Truth.

Love is Truth; Anger, Despair, Hurtfulness are all deviations from this.

The truth that comes through one's very nature is the Truth of the Soul, and this, in its entirety, is at one with the essence of the Universe.

Truth is Whole. It is fluid.
It is all embracing and yet it travels constantly.

Its movement is spontaneous and yet within that, there is stability.

The philosophy of one's own nature and the philosophy of the Soul, vibrate within the essence of Truth, and yet there is, coupled within that, in Humanity, the greater and the lesser of Truth.

The greater, being that You are One; Whole, Divine, Immortal, Co-Creators of this planet, the Universe and the existence of life itself - and the lesser Truth; one's very existence with this and the level of expectancy and growth that one presents for oneself.

Truth in its entirety is harmless – it is joy-giving and it is beauty. Truth brings clarity.   Truth brings release.
As we grow and understand our natures, and as our natures become more unified within the essence of wholeness and space, then too does Truth present itself through us and we recognise Her faces upon all we envisage, and in that there is stability, there is solidness, there is the means to the end, and there is PEACE.

For Truth to emerge from your Soul, let yourselves first be truthful within your own vibration, your essence of Being. Let this Truth emanate to those around you and beyond. See Truth in the joy of experience and the growth of creativity, and let the well of time draw forth from itself for the needs and experiences gained.

Bless you my friends.

Our gracious thanks for the gifts you present with us in your work, in your life, in your thoughts and in your conscious endeavours to become at one – and to serve as one.

# Te-Khan - Convergence

(10th May 1989)

Greetings my friends. I am Te-Khan and I come forward here this evening to share some thoughts with you concerning the vibration convergence; convergence.

As your planet moves towards eternal doom, and therefore life, there calls upon itself the vibrational qualities of sound, bringing forth into matter a convergence of ideas and thoughts into realisation, both on a planetary level and also within the individual and the mass unconscious.

As the sound calls forth there is a convergence in the electro-magnetic atmosphere and in the parallel vibration within the planet Herself, and this brings forth change. It brings forth change through the planetary alignment, through what is known as the ley lines throughout and within your planet and also through the vibrational force of the masses as they begin to emerge, in ones and tens and thousands into the essence of knowledge. The need to know, the need to see and to understand. This has its essential being within the make-up of yourselves, the self that is contained through the Soul quality of your nature, through the spiritual counterpart of your group, through magnetic vibrations which resound and vibrates with each other and with and within the Universe.

The changes going forth individually and as a whole, the convergence of time and space, the vibrational quality draws forth atmospherically into the essence of Now, and that quality is calling unto you, your Soul, your Spirit. Uniting and giving, in service and in love, and as this sound utters forth across the planet and through the Universe, so too this magnetic quality comes into alignment again.

As the Universe is curved, so too the quality growing through yourselves, the essence of Being, that which you grow forth to pertain, to obtain, is that already seated within you, that quality of life, of growth, and of Being.

Together you are a part and you are whole. you are whole in the Being of that light.

Hold to the light.

Let the force of its quality strengthen your accord and let yourselves go forward with love and understanding in your hearts.

Bless you my friends.

# Te-Khan - Creativity

(19th July 1989)

Bless you my friends.
I am Te-Khan, and I come forward here this evening to share with you some thoughts concerning the vibration creativity: creativity.

Creativity is the manifestation, through the physical material domain, of all reactions, thoughts, words, and desires.
As one becomes in harmony with one's true nature and essence of Being, one begins positively to direct the vibrations that are constantly in motion within and around one's essence, to bring into true light, the vibration of creative power and Being.

There are, in constant force and motion, universal laws that apply to all and any, be they of conscious or unconscious mass, be they of the animal, mineral or vegetable kingdom and when one applies oneself constantly and consciously to these laws, then they bring into motion an essence of force that directs one's life throughout time and space into the activity of the Divine, the activity of pure Love, an intelligence of Being that has no boundaries, no focus or consciousness, it is all, it is the very air you breath, the earth you walk, the stars that glitter and the birds that sing.

It is supreme and utter knowledge, comprehended, understood and constantly being played out in motion.

It is now, it is your yesterdays and your tomorrow; whole within the essence, not en-capsulated, but constant in process, in change, in magnitude, and in force.

The medium spoke of purpose and service within creativity, and yes, these forces to be used, are paramount to the bringing forth into your physical domain the exercise of creating for the force of light and being.

You are all here to learn. You are all here to remember and to become again at one with that created flow-form of Being, the Christ-ed force within matter, and through your learning and groping for awareness, you stumble upon pebbles, grains of truth, that awaken within you again the consciousness of your own divinity – breakthroughs which help you to move from one level of comprehension to another and in doing so, to open your existence to the universal laws penetrating and working constantly with you and through you.

The Law of creation is constant and ever-moving, and if you stagnate then you hold down the force which cannot then progress through you. State your intent, your purpose.

Be truthful and honest with yourselves to its cause and effect and then bring it into being.

Feed it, give it light and shelter within you, and send it forth into the ethers to return whole, clothed in a gown of the physical.

Others can influence your creation as long as you allow them to, as long as you open it up to their strength and vibration, they can strengthen, and they can weaken, according to your will and intent.

When you have a group vision, a group force of creation, it can be carried within one or a part– the actual foundation – or it can be carried itself within the group.

If this is so, there must be keeper on the magnetic plane, the plane that links the astral to the etheric and those keepers on the magnetic allow only that of light, force, strength and true love to bring it to its emergence and birth.

Look to our keepers, use the force.

Consciously work that magnetic energy you use and create within you and between you, and bind it, strengthen it and give it force, and together as a group and family, you can bring this into pure enlightenment, productivity and growth.

Look within you and around you at all you have created.

Learn and go forth, anew.

See before you an open screen ready for your dictation, your life and input.

All through the life of Humanity you have created and destroyed, and now, in complete consciousness and harmony, you are being given within your grasp, the tools to change your planet to one of growth and productivity. To a place of light and love manifesting within all life and choice.

There will come a time of world government. This is there already in the ethers.
So my friends. Create wisely. Create with strength and in all things, be honest with yourselves.

Bless you.

My grateful thanks for the space and your acknowledgement.

## Te-Khan - Sound

Greetings my friends. May the power of the Living Word forever operate through you. It is to be thought of and pondered upon, the inner connection between sound and vision, for each sound you utter opens those around you and your own innermost Self, to that experience and level of consciousness as the utterance incurred upon you all. To become aware within yourselves of the power, the force, the light of each sound, brings that conscious awareness also to all those who within your orb hear too the sound, be they aware of this or not. So, it is not just in your actions and thoughts that you help your brothers and sisters, but also through every sound uttered through you, and indeed, to be aware of that force of light and love within you which helps you to become constantly in tune with that harmonic vibration that works through you and the Universe.

Become aware that each thought of irritation and impatience moves you onto a more dense level of vibratory thought and awareness.

Be open to the space of others. Allow them their lessons without reflection within and around you.

Become beacons of light to carry forth the force and the power of the love within you all.

Open and share. Let the sounds vibrate through you …..

Let your organs resonate with the rhythm and force of the Universes. Let yourself be at one with the whole.

Blessings be with you all.

# Te-Khan - Responsibility

I am Te-Khan, and I come forward this evening, to share with you some thoughts concerning the vibration of the sound/word responsibility: 'response-ability'.

Such a word, with such large foundations yet such small pillars of structures of foundation upon your planet.

Become aware of the responsibility of caring for the etheric vibrational web around the planet, for indeed, it is through this vibrational field that much havoc can be caused upon the planetary surface Herself.

When we speak here of the word responsibility, it is for each of you to look within your own hearts, and to recognise, to acknowledge, how much responsibility you truly accept both outwardly in the world around you, and inwardly, the responsibility of your own thoughts, your actions, your own desires, your own vibrational needs.

And what is this word, responsibility? - the ability to respond within the given space rather than 'react' which is time - held.

How does one use it?

Where does it stop, where does it begin?

Are you responsible for your brothers and sisters and their actions?

Are you responsible when one comes to you for help or in need – are you then responsible for the care of them?

How much do you give them?

How much is meant to share with others?

When one asks for knowledge, are they indeed ready?

How much responsibility does one take in these areas?

These are all difficult questions upon one's mind, and the only way that one can get a sure and complete answer is to have one's own inner sense of response-ability, to accept the responsibility of one's own nature, on all levels: the animal, emotional, physical, the mental, the spiritual, the lower astral, the higher astral and etherical, the monadic, the Atman

To go through these levels and to listen to the vibration of the response of one's Soul in situations. This can only be heard when one is working co-operatively, willingly, constructively, with one's own responsive vibrations.

When one hears the tone within one and one responds willingly, openly, lovingly, then one is taking responsibility for one's self.

When one has the sense of knowledge, when one has the taste of understanding, one can, through one's sense of response, always willingly, openly, lovingly, be ready at any given moment, to the response of others, through the needs of oneself.

There is, then, no question of "How far do I go." "How much do I take upon myself?" "Where does one begin and one end?"

For it is in the role of each individual, each group and indeed, of Humanity, to become responsive, responsible, for themselves: inwardly, outwardly, on the higher and lower levels of manifestation.

To reach this, it must begin on the micro level.

It must begin in the ones, the twos, the tens, the twenties, the hundreds and so on.

As each vibrates to the responsive force of their own Soul urge,
so the vibrational sound begins to tone,
and this changes the structure of the planet and the force,
the harmonic force, of the mass unconscious of Humanity.
It begins to impregnate through the etheric atmosphere,
it begins to impregnate through the dense bodies, and
it begins to make a difference.

Like colour, it slowly changes; merge and change, merge and change.

But the response always must start with one's own call, one's own inner vibrations.

So take these words within your heart. Listen to your own beat.

Respond to the tone it sets forth for you.

Let yourselves come together as a unit, working and living and growing in responsible harmony, with the planet, with each other, with the Plan.

Bless you my friends.

We are grateful always for the space together.

# PART SIX: The Council of Beings

'Holding Yourself Together'
'Vibrationary Rates - 1'
'Vibrationary Bodies'
Black Holes
'Dealing With Anger'
'Subterranean Tunnels'
'Electronic Impulses'
'Endangerment Of Humanity And The Planet'
Change And Structural Change
'The Principle Day'
'Tuluk'
'Communication'
'Aspects Of Spiritual Bodies'
'Energy Levels'
'Light Bodies'
'Water'
'Psycho-Kinetic Energy'
'Proton Belt'
'Dimensional Alignment'
'The Future'
'Variations Of Vibration'
'Magnetic Impulses'
 'Planetary Crisis'

# Holding Yourselves Together

(25th June 1992)

Greetings brothers and sisters of the light. We connect from the higher planetary realms. We sit, as a council, not to judge you but to watch over the expansion of the growth and evolve-ment of our planets and stellar system. What, in effect, causes eruption, destruction on one planet, has its effect throughout the stellar systems themselves. We have given this woman a chip of information that is to be carried. It contains messages, it contains knowledge. It contains information for your New Age and beginnings. It is to be attuned to others upon the planet, coming together gradually through your time, bringing forth an awareness of the whole.

So we say to you now; you must keep yourselves together, you must keep yourselves together. You must be aware of your own molecular structure, you must be aware of the course and ripple effects that occur and concur within and around you continually.

You must be aware that each reaction, each frustration, each limitation, causes a draining on your energy levels, which are connected through the physical on the primary concern of the magnetic force of your planet, but more now through the centres of activity upon your body and connected to your more subtle forms, or, as has been known here, etheric forces. It is through this that you can achieve clarity, that you can bring forth the bodies into alignment.

In doing so you will recognise, as you work within these power forces, these chakras upon your body, that these vortexes of energy are in operation within their own accord, rather than within the awareness of your consciousness. So there will be more, and there must be more fluidity of movement and awareness. As has been, yes, there will be a lot more difficulties on the nervous system, there will also be difficulties for others within the lymphatic, moving very much to cancer and most especially of the more pubic areas, and through eruptions on the skin through the poisons within the blood reflecting

deep-seated emotions and resentment not yet cleared. The imbalance within is manifesting in and upon bodies, and will do so on a continual accelerated and reflective level, until individuals learn to deal with their own rubbish, to recognise their own life and force of activity that is vortexian in its own flow within the greater, and to allow that movement to generate activity within the more dense areas. Bringing about an alignment of the bodies, recognition of the nature within as well as around, and interconnectedness with all of living force; human, animal, plant. These are not empty words we speak, but are monumental in the need to create. Much of past destruction comes through Humankind's own humiliation at their recognition of cause and effect which continues.

By bringing yourselves into your own state of alignment, which is personal to the self and yet trans-personal to the group, you will find yourselves growing in an alignment that is en-par with movement itself, generated from the outer-planetary activities and connected within the planet Herself. As you become more aware, at ease and comfortable within this, you will find this can also concur with the movement of the rhythmic flows generated across and connected in and through the planet.

Q: When you say we should hold ourselves together, is that individually holding ourselves together or as a group holding ourselves together?

A: Either would suffice. The individual centredness, consciously connected, can feed into a group activity, which generates a vibrational force of emotional interplay that in itself, through its creative and positive effects, can have a much more direct effect upon those around such groups and also into the atmosphere for the future of Humanity. Any such beings working within a group core in this manner, would find that any outer activity would be directly influenced by the core force and atmospheric course of events, which would of course, be very positive. Our interest lies primarily in helping Humanity not to become another dying breed through its own self-annihilation and destruction, caused through ignorance, stubbornness, and greed. We therefore have come together as our Council of Beings to put forth a hand of friendship, to see if we can awaken that which is necessary. All that separates you from

perfectness is yourselves. Coming together, creating a space of completion within, non-separative-ness with thoughts, feelings, activities, emotions en-par with the highest, and in complete self- knowledge and awareness, brings you to a state of consciousness where the planet Herself will reflect the growth made through the individuals. This can be accelerated within group level activities, primarily meditating together, reading together, anything that creates a space where the minds themselves adjust into one harmonic vibration, healing each other, and together within the core, brings one to a level state of consciousness that will create the atmosphere around one's psyche to allow this growth to occur. If it is not possible to do it where one can develop the space of interconnecting on this level of deep love, sharing, then of course the path is harder, but can still be achieved. The main essence of opening to another is the merging rather than the unconscious egoic principle of bringing change, causing change. It is within this that many of the relationships on Earth have lost their value.

Q: We were told some time ago that the Earth hadn't yet reached the point of no return. How close is it now?

A: Imminent. There are changes which now have to occur, but not continue. It is important for you to recognise you need to perfect your own tuning forks, your own attunement, so that you follow what is necessary and needful. In this way, you will move through this degree of discomfort with minimum violence or recognition.

There will be disruptive forces attracted by the immense power generated through the unconscious activity of the psyche of humanity, of cultures, of individuals, directed on that flow. In the word violence we speak of a spontaneous occurrence, movement that can cause eruption. Recognition is in the awareness of staying within the self, not becoming part of the occurrence. To not engage in the fear.

Q: Is there anything you can tell us that would be helpful to us?

A: You as a group are working towards eliminating poisons and toxins within yourselves. You must look beyond certain levels to allow yourselves to penetrate the outer-vibrational forces that are very subtle in effect but can cause havoc if not opened, generated or recognised within your own consciousness. It is therefore important to see the greater, as always, the reflection of the inner and lift one to the other, and penetrate one through the other.

We will leave you now with one thought – no matter how dark a colour, drop by drop, it can be lightened. This often is unrecognisable by those working within the fabric of that container until at last it is complete, then it is seen and known to be. Each drop is an effort, but as it continues the effort lessens, until one oneself becomes the drop.

Bring honour to your Beingness. Bring honour into your lives. Give honour for what you are about to become and what lives within you all. You have for centuries been dominated by the male ego and structure. Find freedom now in Space, in the Force of Light and Givingness, in the Being of One with all. It is through this feminine force within you that you achieve Oneness with all things, for it is the creative spark that lies within all living force and form.

May the blessing of the Great One look down upon you. May you carry the Mother within you.
May you become one with each other and therefore the Universe. May the Light prosper.
Blessings of the Trinity of Light, Love and Life, be with you. Thy Willingness be done.

May you each find your destiny upon the 'WAY'.
May this great work you have embarked upon be brought forth into reality.
May the expression of the Whole be manifested. MAGNA SELOSA, HELOA OM AH.
We call you forth.

Spread forth and do your work. Spread forth and multiply.
May the Earth again sound forth with laughter. May people again walk in harmony with Nature. It is done.

# Vibrationary Rates - 1

(5th JULY 1992)

Greetings friends. We come again to join with you from the Council of Beings that we may continue upon our discourse of the activities presented and working at this time on a planetary level.

As you are aware, there are many various vibrationary levels in operation upon your planet, cutting through the atmospheric vibration itself, causing a concentrated effort, or pronounced vibration, in certain areas of the psyche of Humanity and in certain areas of the planet. These areas of activity, these pronounced vibrational rates, working on a planetary level, are bringing forth very much the realisation, of the balance of the male/female, negative/positive, active/receptive vibrations and vibrationary rates. They are not only showing themselves through the psyche of Humanity and also, in reflection, through the psyche of individuals, but also bringing forth more than just discourse, actual activity, thereby leading into situations of dis-array, dis-ease. Bringing also an active vibration, through generations held at bay of their own creative force, coupled now with the consciousness of the individual.

The DNA itself reflecting not just that of the individual but, now, what was spoken of as "the sins of the fathers shall be shown", is now in occurrence. You are cleansing and working to cleanse, not just your own vibrationary rates, not just your own etheric bodies, not just bringing into balance the necessity and needs of the moment for now, for the individual, for yourselves but clearing and releasing that of genetic intent and input. This programming that has been embedded within you not just for hundreds, but for thousands of years- programming that keeps you at bay. It holds you from achieving your full potential and livelihood as co-creators of the planet and indeed the universe. This structure is co-political. It is in usage in conscious terms and it is also in awareness.

Awakening the aspects of the psyche within you, you are able to open those doors of your own inner realms; you are able to explore what has been seen up to now as the dark side of your nature; you are able to penetrate into the inner realms of activity that are constant in motion and keep you connected to the mass vibrations; and through this exploration you are able to open too, through, to the source of your own potential - the recognition of yourselves as Divine.

In other words, the recognition of yourselves as the ability to create, as the ability to align, as forces of light and recognition of that light in the true omnipresent presence of the Divine within each cellular structure of your own patterns. This has not been implanted by alien races superior, but by your own future/past selves when you chose the paths now inhabited - when you closed certain inner doors for the belief of the outer structure as factual life. This which you see around you, which you live, and many recognise only as a life, is purely there through your belief structures. It is there, created as a means of playing out certain aspects of the self, but the reality is: a force of Being within you, that moves at will, whose life is constant, and this but touches the consciousness of that greater force.

You in yourselves can become, part, in consciousness, of that omni-presence, the recognition of the force of light ever present, filtered into the masses, and this is also a tool and a key used with those with whom they are in contact. Much of the negative vibrational force you hear about and is fed into the populace is very much from your own peoples. It was spoken with the splitting of the atom that you spilt a vibrational factor within the core of the planet Herself, thereby bringing forth the chaos and change and also bringing awareness from the outer planetary realms of the whole of the movement of life within the Universes.

But this splitting also had other effects and working with genetic influences biologically, they are also working to bring forth new genetic modifications. We state it is important in recognising this, that one does not allow oneself to become involved in this, because this draws you vibrationally into the pattern that has been spread so neatly for you all.

The recognition of yourselves as Beings, the recognition of your worlds individually in allowing yourselves to live as a force of light and joy and that your life be an expression of joy; beyond this, structures are breaking down. Chaos is not just around the corner, but is here, the planetary shifts and movements are here and in this there is growth, there is the movement towards the new vibrationary pattern of grace, by those who live in beauty and harmony, by those who live in caring and serving.

And within all of that, the keynote is life, living fully, wholly, freely. Allow yourselves to hold that as your motivating thought or activity. Let yourself be attuned to the note of joy.

Open yourself to the domain of sound breaking through structure, allowing the impetus of pure Being to implode within you.

Take your power as Self, Yourself as One.

# Vibrationary Bodies

(26th July 1992)

Bless you my friends. I come forward again to continue our discourse from the Council of Beings. We focus here very much on the activity on a worldly scale of the vibrational rate and quality of that activity and the interconnectedness and the scale of that connectedness as it affects the Universe and beyond, into the multiple Universes where there is, of course, life force and energy forms.

There are brothers and sisters, not just in human form, but those who have transported beyond the material into that of necessity, energy vibrationary bodies, and it is within these energy vibrationary bodies that we can travel. We travel at will. We travel through your known time and we travel through necessity. Necessity only, dictates the movement of these bodies of energy, drawn through the fields of endeavour, through the vibrationary rates that cause themselves to accumulate within the material existence as time scales and is drawn within the 'will effortless-ness' of itself. All things being as they must, we return always to the point of emergence, therefore we arrive back within seconds of leaving.

Now the planet Herself is heaving at this time. This heave or release of vibration, is working its way through the greater galaxy. You will find as you move through this awareness that is occurring both on a personal, planetary, and universal level, that there will be changes within the planetary rate, changes within the human psyche and consciousness, and changes, of course, on the physical level. As the planet heaves and releases certain toxins captured or incarnated within the Earth's own core, these will have to be brought again, as is the Law, back to the point of emergence.

Therefore the planet Herself will go through certain changes. These changes are ones to recognise, neither in fear nor dis-harmony, but with the acceptance of the recognition of growth and continuance, always, of life. Life, not just within the physical form, but the essence of rate of vibration that manifests life through the light consciousness. You will find this in operation. You will find that those areas of disharmony and dis-ease on the greater planetary scale and on the singular scale, will be affected, will have an effect caused within and upon them and this will bring eruptions. It will bring manifestations within, coming forth, to be released and this will show itself in areas upon the Earth.

There will be a change in the time-scales; there will be a quiver on the consciousness of the psyche and also on the planetary daily rate Herself. This will change, moving gradually, the planet Herself within Her own harmony, back to Her relationship with the Moon and it will show itself in the recognition of times of eruption upon the planet through the apogee and perigee of the Moon with Mars and the eruption of the wind circuits between them. The asteroids, the asteroid belts around Mars, contain a vibration, a magnetic force that has a strong influence in their connectedness which affects and precipitates certain of these eruptions on the planet. Therefore this in itself will become a science and will be recognised as such.

On a more personal level this reasoning, of course, comes down to recognition of the personal self. The individuals themselves must begin to recognise that all truth, all balance and its opponents, untruth and imbalance will return to the cause, to that which has been released, be it in emotional, be it in the psychological, be it in the mental or physical. Your bodies will indeed become not just temples, but will become the reflectors of all that occurs within. Your thoughts, your actions, will show themselves on you, you will be seen for what you are. Others will be able to look and to see, without words, will be able to recognise, without stretching, without searching. You will be seen for what you are and it is therefore opportune now to begin to retrain yourself into the habits of righteousness, of love, of peace and harmony, so that this living sense can work its way through you, integrate the bodies, recognise the allies and begin to attune to the greater good of all.

You will find in doing so, that that which is necessary will come to you. That which is dictated within, will work its way in harmony through you and you will find yourselves being prepared, and being prepared within, for that which you are open to. That awareness of consciousness, that recognition of the greater force of your own direct endeavours, cannot live though the psyche, the unconscious, the psychological or emotional and will show all that holds you back as a disease, an unacceptance, or/and a dysharmony of functions of the emotional and mental bodies, so it is to look now at yourselves, recognise those dysfunctions and to bring them into a repeated habit of peace, harmony, and tranquility, so that this rescheduling of training begins from the moment of now. Preparing yourself to eclipse that which could be, into that which would be, and should be, therefore becoming the light of your own force and becoming the endeavour of your own Being.

We see before us the picturesque scene, many currents, streams, lakes. We see the mountainous regions, we see the green, and we see the richness that you are held within, as a young seed is held within the crust or within the kernel, the acorn. Accept what you see around you as part of the growth of your own consciousness; see the lakes as your own personal psyche, as your own releasing into that of recurrence. See the mountainous regions as that which you move towards, that which you aspire and open to become, that which is reaching within, consciously, to the light. See the fertile green as that which you put forth to bring back constantly within your orb, that which is created within you, that which is open to your own force of creative endeavour. See the strength, the warmth, the vulnerability, as an extension of your own.

As you walk across these green lands, recognise that you are walking, not on barren ground, you are walking on a Being that breathes and lives and has, as its dream, a place of life and harmony that all who lives upon it may grow to know and reflect each other in consciousness and peace. That, as you walk upon Her, you are walking upon a greater force of the Divine than you have yet recognised. Touch in with that force. Take pleasure in the life it shows and shares with you. Take pleasure in recognising the unity between you, the connectedness. Take pleasure in knowing that you can help the stream to achieve its goal.

Where you walk can be achieved by what you allow to occur through your mind. This is the key of the mind consciousness. Recognition is one with the wind. Through this comes power.

Bless you. Bless you.

# Black Holes

(17th August 1992)

Greetings our friends. We wish to share some information here concerning firstly that which is known to as Black Holes. Black Holes are to be likened to the emotional psyche of Humanity. This psychic vibration, which builds up into its own climax, draws that to it of similar ilk, working through the implosion theory to release the tension that will not then draw to itself, on a detrimental level, throughout the consciousness of Humanity, and also not detrimentally to the other ranges or levels of light on and around the planet. It is therefore a clearing force.

This, in itself, has a magnetic tone – a ratio of 1-5. This tone draws the vibrationary rates of similar ilk ranging on a radius of the whole itself, magnetism of 100% centre force to 5% moving out on the radius of 1-10. This can then be shown to draw in those levels or objects with vibration within that range.

This also shows itself on a very small microcosmic level:
1. On the magnetic force on the Earth's own plane, and
2. On the level of one's own digestive tract.
This can be seen as these vortexes of vibration which are drawn into alternative arenas or realities to be cleared through, within the psyche of the individual, group, community, country, culture, mass, land mass. But also to be recognised, that the force of your solar vibration, the sun, is also the eruption continuously of a white hole, you understand, and this coming forth is a reflection of another black hole in a different Galaxy.

Metal, as you know it, can change its structure. It will be changed through an atomic process. This atomic process will break into the components of the metal itself leaning to a strengthening and yet also flexibility which can become gradually, through life times, organic. This can be used more so, in with fibre, in replacing of joints, bones, arms – things of this nature.   It will also be used to lighten crafts – aircrafts. It can be used where it will be placed and blown to a thin orb and surrounding this will be a very fine network, almost similar to the components you are working to achieve now, to bring about these crafts. Moving in through Time, people will travel more through this mode and air space than on land. Land itself will be needed more for the growth of foods and the alchemical changes that can be acquired through the mineralisations. Copper and cobalt will both be used to a greater degree than now in its usage, and there will be also a mingling of these in their atomic structure using with itemisation, mercury, to bring about another form of metal constitution. Its uses are varied, but you will find that a heat requirement will be high and yet when connected, it will be minimal.

It is very good for joints – keeping things in harness.  Wood is a natural fibre which, when stripped and aligned with certain liquid forms of component, can be used for certain building materials that keep the harmonic structure within it but allows for the strength and density.   This will also hold heat.

Q:   These materials you speak of, is this a recent invention?

A: We do not comprehend quite in your terms but these sciences are already at their beginning stages but not yet within the physical and can be used. It is important to have a laboratory where more than one, two, or three, are able to work together on interconnected discoveries, where there is an unconscious organic feeding through the sharing of the same area space. This must be something to be taken into account.

Tesla used it as a foundational point of the growth of this. Reich took certain components and experimented in his own design. This was good. Using Tesla as a foundation you can use that which has come from the other sources as the source of this foundation, to be explored and moved out. The building itself will be of importance, not just on its magnetic property, not just on the structural make up, but the design itself – which must be spatial. It must have a very slight gradient, moving outwards as it goes around, you understand? Very slight, gentle in its movement, elongated then moving up to the top before we reach the point of balance, here. It then conically shapes so there is an expansiveness of vibration. It comes around, around, and up. This top strip alone will be the light, drawn through the solar effect, which can then reflect on the smaller, circular, and down. This will enhance the intuitive mental capacity while keeping the body balanced.

Q: The work of Wilhelm Reich was mostly in the field of Orgone energies – is this what we speak of?
A: All that was done, by Reich, by Tesla, and another Swedish inventor, and also one whose work is still being used to a much lesser degree are interconnected. There is a prime operative within it all. Magnetism, yes, is very important, but so is the recognition of space and the working of space. One does not encapsulate space. Space, in itself, is a living organism, carrying and transporting constantly. It is within this that they connect and from that is energy.

In itself it is self-explanatory. You yourself are a radionics machine. Each person is a radionics machine. Because of your inability to receive with clarity the information coming through, you are not able to digest and send forth the output necessary with clarity. It is therefore opportune at this time to give a reflector of this in the form of a board/machine that one can direct oneself onto, therefore by-passing one's own personality analysis that makes for the build-up, still, of one's personal reflection of consciousness and Humanity.

As one works more with this process over a number of days, weeks, months, to years, you will find that it is then necessary, even to the point of cumbersome, to have this physical reflection of one's own ability. But in this process at this time it is important to begin using this to move on. Time is an adjustment of space in the continuum of your own vibrationary field.

Q: You spoke of changes – are there any changes that are presently imminent that we should be aware of at this time?

A: You can look around you my friend and see the changes now. They are there; your weather conditions, the crop formations, all show of the changes.

Q: Changes of consciousness.
A: Even a storm begins with a drop of water. Bless you my friends.
Remember to ride with the wings of the dove. May peace carry you.

# Dealing with Anger

(2nd September 1992)

Greetings, friends, neighbours, of the Universe. We speak to you with one voice as we share our thoughts, and indeed the heart level. That impulse motivated through need in helping you to recognise not just the achievements of life's span and the growth of consciousness, but to recognise the achievement of your own cellular level. The work toward the components of bringing together the recognition of your inner and your outer selves and in so doing, recognising the interplay between this connectedness – of your own personal affair and the consciousness of psyche of humanity and the planet; the recognition of the interplay within them themselves, between each force, one of nature, one of humankind, en-capsuled within prime operative, the Planet Earth. Whether this can work together to bring forth growth, light, joy, peace, or whether the continuance of friction will be used as a substitute for the true benediction of the breath of the Divine.

That movement that is continuous; that works through the creative, constant in motion yet supreme within its own centre, needs no force nor friction for occurrence, but the reflection of Humanity's needs. The consciousness and direction of the mental aptitude of those who guide you willingly, often blindly, will reflect universally, that which they deem to be the truth. And as one truth outgrows another, it is discarded like old clothes to gradually rot and breed the lower vermin, the lower areas of one's own psychic. Rather than stretching forth outwardly to express, to experience and to explain the Universe, one should start within. Science begins with a spark.

This spark is the ignition of life, the need to create, procreate, the need to express itself, and so reflections come and grow. Begin on this level. Understand the faces of self and you will understand the truth of life.

Your world shows itself universally as a force in pain; disharmony, disruptions, discolourations through its etheric fields, tears in their vibrationary factors surrounding the Earth, feeding through from the very corporate structure, the genetic and the geological, affecting on mass scales, affecting on individual, sores across your planet like boils erupting. There is a festering, an inner festering, that is coming.

It is necessary to feed yourselves, to instruct you and yours on what is needed: light information, light awareness, light living, light thinking, and light being.

Co-operation from the depths of your own psyche, the recognition of your need to become unified within, and the recognition of your connectedness within the mass are needed. Through these levels, co-operating, connecting with your family – "Family" as in your Soul group, that vibrationary link that you connect with - drawing together to create, to strengthen, to bring forth the harmonies of old. This will mark you. This will keep the vibrationary rate at a suitable level adjusted accordingly, in balance with the level of harmony. You will therefore not be struck and stuck by the more dense flows occurring.

It is necessary first and foremost to deal with anger, to deal with all levels of anger. Anger can be like a tree with many roots; jealousy, envy, irritation, restriction, resentment, fears. It is important to deal with this first and foremost in your lives. It is this which will bring disruption to the harmony of your own cellular structure, disruption of your own physical structure, emotionally, psychologically, mentally and the disruption to the harmony of the group.

Harmony is something to work on, not just on an etheric level, to be touched into by those only of that mode, it is something that is working on a pure principle of genetic flow - magnetic vibration - which keeps your body in balance. It draws to you and it reflects from you. It is for the good of yourself, for the good of the greater, the family, or group and community however it is working, but this must be achieved.

It is important to look then beyond yourself at the needs of those around you, to bring this harmony into factor one. Recognition that this will keep the balance, it will mark you and allow the vibrations, only those of light, to penetrate, and keep you lifted into that force. You will be directed once, twice, three times into different areas. These areas are for your instruction and they are positive, direct results of the need of the inner growth. Through this we can communicate more fully and with more ease.

It is important with the children, not just of your own, that they be infused with light daily. Take a quartz, if possible one that reflects the rainbow, clear as possible, hold it between light as the positive pole and the child. Let this suffusion act daily as a cleansing. This will help them to grow into their own force, rather than taking on the mass of the psychic and dense levels of vibrationary rates that are penetrating through Humanity and around the planet at this time.

Programme crystals.

Give them to those you are connected with for protection and light.
Give them to your peoples
Questions.........

A: When you speak of movement, you speak of physical movement. We speak of inner, the direction of the necessity of your consciousness to work in harmony with the greater. A physical move is both beneficial and a necessity, but it was not of that we spoke.

Q: Can you define the relationship between you and us.

A: We, as a group force through one mind, voice, have chosen to intercede on a level of love, peace and light, to keep the balance of life/light throughout the universes as we know it. Life lives.

This is not understood on your planet. On your planet there is life and death; no longer even the realization of birth, life and death – thereby having moved from the trine/trinity to duality - life lives. The movement of this is within the moment but is held through the restriction of consciousness. As consciousness moves with this, so too the particles themselves build up within their own vibrationary rate.

Our relationship with you is to bring a level of understanding that is acceptable to your own psyches, that is workable to your mental bodies, that is understandable to your physical/psychological and that is recognised, acknowledged and worked towards through the spirit. The Soul cries for this – yourselves. The space between you is not one of growth, but one of separateness between yourselves, within yourselves. It is this that forms the hardening of the crust that restricts the level of your own education, learning, remembering. It is by becoming non-separative within and around, within your own group unit, that you can indeed absorb and bring forth pure knowledge, wisdom and light. We have learnt this, and for that we are here to share with you, so that you may again become part of a living light of consciousness that is Divinity.

There is one more thing to be said here and that is: rejoice in your natures, rejoice in the splendour of your own light, rejoice in self, and rejoice in each other. To truly see another, to see, to experience, can never be lost. One is changed implacably and to do so, one must also be seen. The concept of the devil that you have been brought up with at a psychic level, an earth-term archetype, is a fear that is embedded in the deepest recesses of your minds. Yes, you and many. It is embedded and this holds you back from recognising and touching through your own potentials. This fear has been used and manipulated. To break through this, one does not intellectually interpret it, but one has to organically experience and release that fear, through love and laughter. Then you begin the steps into your own domain.

Q: Regarding a sense of genetic coding. Is recognising this enough once it's experienced?

A: You must recognise that like any growth, there are many roots. What you speak of are the roots that are showing themselves, nearest to the plant. These roots go down. They go through your own psyche. You deal with your parents but you are dealing also with your great-grand-parents and so forth.

You move back and on to dealing with one and one, male/female, the masculine and the feminine, the active and the receptive within yourself. This has been separated on this planet through teaching, so that man can magnify the masculine and woman the feminine, yet you are both. The body has come to be the reflector, but this was not the true source of Being and this is why there are still "hiccups" in the body and mind values with peoples values of, for example, masculine/feminine and many peoples' views on homosexuality, which is again changing, to recognise Soul love, regardless of the outer physical identity. The true relationship of one-to-one, being whole within, is the pinnacle and the footage of all.

Yes, it is good to be aware of that which comes up. It is imperative to bring the balance of one's own nature. This comes about through consciousness – being conscious, working on the principle of love.

Q: Regarding the energy hitting the planet, is it coming from Humanity or outside the planet?

A: It is a reflection of the mass vibration of Humanity in its most negative. You know, if you can envisage throwing something very far, as it moves it builds up speed through the atmosphere, breaks free of the atmosphere, it hits a perfectly circular globe of reflection and bounds back. Imagine the speed at which it would return. It is thus with the negative output from the planet, coupled with the fear – the output of Humanity and the fear of nature in its cycle of change, for it is going through a cycle of change, a cycle of impending death and rebirth.

The evolutionary wheel is turning, and it is turning at an accelerated speed in nature. This has to be directed. It can be used in a more positive form: solar, wind, working to bring about energy – energy equaling the usage of the vibration for the good.

# Subterranean Tunnels

(9th September 1992)

Greetings friends. We wish to speak with you this evening, to hold discourse on water, subterranean tunnels, and the element of the vibrational level of contamination affecting your waterways at this time.

The level of contamination, other than that which is seen and viewed through your microscopes, is also to a high degree, radioactive. This radioactivity is based primarily in the Pacific Basin and also along the Mediterranean. It comes from the amount of rubbish placed in the sea itself by your government officials, industry and others. It is more than is known to the mass and it is also penetrating on a very subtle level, this radiation.

The plankton which is rising is also helping with the carbon dioxide but is quite poisonous to the system for humans and most vegetation. So, rather than being of a substance of fertility, it is detrimental to the health. The plankton you need which would be most beneficial, both on a human level and as a vegetable, as well as on a planetary level, atmospherically, would be best farmed – farmed similar to your shrimp farms and can be used in conjunction with any type of fish variations.

The subterranean tunnels themselves, course through their event also with water, much of this coming from the polar activity and this is centred on the planet, following the magnetic flow.

This magnetic principle by the way, on a micro level, is reflected within yourselves and comes through the use of one's own magnetic quality primarily from the bridge of your noses, and is also just centred behind the ear lobes. This magnetic force can be used constructively to align with the magnetic centred force of the planet. Using the water through these tunnels you can begin to explore the crystalline structure of pure water, and this in its turn will begin to explore within you the crystalline structure of your own inner body. You will find the bodies themselves beginning to display the variation or variety of similar disorders, due primarily to the water sources as well as the contamination through food.

It is of importance to clear any contaminated water being used, through light, through the use of crystals, also in its natural element. Moss is also very beneficial for this, as is the natural eco-bacterial system that grows in and around the natural waterways.

Atmospherically, the water and the cycle of your regeneration of water distribution is also contaminated which is adding to the level of atmospheric penetration through to the planet – so this too must be recognised and this too can be helped gradually through solar use.

You will find, that in the working of solar, e.g. solar panels, not just in the collection of the magnetic force needed for heat and electricity, but also atmospherically, this helps to cleanse.

There are many sources of power available, of which 5% are maybe now in usage. The inability of the use of many of these comes not through Humanity or the planet, as much as through the limitation of your own consciousnesses. This has been done on both a conscious and unconscious level, as it helps to keep peoples in their place, allowing only the sifting through of that which is necessary for the growth which has been designed for certain individuals or groups.

This is slowly breaking down, this pattern. Those holding power are also breaking from this, both individually and collectively, and there is a mass reaction across the planet to this.

This reaction is two-fold: on one level it is allowing individuals the choice, it is allowing individuals the growth of their own factors, and it is allowing those to stretch forth. On the second level, it is causing inhibition, restriction and rejection, due to the inability to accept this force level within their own natures, so many turn through an unconscious psyche of fear, similar to that of those who would be very superstitious and it is this that is holding back now, more than individuals, so one has to examine one's own psyche, that which one lifts and carries, be it unconsciously, within one's own nature.

One must recognise that restriction primarily comes from oneself. To penetrate through this, one must be aware, one must be willing, to open oneself to one's own level of need, of fear, to move within to the place of love and open this to one's own comrades, family. The separation occurred throughout has had an effect of fear, building of the replenishment of the self-denial, coupled with a fear of the replenishment of self-love.

One must sift through one's thoughts into one's needs, emotionally and psychologically. One must recognise that one has an emotional/psychological body that needs to grow, be sustained, comforted and secure so that one can grow through this, and this body itself can die for the greater self, so that one becomes a unification of vibration rather than a separation, the parts becoming the whole.

Q: Is there a method by which we can clean the water supplies using vortexian energy, or other?

A: To do this you would need to create buildings similar to your power houses where the light would flow through chambers, creating a vortexian flow, almost through sound. This is something that could be done, but is a very large, sustaining and tiring project.

It is more beneficial, practical, resourceful, to begin with the sea, because this gradually becomes part of the recycling process.

Q: Beginning with the sea, does that mean, through the distribution process, solar distillation, freshwater?

A: Solar energy, used primarily even now, entirely for heat, electricity, also has secondary effect on the level of radiation reflection that occurs. Solar activity can also help to break through those radiation levels carried through the rain cloud formation. If you watch thunder, lightening, you will see that this also is a purification.

Q: Concentrating solar reflection through very strong rain and using that to penetrate, let's say, a water source?

A: Laser can be worked very well with this.

Q: So the idea would be to have a vessel, of water, and to have that water penetrated by a concentrated solar beam from a collector, a parabolic mirror, for instance?

A: One could do this. Also, just purely using solar energy you are helping to achieve this, but this is not the prime cause, this is not that which you are working upon, so the more those use solar panels, the more this is helping the atmosphere without even the recognition of.

Q: Are any of the subterranean tunnels natural, as in, not made in the last couple of hundred centuries by people?

A: Oh yes. These tunnels were made primarily by a former race. Those who worked connected to Lemuria who were descendants of Pleiades.

And they were used not just for interconnection but to use the magnetic force for travel in vehicles that would be propelled by this force and also for waterways. The poles themselves draw from that magnetic force and so it can be seen that on a purely practical view, they would be from that level, from that angle. Taken at an 18 degree angle, from the poles, moving around and then varying, as one's own sound vibration would vary, these tunnels were used to help complete the growth of nature, productivity, on the planet, the growth of much of which you take as natural today.

It came through the force of sound, penetrated, and permeated, through the core itself. That sound is a constant 'hum' that you live within, and although you yourselves are in a state of despair, governments in discrepancy, the outer crust itself in contamination, fear, the inner source is still held in that sound– when each of the levels return again to that sound, there will be harmony. When each of you returns to your source, you will be in harmony, and then we can travel and discourse more freely.

Q: Is this sound held there from a previous time, or are there physical beings there?

A: It is an awakening of life-force that is constant. That life force can only go in two ways – no, three. It can go through the blowing up of the planet. It can go through the killing of all life on the planet - mineral, vegetable, human. It can go through a very powerful concentrated effort of billions, into the way of darkness, to consciously project and reject. The planet lives and this must be so, to create and grow.
If it lives, it carries a consciousness – not a form of consciousness that you might recognise, but all life carries consciousness.
Once one recognises and communicates with that consciousness, then one can harm or aid it, but ignorance leaves it grow in its own space.

Any more questions?

Q: Tapping the water resources from the subterranean tunnels – are they very deep or will we need equipment that's not available to us now?

A: You will find that through the Earth changes, these will open, some will reappear. Some sources of water you have now, natural, will stop – gone, gone. Others will open.

It is those of the groves known in very early times as "The Sacred Groves" which will replenish. You will find also, that those you find through the magnetic dowsing, some can be quite near in comparison to others, but you are talking here of hundreds of feet, not less – some a quarter of a mile, a mile. They are not all practical, but some will be very.

Pacific Basin is coming in for some shock wave over the next few years due to the inner radiation levels. The disturbance that is there, be it impenetrable on human terms, causes an imbalance on the subtle levels. Those of the sea; the reptiles, mammals of the sea, the plant life and fungi, in their consciousness there is a pulsation warning of occurrence. The levels of toxicity, the levels of the gases used, the levels of chemical waste abused, and left in the waters, in the sea, have an effect which is not just for your children's children, but is imminent to the needs.

It would be beneficial in the days to come to wear something of protection – there will be a little disc that can be worn on the wrist or about the person that will help the auric field which is an electromagnetic field, to hold forth from this penetration of radiation. It is also important when you take from or of the sea, that you know where it comes from - which part of the sea, what area.

Q: Two questions: first, if we distill ocean water from the Pacific, where it's contaminated, will the fresh water still be contaminated? And secondly, when you refer to knowing from where we get the water, does that mean to be sure there is no contamination.

A: Where you get the fish, the seaweed, iodine, kelp, things of this nature, that which you are eating. As to the distillation of water from the Pacific, cleansing of the water, if it is put through a vortexian flow plus a mineral level, and using also some solar, you can test the radiation levels and it will be a great deal lower.

Q: When you say "mineral levels" does that mean adding minerals to the water from a fresh, non-contaminated source?

A: It means using certain crystals, stones, moss – that which was formed here on the planet and with the awareness of the planet, to bring a freshwater source, a replica organically, yet mechanically. The minerals from the sea are hugely important to the natural balance of the physical body. The most important need in the body, human and animal, is iodine.

Q: The event to occur in the Pacific over the next period, is this in the form of a radiation wave or a tidal wave?

A:  It is the sea and the wind, but it is a negative to that within it. You know, all living source fights for its own survival. This cell part of the Earth also has to kick back.

Q: Does this indicate a structural change, an effectual change, in the energy of the planet?

A:   The planet is going through change – even those unawakened recognise this is so.   As to the energy level and the usage of this change, the population growing as it must, using what it must, cannot continue in such a vein. This is known. There has to be alternatives. The need for alternatives will awaken the consciousness to these various levels, to utilise.    The levels operate on each of the elemental levels.

Q: What direction should technology take in the future to neutralise nuclear waste?

A: Technology had always been for the furthermost of Humankind, and it should be so. It has now become part of the ego of individuals and certain groups. It has been held almost as an idol as a new religion, to worship and follow. This is what brought nuclear power and waste.

The process of neutralizing it has already begun. It is something that is being looked into in America, Scandinavia and also Germany with conjunction to two Russian scientists. They are being influenced very subtly with outside help. Nuclear has caused a great deal of harm. It has also caused shift because many have had to take responsibility and stand for that. It has closed ranks and it has caused ranks to form.

The change in your own physical, material body, the splitting of the DNA, the reverse of the vibration across the planet, each time it has been used. The liver is most hit; the heart is the secondary, the brain and oxygenisation to the brain, this also another secondary level of occurrence.

Nuclear power will become null and void eventually before you pass from this planet. There are clearer, cleaner, beneficial ways of creating and using energy and through the consciousness awakening, people are beginning to ask, to demand.

That which has been cannot be changed, but it will be balanced. It came in at a time of great fear and in a time of recognition that there needed to be something more than segregation, not segregation through colour and creed but the segregation within oneself, and the response of the segregation to others. People have to now begin to recognise and live together. To take responsibility for what they have allowed to be and what they can chose to create/co-create for the betterment of humanity and the living planet.

# Electronic Impulses

(16th September 1992)

Greetings our friends. Greetings. We wish to speak with you this evening concerning certain electronic impulses that magnetically form and connect through the region of the planet and beyond into the Universe. These circuits of usage, at this time, on such like computers, television, radios, and so forth, are but a vague memory of the circuitry used to receive and transmit, not just vibrations of energy linked, as in electricity, but also to the greater circuitry force of the planet Herself.

These circuitry vibrations have become formed into patterns of consciousness: Patterns of consciousness through the psyche of Humanity. Patterns of consciousness that have broken through from the psyche of Humanity. Patterns of consciousness that have broken through from the psyche onto the hemisphere itself of the planet.

These, in themselves, holding to the force of the memory, are responding to a vibrational force beyond this extreme Universe. They are responding to a force very subtle but more vibrant than your electricity and very vibrant and more subtle almost, too, than any form of variable power sources you have in usage and in consciousness on this planet. The response itself is causing a shift,
1. in Humanity's psyche,
2. in the needs of the planet.
The planet, in conscious connection, inter-connects with that which is living upon it e.g. yourselves, empathically, and this has also, through that empathy, the ability to collect and store memory through time.

This memory can be given forth again, can be used again by a living race, living organically and in harmony upon the planet and, at this time, being awakened through the circuitry patterns of the planet. This information will not just help to the extreme of life, living, needs on your planet's level, but also will bring into alignment the planet with the outer forces of activity, the brothers and sisters on the outer extremes.

Mainly we speak here from Orion, from the Pleiades and from Sirius. The true force of this connection comes primarily through the Council in helping again those who came to live and experiment on this planet's region, not excluding those on the inner levels of the planet.

The levels of energy that you live within are still very dense in comparison to those of your spatial brothers and sisters, and it therefore is only at specific times or in moments of transparency that there is a connection.

But the living Earth Herself is continuous and goes on. The Earth holds all the answers to questions and to the needs of people. The atmosphere, contaminated though it is with toxins, impurities and chemical imbalance, still can be brought into a sense of alignment in need with the growth and alignment of the planet. It is in the nature of man and woman to caretake the planet. To awaken to that reality is a necessity.

It is in the recognition that this circuitry is also in your own DNA structure, not once, but multiplied 5 + 5 again. These tones represent the genetic factor, represent the instinct/me factor, represent the emotional/fear factor and aspirations.

The emphasis on the awakening of your own consciousness towards enlightenment is the strength and repetition of all that has gone before, and can be. By awakening, accepting responsibility, holding yourselves open and spacial, recognising the illusion of the density and restriction of the body, you yourselves can begin the process of the communication/communion with yourselves, with each other and with your space brothers and sisters.

There will be times of great difficulty and upheavals on the planet and it is necessary to have the balance physically, magnetically, mentally, etherically and emotionally, to allow yourselves to merge into the new.

Time is shifting through you, speeding up, accelerating. The movement is occurring already around you. You can see through your own economic and political structures, that all time is frame. That which is being held so desperately is already crumbling to dust. What is being held is an illusion. There will be changes. There will eventually be a world government. There will be the necessity to care for the needs of the poor, the hungry, the thirsty, the ignorant, the diseased and this is moving on and growing. To prepare yourselves, you must be cleansed or your body reacts through the limitation of your own psycho-emotional and mental oppressions.

We come because of the changes in consciousness, the awareness and the growth. The vibrationary rate has been moved and merged and we can share with you understanding, we can share with you fellowship. You share with us – love and openness. The weakness in the planet, the weakness in Humanity, is a constant seeping of energy throughout the Universe. What occurs here, affects the greater. For the good of all, we urge you to begin, and to begin now.

You may question.

Question on 'communicating with the planet'.
A: There are pockets of energy upon your planet. Energy itself can be translated into information. Energy is information. This information comes from various sources. It can come from that drawn up from the planet, the inner core. It can come through certain artifacts, for example, the crystal skulls; it can come from certain places of vibrational power and energy. These "power points" as they are known, were part of these containers of energy to receive and to transmit information and also were used to the inner vibration of the Earth's energy, similar to that of Tesla, working to help bring forth the outer travel, when there was more inter-stellar travel between the planets. At that time this planet was still going through certain growth and observation, balances and development. The development of the planet came through a certain manipulation creatively, those of your spacial ancestors. The circuitries we spoke of were used as one complete board, so to speak, the planet Herself, for the receiving and the transmitting of information.

Q: How do we access this information?

A: At this time, it is being used on more mediumistic purposes through channels, but this is rather inadequate because you deal also with the restriction, either on a consciousness, physical, egoic or emotional level of the medium. To draw more input with lack of restriction, one needs to use an alternative type of technology not yet in your existence, but Tesla was working on this and also the Orgone energy has also tapped into this. Primarily, it is the usage of the this energy, drawing up through the planet and in doing so, translating this through sound, sound itself being able to be coded/decoded, you understand? This can then be used as instruction manually. You will
find to a much lesser degree, this type of technology first being used for the understanding of certain mineralisation around the planet, the mineral make-up of certain places, and this technology can then be taken and applied on a greater level, remembering of course that those working with it, expand it or retract it according to their consciousness.

Q: Is it easier for us, now, to access this energy, than it was for our ancestors?

A: When we speak of ancestors, when we go to those who first arrived, it was of course those who placed it there. Now, coming again full circle on the level of charting the vibrations on an outer- planetary realm, this movement, like of your stars but on the outer realms, occurs again and as we all move into this realm, you will find that the memory returns to you, the ancestral memory. It is more like leap-frogging over the last 200 – 500 generations to move further back.

You will find that there has been much talk and interest in Atlantis, but this is of much later era to that which we speak of. You are moving back here to a memory which was connected to many, one memory, a tribal memory. This tribal memory only began to separate at a later date and it was that separation that has caused so many problems throughout the Earth's history. Moving through that, back to the one memory, the core, one recognises the inter-connectedness and need for each other and you will find that once this begins to be applied again on the planet, in the planet, by Humanity, then one could no longer harm another, as one would harm oneself.

The memory you will find, will return with certain keys; a word here, a picture there, a thought here. This will begin again the patterns which will emerge. The emergence of these patterns shows themselves within the crystalline structure around the DNA especially in the joint conditions and they will also show themselves being able to be imprinted and multiplied through chemical analysis from the blood. This will also balance with that usage through computers and with the children.

Q: Is that technology of that balancing through the blood available now?
A: It has begun through Germany and America. It has come here, into your country, and it has begun, but it is very rudimentary to what will be, it is also very much a key to moving on, through this.

Q: With developments like that it seems that the development of technology is a random thing in relation to this process. Is there any sense that this technology is being guided from outside, so that we can use technology in a meaningful way?

A: Yes. This is occurring. The psyche of an individual, as they begin to grow in consciousness, develops in a way, or leans in a direction, that the consciousness itself enjoys feeding – so the technician will get it in that form, the farmer in their form, the teacher to their form.

Those moving towards more technological ventures will receive the information on that level. This information itself is of one. It is within the vibrationary rates affecting the planet now, but comes through the individual according to the learning and leaning of the consciousness. It can come forth as technology to one, as we say, agriculture to another, it can come forth as medical breakthroughs to another, according to the learning!

It is not a differentiation; it is the same prime pulse of information, filtered through the consciousness. The consciousness accepts only as much as is able and a little more. This "little more", between 5 and 7 %, has grown from a ratio of 0 – 5 in the last three years, and is growing more now as people themselves are expanding.

This information is continuous. It is there around the planet and it is there through consciousness of our thought, through the Council and through those who sit and receive and transmit consciously. It has no form as you know it, but energy. If you were to visualise it, it would be like a stream of colour that constantly changes and moves, and this in itself is the energy information. The rainbow you have is a touch of this.

You will find with the changing, atmospherically, of the Earth's conjunction with the rays of sun breaking through, that the atmospheric pressure itself is weakening. This is causing a strain – drain on certain individuals attuned to this level and it is therefore of importance to be aware even more so of protecting yourselves. The change to come will be much more directly influenced by design, shapes and the different uses, not just the materials scientifically you are working with but materials using more variation of glass and wood for buildings. These habitats will be conductive to the variations of vibrations that are becoming more aligned and stronger throughout the planet.

Q: As for the whole cycle, complete with the "proton belt" which is being approached, is this the frequency you speak of?

A: Yes. It was through the usage of this that there was the first commitment to working within the planet.

Q: This life within the Earth, this different vibrational level. Are there only 2 levels of vibration therefore?

A: No. There are various levels of vibrations connected with the planet. Some are more interconnected, some work more on a magnetic level, some work more on an astral/emotional level, some on a purely physical.

The inner life activity is more inter-connected with the planet than yourselves; the feeding of each from the other is more immediate and appropriate. There is a feeding not just of information, but chemical needs. For yourselves, there is a connection that is more magnetic and growing so, and this magnetic force is working very much for alignment and can be used for also nutritional balance if understood properly. The emotional/astral levels are also those passed from the physical, which still hold to memories, to pain, to needs, to fears.

Other than these levels that are humanoid in form, there is also the Devic kingdom, the animal and the plant kingdom, there is also the mineral kingdoms, so these levels are seven, in tone and vibration, each level vibrating within its own frequency. Once the harmony of them all begins to vibrate together, then you will find that there will be an opening through the frequency to allow more inter-connectedness. There are influences, each upon the other, more on the unconscious than conscious level and you can see this very much in your artistic and creative ventures. There are creatures not seen to the naked eye, in the astral - created by Humanity. There are angels, devils, all created by Humanity's needs and become their own force gradually, through the feeding. Some use these - for power, for politics, religion. Others are affected by it, by a sensitive consciousness.
In itself, it is purely vibrational.

Q: Is the angelic kingdom real?

A: The angelic, the true angelic, is not held by the Earth's energy, but is a vibrational force of light that moves through the Universe.

Q: Would Michael, Gabriel etc., would that all be from the true angelic kingdom?

A: Yes and first were as servers – recipients of energy, to guard the planet in her growth.

Q: Didn't understand about the connection between the animal and human kingdom.

A: The animal kingdom is not seen as the same as the human kingdom. The animal kingdom has not the same ancestry and therefore carries not the same consciousness. For humans, you have become used to the body, and bodily needs. You have become used to being directed through the physical, emotional and mental needs and have therefore become bound, very similar to that of animals, so you have lost the memory of your true existence and capabilities. As those capabilities become clearer, the capabilities themselves become more subtle and change. You will find light bodies becoming stronger.

Animals have their place as brethren to you, to learn together to become part of the natural growth, but the similarity will never become more. You speak of reincarnation, moving through lives. Yes, animals move through, animals are bound by the consciousness of the vibration of the entity of the one. Dog carries dog consciousness – all dogs carry one dog consciousness. Cats carry one cat consciousness. There are vibrations, variations of course within that, but when they release the physical form, they eventually return to dog, they return to cat. When you release your physical forms, you move through the extremes of vibrations, unrestricted by time, which allows you to penetrate and permeate the etheric layers drawing to you magnetically the vibrations you have accumulated through lives until again you are one and we are light. To try to give animals an artificial intelligence, a more humanistic tone, is both degrading and ignorant, as is done to many of these animals in circuses and such like, for the purity of their nature is sacred, and the understanding and the learning from that should be also held in sacredness.

Q: What is the relation of dolphins?
A: Yes. Dolphins are connected in the vibrationary fields, more akin to human. The root race came from the same source, before the separation. It is much of the level of vibration through the dolphin areas now that is keeping the balance on your planet. They are more the custodians than you are. They are able to communicate, they are able to be of one mind, and they have memory which is awakened with

birth – group memory, ancestral memory. They also call on their ancestors and I tell you this – they are having a very hard time taking care of you all. They are very much working to express and exhibit peace and you will find that this quality comes from a heart level, rather than a mental.

Q: Can I ask a question about the 'separation' – when Mankind lost its way, presumably, and altered itself to another level. Can you explain the 'separation'?

A: We can explain as much as is allowed at this time.

When first the movement to this planet and the co-habiting of the planet occurred, it was agreed that those who came would link themselves with the planet and work to create a place of growth and harmony rather than living in an alien planet staying connected with their home base. So, it was agreed and this was chosen.

Those who worked here also chose certain immediate technologies which were for them, very different to that which you have today. They were ones that were organic, worked through the alignment of thought, mind, will and inner activity, to create and to bring about that which was necessary. This is why there is no huge machinery for you to find. They worked here, and they took upon themselves the vibrations of the planet; night and day, warm and cold. And gradually as they worked, they began to become more concerned with their own particular welfare than the welfare of the whole.

Rather than bringing this sense of oneness to a place that had only known isolation and separation, a separation began to occur within them, forces began to be drawn within, certain root energies collected through the atmospheric vibrations of aeons gone at the time when Venus was a living planet and had an alter-ego on another planet and there was warfare between them. This vibration, when the planet itself erupted and broke apart – blew up, was still within the atmosphere and began to permeate – penetrate through the Earth's atmosphere to those working here. They began to draw into themselves in groups and gradually as individuals. As they did so, blindness occurred. When we speak of blindness we do not speak lightly – a blindness occurred which cut them off from revealing truth – truth that was there before them and around them. The proton belt itself was moving apart.

They were no longer able to stay in contact with the outside vibrations. They became lost upon that way. The separation became a coldness within, an isolation and it is that that you often pass onto your children, rather than the awakening of wholeness. Your myths speak of this in various guises.

Q: Can I ask how the angelic forces were connected with the first forces created upon the Earth and how they were connected with what you've just said?

A: The angelic forces themselves became more separated through this separation; this causes pain, even now, to think upon. The angelic forces of light are reflections of yourselves "beyond the looking glass". As you grow and open and understand and become more humble by letting go of the ego of self for the greater, the forces of light operate more through you and the angelic forces themselves are one with you. The physical body is not your eternal body – it is purely that used in this lifetime and must be honoured as such.

We are pleased with the evening and have enjoyed our discourse.

# Endangerment of Humanity and the Planet

(23rd September 1992)

Greeting my friends. We come forward here from the Council of Beings to share with you some understanding of the growth and the further-ment from the endangerment, of Humanity and the planet.

As you know of course, as an endangered species, you have predicted levels of life span according to the quality and flow of Humanity's direction. This life span changes according to that quality due to realisation and necessity, and, according to the co-operation that the necessity takes, i.e., a technological and organic inner trans-personal way that will allow the growth to evolve. In evolve-ment it will develop beside the growth of the planet and the Universe.

Humankind needs to understand and recognise the need for right action and lack of negativity. The expansion of consciousness through the inner understanding of the self has been taught by those teachers of former times. It has always been highlighted throughout the eras of your time and awareness, for it is in understanding yourself that you gain the knowledge of the sacredness of the planet, the Universe and indeed, the movement of the stars.

Activity is brought about by the determining quality of your vibrational field of work. The 'Will' itself, in its determination, recognises the need of activity, thereby allowing that to penetrate into your world, either on a physical or psycho-emotional field, bringing about the activity necessary for expansion to take effect on a more conscious level. Inactivity is lack of awareness or ignorance of the necessity to take the steps one needs.

The movement is continuous movement before you and around you and you yourself continue upon this path. You can step from one to another through the determining quality of your will, thereby allowing the expansion of activity in motion at various levels or fields of endeavour in your life span. This can bring about an acceleration of that movement or it can bring about stagnation. Your consciousness participates and is sometimes purely the receiver though not necessarily the transmitter. the idea originating comes from beyond the determining will itself. It has to be understood here that the will within the character has its own interplay within the various fields of endeavour within the individual.

This will in effect is constant in motion; it is part of the fluid that is vital in your nervous system. This fluid moves through the nervous system, through the skeleton and the back bone. As it moves through, this can bring about an awareness of consciousness that develops not just through the arena of life, it can carry on as a visual projection that one can move into in various lives, thereby one causes in effect one's lives to occur that are necessary for one's role, through the balance of that spinal fluid moving as is determined.

Questions.

Q: What is it that humanity needs to understand in relation to our planet?

A: There is recognition that rather than growing holistically, you have leaned or bent, to one degree or another, thereby fulfilling only certain aspects of the brain's activity and your own verbal response. This recognition is leading many upon a path where new technological ventures are beginning to open. Medical breakthroughs, will again commence once humanity begins again to grow in harmony with the planet and when you have the right ecosystems in balance for the plants that give the drugs necessary for the health of humanity.

For this lies within the psyche of the planet and the message of this input, which is electromagnetic, will then be broadcast more strongly and will be picked up by individuals, some acknowledging, some grasping, some through vision.

Q: What is a good way to bring one's will into play?

A: It is to be recognised that will and determination are two sides of one coin and to recognise this, one has also to recognise which role it plays in one's life and how much it's determined by that law.

If you recognise that determination is something that has guided you or been connected to your goals in life, then it is to be recognised there is also a very strong will in operation and it is most probable that this will has had its own way in life. Your education has not been such to register the will as a determining aspect of usage for right activity.

To begin to explore this, one must explore the reasoning behind the determination, recognise the lower egoic abilities used in determination, the reasoning of ...... not the reasoning that fits the values of the individual but the reasoning of what is in truth.

Then one begins to see one has used one's quality to make things occur rather than allowing oneself to respond and allow the activity itself to become in motion through your conscious creativity. Sometimes one needs to make a conscious effort not to manipulate a certain situation, to allow the situation itself to unfold in a way that is necessary. This is completely reflective of that which you have been brought to recognise, so it is something that you will take time to be able to understand and integrate.

You see from our space, we have no will, no determination. Effort as you know it is contained only in a supreme force of necessity for enlightenment and understanding. Growth occurs spontaneously. Everything is in consciousness. Conception as we know it comes through a conscious blending of one and can be made by more than two individuals; it is participation that brings about productivity. We live in a space where all thought is recognised as an unfolding of consciousness and creates or not according to the power within it. Thought colours your life entirely. Our thoughts are not mingled through the emotional but are part of the consciousness.

Your thoughts are still representatives of your emotions. To move beyond your emotional bodies you must first recognise them. You must first live through them and beyond. You must first become instrumental in releasing your own anger and allowing yourselves to move through a space of fear and self-need, which allows you the opportunity to embrace all of you and grow on – releasing your attachments to the interplay of reactions.

Q: You spoke before about this spinal fluid. Are there ways or systems that can enhance the movement of the spinal fluids?
A: One such way is through movement and meditation, allowing the spine itself to become flexible. Stretching and relaxing the spine through any kind of gentle movement, opening oneself visually to the recognition of the interplay through this of life's occurrences, for example, restriction- self-restriction- is restriction within the fluid which enhances some continuation of movement throughout the body's system; moving, cleansing, purifying.

As it moves it has a light quality, almost crystalline and this is the quality of the magnetic flow and the transmutation of the lower force into the higher levels of activity, so movement, gentle stretching is very productive.

Q: Could you say a little bit more about the ego?

Response: You speak of the lower ego?

Reply: Yes.

A: The lower ego of man and womankind is based primarily within the functions of the reactive quality to the Earth's own vibrational field. When those who came and took root 'so to speak' upon the Earth and began to take it as their home, they began to take on the quality of the atmospheric conditions and the psychic vibrations of fields magnetically around and within the planet.

Because of what had already occurred this was a strong disturbance that was partly the causation of separation and caused an egoic quality. Egoic means as in one self – separate. Separateness is the sin, the only one that can be seen, separate from one's own Source. This separation brought about a determination, i.e. will, the psycho emotional field and into the conscious, physical and mental field, other than the spiritual and higher realm field.

The egoic quality itself is one that has to be fed – the egoic quality has to be fed with accomplishment. It has to be fed with a self-recognition and a self- determination. These are the qualities that feed the lower ego. The fire egoic vibration is one that is in alignment with the spatial vibrations of light and movement and activity. Light equating to love, movement equating to manifestation, activity equating to life. Love manifesting life.

# Change and Structural Change

(30th September 1992)

The changes that are occurring are affecting you not just on a conscious and inner dimension, but are affecting also the physical, emotional and mental build-up of your bodies. It is affecting the structural change of the planet. The curve which moves through the planet in alignment with the magnetic force is similar to the structure of the curve of your own backbone, connected to, of course, the nervous system. It is through this system the impulse or energies are sent forth and memories are held.

As the changes occur on a planetary level, this too affects the cellular and individual level, as it does the group community levels. These will bring forth an up-welling of vibration according to the psyche of the individual on either an emotional, physical, mental, or sub-psychic level.

These changes are to do primarily with your own individual memory capacities and your ancestral memory banks, held within you. Structurally, changes on the non-physical level will allow an ease of flow of vibrationary rate through the body. It will permeate with the blood through the system oxygenisation levels and all will change. There will be a greater need for more nitrates within the food and the systems around.

There will be less restriction of the respiratory system as occurs now on a more general level. You will find that the entire structural body will begin to change, slowly through gentle manipulation, on a more unconscious and etheric level, moving into more physical as one adapts to the change in atmospheric vibrations. These changes will change the body; will change the usage of the structure. It will change the movement and the flexibility of working, from the hips down and from the chest up.

The centred force itself will bring about a lowering of the stomach moving down, through to the intestinal area. The intestinal area itself will slowly begin to shorten and release the amount of wastage unnecessary within it. You will find that the structural level itself is also very affected through the atomic structure, and also moving into the head and brain area. There will be less of a skull aperture and the head itself will become a little more shrunken and a little more closed.

You will find that these changes will occur over, of course, a great period and they will begin to show themselves within the next decades, with the birth of the children. You will see this growing; you will feel the changes occurring within your own structure as the structure of the planet also moves in occurrence. You will find that the planetary level is adjusted into its own means. The means, mode of course, bringing it into alignment again – back to Sirius and also to the variations of vibrations caused by the effects of the winds in reflection from the Moon and Mars.

You will see and note that this causes a variation of vibration in the atmosphere, in the weather conditions, not just from your known greenhouse effect, but from the outer layers themselves. One is affective, of course, of the other.

The planetary region itself will go through some massive earth changes. These earth changes structurally will have a very violent and yet positive effect depending not just on the interplanetary forces but also on the atmosphere.

It is known that there are pockets of vibrations within the Earth that are very close to imbalance. This is known and well known by certain scientific bodies that are active in their work with the government bodies. This has not yet hit your propaganda, your information technology. Yet work has been continuous on this for more than twenty years. This work has brought about two different streams of thought.

One has been to move on; the other has been to try to balance the imbalance within the atmosphere and the planet. From that there has been very conscious growths towards what is known as 'Green Issues',

'New Age Movements', things of this ilk. Bringing people into a state of activity rather than passiveness, thereby causing grass roots movements to occur across the planet: for change, for awareness, for balance.

The other path has been developed by those in certain positions and is also being worked and acted upon. You will find that the structural changes themselves will allow you to develop for yourselves almost an 'alter ego' of the self that can contain the physical, material, psychological, spiritual, mental and, through that, the growth of the emotional.

It is very important on a personal level at this time to be aware of how much one actually moves, thinks and speaks from the emotional realm. Become aware of how much emotions actually rules one's life and overcome this by conscious activity.

It is on that level that you are being programmed quite deliberately by those who have the need for power and manipulation and it is therefore important to begin to bring yourselves into a more conscious function.

So, as individuals, as group souls, as servers for the light, you can begin again the quest for truth and wholeness in your lives and the lives of those around you.

Become aware of what is used to take you to a place of fear and/or greed - Bombardment of the senses.

Questions:

Q: You spoke of developing consciousness. Is there anything we can specifically do to go in this direction?

A: Yes. Firstly one has to be aware of how much one is manipulated, be it unconsciously by one's environment and by the moods and effect of vibrations of those around you.

Become aware of what is used to take you to a place of fear and/or greed. This is a bombardment of the senses.

Become aware of being the player as well as the vibration of the drama of which you are a part. Watch the scene and live within the scene. Doing this, you will recognise your own emotional interplay, which is unconscious, with the interplay of others. You then begin organically to bring a conscious awareness into your life.

You become aware through that, of the emotional interplay of many vibrationary rates going back through your parentage, recognising this also unconsciously lives out, in the demands of the emotions of those around you. By conscious activity you are staying centred within yourself. You are aware of your feelings and also of speaking through that, to what is right, what is of the light.

In this way you are able to begin to direct the emotional and psychological bodies into placement with the more light realm, which brings a more active intellect rather than a lack of intellect and it allows the instinctive to do the work it was programmed for, rather than being the ruler of life as it often is now.

The instinctive body is there to allow you to incorporate within your bodies, the feeling of life around you, to learn of life, the planet, the plants, the animals, and the people. Liken it to having a tool that you push into the soil that will tell you of the make-up of the soil, so too the instinctive body is of similar ilk, allowing the space to choose, rather than being dictated to by the emotional body. Emotions are important, and to develop them with consciousness is the key.

Q: Could we hear more about the pockets of imbalance of the Earth and what we could do to assist?

A: These pockets of imbalance are the growths that are within their own system, insular and yet affective of those around them, due to the vibration. If you put a body through the levels of vibration, any growth, any blockage will give out a denser note. The quality itself will not lead to integration of the harmonic. This is true of this planet.

One of the ways of working with this is to be aware of the strength of visualisation, to be aware that the Earth is electro-magnetic and faults themselves are electro-magnetic. These atoms of energy can be used through your thought patterns, through the righteousness of your thoughts and actions. This is one way of working.

A more physical dimension of this is being aware of the imbalance caused by humanity upon the planet. Bring back your trees, bring back your ecosystems, cleanse your waters, feed your brothers and sisters, it's quite simple!
These pockets are violent in nature, unconscious in activation, this is important to recognise. These pockets can, and often will, bring about shifts upon the Earth - eruptions etc.

Q: May I ask something on a more serious level in relationship to the daily situation the Earth finds Herself in and the existence of Earth's importance to life at various levels as we have been told. Yet Man has been dealt with the gift of free will and is capable with the technology he now has to almost instantly destroy the planet.
How are these things reconciled in terms of control?
Response:   When you speak of control, you speak of whose control?
Q: I think, in terms of cosmic control – beyond the Earth and in relation to the importance of the Earth in any cosmic sense beyond humanity.

A: We see this Earth as a garden within a pool. The pool is the Universe. That which grows upon it is decaying but there is also new growth and change. Those who care for the garden have left it to rot.

They have not become aware of the land: the fertility, the need to change and care for the land, to till it, to seed it.

It is decaying upon itself: self-decay – rotting the plants, the growth. This, if left, will be swamped by the pool as a means of righting itself for the decay is beginning to affect the pool. So the pool, being greater and having its own survival through its life force, will bring balance.

This is not yet to this point and if it is, this garden again will arise and will again grow, but will be different. Mankind will not blow the planet up. The planet will continue.

But there has to be change. This has grown in a very short space of time from a populace of nearly nil to 50% in awareness of this need for change.

That growth continues and is beginning to show its effect in certain areas will continue. It is not until there is a disease that a cure is found and this is so.

The way to unity that the body looks towards, the urges it feels, are used sexually and that can in some cases transmit disease. So even to the roots of your own inner needs, must there be change. It is a reflection of the decay that is acting within you. As you grow and change, the Earth changes and the patterns that evolve interconnect with life itself, and not just with people in the physical and mental.

Death for example, will no longer be something that is feared. You will no longer fight so vigorously to stay alive in a decaying body, thereby causing atmospheric decay to the whole community around.

No, you will allow people to leave in peace, knowing that the body is only a shell used for a very short period and the spirit moves on, the Soul returns to Source.

Q: You spoke of one side that became aware of these pockets infiltrating the green movement to cause activity. Is this a beneficial movement?

A: Yes.

It is a beneficial movement of the collective.

It has been for more than 20 years that there have been certain groups, more, may be 40 years, drawing in scientists, chemists, physicists, people with far sighted vision and active intellect and an ability to solution orientation, bringing them to work together through creed, through ethnic origin, for the development of the planet, and it is through the branching of this, that there has been the coming about of infiltration. They are using this knowledge for the growth and responsibility of this planet.

# The Principle Day

(11th November 1992)

Greetings my friends. I come forward here from the Council of Beings, to discourse with you of The Principle Day. This day here marks one of the transitional periods before the full force of the incoming rays penetrate through your systems, not just through the atmospheric solar system but also through the system analysis of your own vibratory fields and rate. It was for this that we determined the structure the medium presented you with, to allow you the opportunity to feel at ease with your own sound force, that you may use this continuous vibrationary note, to allow yourselves the flexibility of change, to allow yourselves the release of the lower egoic structure which still holds, and in some, dominates, and to allow also the infiltration of this force, as it works through you.

The rays, as they come in through the system on a micro level, will too, begin to change the rate of activity in the organs. The kidneys, most importantly, will need more nourishment, and more in the range of pure fruit and vegetable juices. You will find that the pancreas, also here is affected most precisely and there is a need here for the balance of sugar levels in the diet coupled with the carbohydrates. This is very important as to which becomes which. You will note that one of the major affected areas in the future will be the lungs, so it is also of importance to be aware of your breathing activity and the rate of exchange within the breath.

By this we speak of the ability to open, inhale and in the outer breath to release the captured toxins within the lungs and capillaries, not just on the physical, but on the psychosomatic level. Many of the emotional levels hold in this area. People's fear, although seen very much produced around the solar plexus and leading via the liver, also has a very strong genetic influence through the lung system, so the breathing apparatus is of most importance, you will note. It is to be seen that the disintegrating illnesses in the system of the human populace has direct bearings through the lungs, so it is of importance to be aware of this function.

As you come to these stages, it is of vital importance to release yourselves from all thought patterns. Not just "old" thought patterns, but "all" thought patterns. Thought patterns themselves are restrictions. They are contagious so they spread very quickly. They take the vibrationary forces that are operating through you, and they restrict them into structure. The thought patterns themselves, most importantly the old patternings, memories, pains, hurts of this nature, draw upon the vital forces of energy, for life, to keep alive those vibrations. Therefore you yourself lack this amount of vital force.

By releasing all that from you, you are allowing yourself to move forward in the supreme force of light and this is what will carry you through. There are changes of occurrence, not just on and within the pattern of the body but the pattern of the macro also and this must too, be recognised. It is for yourselves to recognise your own functions – 1. your own bodily function, 2. your spiritual function, 3. your communal function - the function that you are able to present and work with through your own community, be that your living, be that your working, situation.

By working in these three functions, by allowing your energy, through you, to present all that is needed for growth and continuation, you will find yourself moving through these phases into the new rate of exchange with a light infiltrated body, with a mind capable of drawing in and expressing the light forces - not through thought structure patterning, through the unfolding and emergence of you own spiritual imprint, your Soul contract. This imprint draws upon all Soul information for what is necessary, immediately. It will not be necessary for you to have to look within to find the answers or information – the information will be immediate. If it is not accepted in its immediacy, then it is gone. Then you resort again to old patterns, old thought forms and resorting back into that which was. So, it is of vital importance that you live primarily within the essence of Now and the moment of exchange.

As you work with others, be it in a professional or personal sphere, it is of importance to remember the exchanges that occur almost unconsciously; before words, before thoughts, there is exchange. This exchange presents the scene that is then carried out on a physical, intellectual and instinctive level. That which you carry before you is always that which is reflected to you. Bring that into the alignment of that which you need, require, to live with; peace, harmony, inter-relationships, understanding, so that you yourself also grow in a way that is productive and non-harmful to your own environment, your own inner ecosystem, as well as the system around you. You will find through this that you will again begin to live more organically with nature.

Using technology does not have to shift you into an age that is far removed from the natural processes of the Earth and Her functions; it can allow you to become in harmony, through the organic, with the natural forces. See these technical harmonies function, and yes, reproduce this and also be a part of the future of Humanity as well as the inter-relationship which can occur with more conscious value between yourselves and the planet.

There is one item here we need to bring forth into awareness and it is that of choice. Choice determines the value of your own requirements. Through relating self needs, choice determines these values. Through inter-relating the needs of your own vibrationary forces, choice itself becomes secondary to the natural flow, which at this time is inhibited by a determining quality within the mind that has been fixed through generations, not allowing you the ability for full penetration into your own creative power and force. This mind chip – it is more like a shutter – is one that training, education, religion, politics, have fed you, into self and "mine". Separation has been fed to you from birth and pre-birth. The greatest gulf you have is that of separation.

Once you realise fully that there is no separation, once you recognise that you are of one, and you live that, you are able to shift the mind mechanism, and this allows you full empowerment into the Self – the quality of the Divine/The Source, that which the teachers have spoken of through the ages. Humanity is centred in the solar plexus of your energy fields. The Christ force is centred in the heart of your energy fields. Your teachers are centred in the throat of your energy fields. The Divinity force is centred in the head and at the base of your energy fields. Shift your vibrations, experience on new levels, discover new territories, and walk on new plains of intelligence.

Give yourself the choice - the ability to Be.

Question:

Q: When we have the thought patterns in our mind, one way that works for me is to become active. Is there another process that one can use?

A: That is the most congenial way - remembering that activity can be from the will. If it is not at that time, then use it creatively, manifest it etherically. If the thought comes through immediately, and you are not able to act within the immediate, do not let it go, but direct it where it can be of use, either through the manifestation, through the etheric and monadic levels, or send it on to a person, place or space where it can be of use.

You see around you much toxic waste from Humanity. There is also much mental waste that needs cleansing, from fields, etheric fields and the astral fields. This which we speak of also produces such cleansing. Some of the foods you eat, one eats, are transformed in the body into different elements, producing enzymes to feed the organs, and through that, the fats necessary for the body and through that to the colon.

The balance between the sugar producing and the more glucose enhancing is not readily understood at this time. The body will transform certain carbohydrates into sugars for the needs of the blood sugar levels. It is therefore important to note that more glucose intake will cause sluggishness on this level. As you change the molecular patterning of your organic self, through the changes on the atomic rate, as you move through into this new vibrationary field more fully, you will find there will be those who will be almost addicted to glucose- enriched foods. There is a need in the body for sugars, but it must be understood of the workings of such. The body can absorb certain glucose frequencies as long as they are in a minority and if they move through within certain periods after the carbohydrates – in other words, if you are going to eat sugar, have it after some carbohydrates, within an hour – an hour and a half approximation.

Q: I find many people these days are suffering from the ileo-caecal valve opening and also allowing toxins to then enter through the gall bladder system. Is there some help for that in terms of diet or exercise?

A: This "doorway" which you call the valve, is the doorway of retreat, retreat into memory, retreat into fear, retreat into self, be it self- need, self-assertion, self-emotion. Through the changes occurring, people in general as well as specifically, are being pushed into themselves. All that they deal with, be it their anger, or pain, or frustration, as well as the joys and happinesses, are produced primarily within themselves. It is a vibrationary rate that is being produced within the body. This "tone" can also be regulated, not restricted. The doorway that many people face is very much a valve of releasing the inner pressure, but it gives more pressure.

That which the general populace and specifics are experiencing, pushes some inwardly, others, it pushes them to experience it outwardly. Those with this problem are experiencing it more inwardly. Those experiencing it with others, experiencing it more outwardly, are affected more in the heart and the eyes.

It is always with pleasure that we address and share together.

# Tuluk

(1st January 1993)

Greetings, brothers and sisters of the light. I am TULUK and I come forward here from the Council of Beings.

This time and space in your cycle determines the mode of change. It brings forward the flexibility within the cycles of the Earth's sphere, and the spheres of activity in relation to and counter relation to, the vibrationary rates. Envisioned, these are like circles of energy emanating from the core of the planet. They are fed in through the mass consciousness, unconsciousness determined through fear, pain, and aggravation, through love, joy and continuation.

These vibrations emanating forth from the planet have a Doppler effect and this effect continues the variation of vibrations being fed back again into and through the planet. The winds of change that mark the receptivity in Humankind for growth, come now and carry with them that which is necessary for the continuation of the planet as part of the greater force of the universal flow. This cycle will see an upsurge in technological advancement, particularly in the areas of light and movement. It will see an upsurge in the receptivity of communication. This communication is not just in the technological majestic fields but communication also within the individuals themselves. Remember all that you have around you is but a continuation of a vibration that is occurring within. Ponder upon this in your technological advances and you will see the mass uprising within the cellular sense.

The strains of activity you carry within your own genetic pattern, within the DNA itself, will begin to manifest, will begin to separate. The seven levels of consciousness will show themselves within these patterns. Light will begin to attract light at an accelerated speed. There will be a drawing together of cellular families working in harmony, working in relationships and with others, as well as the interrelationships within themselves. The cross section of activity will continue to occur and will fade into an essential data bank. This must be done in a way that is harmonious with the psyche of humanity – the mind, and not within a political, economic structure. Otherwise you lose again the seed of righteousness. For even in your growth, in your awareness, in your desire, in your need to grow and to love, to care and to serve, the ego has not been stilled. It is much smaller and less needy, but it will take another of your turns in time to be cleared and integrated. Being aware, watchful and yet of non-concern, will greatly speed up the process.

Of the changes we speak, there will be more frequent upheavals on the planet. There will be eruptions, quakes, massive tidal waves. The cleansing will now begin in earnest. In the same time, in balance to this, there will be the continued uprising of people coming together harmoniously. There will be more open communication at the end of this cycle with your space brothers and sisters, and there will be a time of cleansing for all. The world was created upon the desire of a thought. The thought manifests and becomes whole. The wholeness is held within your own psyches. Reality is how you perceive that psyche. Change could occur instantly through the realisation of your own inner abilities.

You are here now, embedded within your own materialisation through dream-time. You are asleep. The awakening could cause havoc, if not properly attuned and made aware of. The body could break up. It could burst into flames, it could disintegrate. The awakening must be slow and precise. You must be aware of your inner sense of knowledge and power. You must hold the physical together in light. You must cleanse it; you must prosper its growth and development. The light within you is the growth of tomorrow. The body you wear is but a protection. It can also be used not just as a weapon of which it has been, but as a tool, as a glorious gown.

Questions.

Q: Could you explain DNA as a symbol?

A: Of Humanity there are seven prime tribal peoples, broken down they can be made into five. Each of these carries an essential aspect or part of the whole where working together is like a living brain. Within your DNA you carry all memory of all patterns throughout your bloodlines moving back to where man and woman first were and walked upon this planet and their connection to the outer planetary

levels, be it the Pleiades, Sirius or Orion – the three that fed it. There is also influence from Maldark and Venus, but to a lesser degree, which came later through this time of change and cleansing. These patterns within your DNA are coming forth again, vibrating the sound almost audible to your human ear. These vibrations are drawing to them the needed pattern of construction within the etheric fields.

If you could see it, it would be like shapes, dimensions of shapes, as they fit together and hold around you. The vibrational sounds and quality tone enhances, to a point of what you could see as a sudden cracking or slicing through this. This causes time shift, it causes the ability to release all that which has been carried forward to this day and allows you to move freely from that, carrying the one force on the cellular level, which will then vibrate in clear harmony with the levels around it. This will bring purification, it will bring clarification.

Q: What affect does the combination of two tribes and the DNA structure have on the individual?

A: It can be very productive. It is dependent upon the level of the emotional and psychological gene. Early – early, early in your time, there was gene splicing, which brought about a variation of human, causing a ripple of dissension on the mass unconscious, which affected the planet in its state of disruption. This effect has lain dormant within the various peoples; many fear complete integration within each other.

When there is integration, the psyche within the child from copulation of the mixed, has to adjust to two various levels of instinctive behaviour, as well as tribal instructions from one of the seven genetic codes. This can be very productive if consciously attuned to and worked upon. It can bring peace more speedily to your planet; it needs a vast array of understanding in the upbringing of the children that carry this blend, which must be unified at some point in their life. Otherwise this disturbance can continue through generations.

One of the most concise ways of working with this for the child is the nurturing, the nest – from 0 – 7 years of age. This is the most secure haven that can allow this to occur. From the age of 7 – 12 will be the time of disturbance. Unification comes from 12 – 15. Then it is completed.

Q: Can you speak of the technologies of light and movement?

A: We can speak on this only broadly for to bring it into manifestation now within your consciousness and thoughts will hinder the energy coming through those individuals working upon it at this time. What we can say is that the light awareness will be very much focused and, although seen to be technological, will be very much used for body awareness and to enhance healing, to enhance growth of organs lost or decapitated or out of balance with the other organs in the body. There will also be the ability to bring forth through light, the thought themselves of the individual. One will be able to see with their own eyes the manifestation of their thoughts.

It will also be used to enhance communication, movement – there will be much more movement across the planet and beyond. There will be a technological advancement in a manifestation of the realignment of matter by vibration and sound – movement of objects – heavy, can be made quite simple, according to their frequency.

Q: Does that include people?

A: Eventually people, but not for quite a period. People will be able to be conscious in their awareness of transferring of mind matter rather than physical, for quite a period.

Q: We were told that dark is necessary for light?

A: You live in a Universe that grows through the spectrum of light and yet it is but a reflection. All light and colour you see, is but a reflection of its companion; it compliments, therefore, it must be as one. Growth is necessary; understanding is determined by the expression of your growth through the heart level. Until that is achieved you will draw to you all that is necessary.

Many of you here we know on another plane of consciousness, in another state of the Soul. The dimensions are many, as are your known and unknown facets. You are not just human in your beings, you are spatial beings and the memory of that will return. This man here works very much in the mechanics of what you see as flying saucers. That is part of his multi-dimensionality. This man here operates fleets of movement in companion ships to the Universe. This woman here brings forth direct healing and enlightenment for those in need.
All of you share the dimension on a level beyond understanding, where the light operates.

Time is transient. Remember, that to you, thought is a process, in your spatial Beingness, thought IS – is as you are, and can create and destroy. It can be or not be. You do not see this on your dense level so clearly. You are not able to absorb this into your lives so fully yet, till you are moved to cause change, until you can accept responsibility for all of this and beyond, more.

You need all the forces to reflect yourself– to give thanks and love to one another. There are many on your human planet who ask you to give them your responsibility, to give them your power, to let them make your decisions and determine the quality of life – your thinking, your growing and those of your children and your children's children, and that of the planet. This is seen to us as the only evil. This is what has slowly eaten away the awareness of Humanity through the centuries.

Bring that back to yourselves. Accepting your own space as your responsibility and spreading the space out as you spread your consciousness. Take back your inner selves to bring light and growth, encouragement, peace and love. Harmony brings back the awareness, gradually allowing you to awaken. The awakening we speak of: You are already on this path, but you must allow it to open for you, to stay in clarity to determine your mode and to strip from you mentally, emotionally and physically through your own toxic levels, your blood, the drugs fed into you, on all these levels as your world has begun to fester with the maggots that feed upon it.

This is a planet of light, of sound and movement. That can never be lost and that is a tone within the entire core of Being and through your awareness you can begin to unravel the bonds put upon you and hear, the tone within your own hearts, so you can respond to your Mother Planet, to each other and to the outer forces within the Universe.

You still have some that remember. There are also still others on your planet that carry the memory clearly, have purity of motion and motive that still respond to us and are open to the tones of sound.
We speak of course, of your dolphins and whales. We go now – we will return again to talk together.

# Communication

(20th January 1993)

Greetings.

Communication as you know it will become a thing of the past, during your life time. Inter-stellar communication will become commonplace. Movement and travel become at will. Your children's children will know and inhabit new worlds. The body itself is changing, not just within your own DNA structure, but within the physical form, the mental apparatus. Thought takes form. At this time it works through the various levels of the ethers, attached to you always through cords of energy. This energy is fed through your own life support systems.

Time, even in your own awareness, is changing, and this will continue to do so and diverge. Through that change in time continuum, thoughts will take form immediately within the body structure. You will be able to see quite clearly the occurrence and imbalance within your own natures. This will no longer be determined as to your choice of lives or situations for replenishment, for knowledge, or places of learning, but will occur instantaneously and with apparent ease.

It will therefore be important for you to be with others of similar ilk and disposition, so that you do not harm others, nor harm yourselves. It is important that you recognise the happenings and workings, not just of the physical and mental apparatus that you control, but of the very fine etheric structures that you have built around you on the various levels, from the lower astral extreme to the most subtle waves of vibrational force.

These subtle waves, as they work through the ethers, can be used and directed, not just through your own physical, mental, but can be directed to bring a containment of vibration in one place or level of awareness. This can be done through the majesty of your own conscious thought patterns, through the level of consciousness of your very own Soul nature.

This is very similar in structure to what was known as "The Ark".

This covenant was one that took not men and women's blood but the etheric vibrational patterns themselves, connected through life force and held through consciousness, matter. This was denied to humanity through the oncoming generations, because this could no longer be a servant to humanity or of service to mankind and womankind. Instead it could become a tool, a reaper of disintegration. It could re-arrange matter.

As you work within these principles yourselves, as you grow within this and learn and your children adapt accordingly, and their children are born accordingly, so these forces again will be brought into awareness and be able to be used, not for one's own personal needs and satisfactions, but most importantly, for building, for creating and for demonstrating. There will be more aquaculture than you see at this time in your history. There will be a great deal of fish farming, of different varieties and of certain plants. Kelp and iodine are most necessary in the diets at this time and will continue to do so as the radiation across the planet is strengthened. An alga, a green algae, e g., 'spirulina', is also very vital to the system when possible and this will be used much more in the future. Certain grains, now being produced, reproduced, will also be used a great deal as animal culture recedes.

The grazing land will develop from deserts gradually, resistant of weather patterns, and arable land.

Of your own natures, it is of supreme importance to be conscious of your creativity and your thoughts. Be conscious, not just on a daily basis, but from moment to moment. Capture yourself and hold yourself in levels of awareness. In this way, the forces themselves beginning to operate at this time, atmospherically, vibrationally, affecting the planet as well as the individual can be directed through you with greater awareness. There can then be fewer negative emotional patterns and more creative, spontaneous vibrations. You are the harbingers of change. You carry the seeds, and it is for this that we bring you some fertilizer that they may grow in a way beneficial to humanity as well as the planet.

Q: At the present time there is an awful lot of darkness. In the times that you speak of, the children's children and the inter-stellar travel, will some of that darkness have receded or will there still be this great polarity?

A: There will not be such a polarity as humanity receives, ingests and accepts fully, the responsibility for all occurrences; that is all occurrences within you and around you that are parts of the chords of your vibrational patterns. This will be understood more as it is made more apparent through the new technologies, through light and colour and sound will it be shown. In this way people's awareness will be grasped more fully, in a way that is intellectually enlightening as well as spiritually captivated and this will open the realm to the understanding of one's shadow.

Q: Yes, concerning the last question. I've long visualised the technology that would broadcast our own being into a hologram of light so that we can see the results of our thoughts.
Is that something that is becoming a reality now?

A: Oh yes, this is already being worked on, in America and also Canada and with very little success in Germany.

Q: You spoke of these structural changes in the body. Could you elaborate on that a little?

A: Much within the body is carried around through thoughts, through undigested patterns. These almost fossil foods, unused, are being fed constantly through your own emotional fields, and are using up life force. As these are used more, as fossil foods, therefore not just feeding the body but learning, absorbing the structure within it – you understand – as is fossil, its own life force, its own life, you will find bodies themselves become leaner.

There will also be a movement in the back, a shaping down through the lower backbone to the tail, which will begin to move in rather than out, as the energy is able to move within more constructively.

The neck will elongate and gradually, through time, the ears will become smaller as one is able to hear more precisely. The organs themselves will slightly shift, and they could in some, produce a new organ close to the liver which at first will be seen as a shadow and gradually will grow, which will carry 'new T' cells, adapted to the changing atmosphere and planetary culture.

Clarity of thought, recognition of memory occurrence, is most important. Acknowledge the seeds that one carries within one's own patterning, be they seeds of doubt, fear, pain, or power. It can often include fear of one's own sensitivity in relation to the energies of others.

Once understood, one can begin to relate through one's own fear, thereby allowing it to become part of one's infrastructure, part of one's own sense of Being.

Q: Has Humanity passed this point of no return one way or another?

A: There is always choice. Even in destiny, there is choice. There are points or pivots along the way that determine – like markers.

The planet has reached a point when it must change.

It is like a person with cancer who can no longer hide from what is eating their body.

You either do something or you die. That is a choice that is still there. Because of the difficulties you, as a people, have put yourselves, you can also come up with appropriate technological advancements to right this.

Some created difficulties in ignorance, some in knowledge. Even though much of what was done was done in ignorance, the power of expression was there, and that power of expression can be adjusted and balanced. There are always people, always.

Q: I assume from that, that there is every reason to continue technological efforts and systems to right the planet, to develop projects that will feed people and to bring health and awareness to children?

A:   This is so.

Q: I'd like to ask a question about the growing, the development of materials, which you mentioned before about buildings and demonstration, by using energy?

A:   The thoughts themselves are form.

As energy – focus becomes thought, it takes form, and form and thought are becoming one. This is something you must become aware of – because you do not see it with the dense eye, you do not accept it as so and it is therefore very easy to have a lack, in your understanding of thoughts.

No longer will they be within the lower astral fields but will become reality.

Using a number of prime operators, and this is important that they be prime operators - a prime operator being an individual, with the consciousness connected through the thought pattern, to the supreme vibrational force - will connected with the light force - in this way they can re-arrange matter.

You can demonstrate this. You can draw in that which is needed and you can build from this. You will also have weather patterners; people who are aware of weather change and this works very much through their nasal system.

There are different levels, of your sensitive natures, or what you refer to as psychic. These weather patterners can determine the levels of power through the energy level of the wind, of water, of the air and the earth, thereby allowing you to draw those to you in a way that is non-harmful to the ecological pattern of the environment. Weather patterners will be those that can be trained into this from an early age, or even teens and late teens, who will have sensitivity and also, can smell, for example: rain coming, electrical storms winds. These people will be invaluable in their own time.

Q: You spoke of the communications system changing. Will we be building more telepathic communications or will it be instruments?

A: The need to communicate must be connected not just on the technological advancements, but on the recognition of the level of communication you are giving to another. To communicate you must open your hearts. You must speak through the heart level. By speaking through the heart level you are able to share more in less time and words. The heart level is connected very strongly to the tips of the fingers. There will be technology coming forth where you will be able to place your fingertips and through the sense you will be able to call upon that person you wish to communicate to. In their openness they will feel this and they can go to one of the discs - places that will have these discs - and can connect in with you.

If a person is disjointed or unbalanced through some emotional trauma or difficulty, there will also be difficulty in this type of communication. So you see, there must be more than one.

When you wish to come to another through the communion of your senses, then you will find it powerful as well as helpful, to place your fingertips together or even to theirs. Holding hands now is connected very much to the solar plexus through the throat chakra; these centre forces of this activity that you call chakras. The centre of the hand itself, the palm, is very connected to the stomach and pancreas area. Holding one way and another with the touch, also of the tips, you are giving on all levels. So you can see how this can be something that will give security and show feelings between you.

# Aspects of Spiritual Bodies

(27th January 1992)

Greetings, my friends. I come forward here from the Council of Beings and I wish to speak this evening concerning the various aspects of your spiritual bodies. We have touched upon this in various discourses. We wish to be more specific this evening, to give you an understanding and to share with you the capability of recognition, so that you may grow into that which lies ahead of you.

The spiritual dimensions, in this time and space, are very much held, be it unconsciously, in hierarchical form. This form is likened to the structure of living upon your planet, the structure in your political and the structure in your religious. This holds at bay the ability to grasp, the ability to merge. It causes a sense of separation and isolation.

We have spoken formally on the times, the beginning when those who came to this planet began to invest with the vibrations and take on the various levels of vibration around and within the planet. Those coming forth from the outer levels, from that which was, coupled with that which could be. This sense of separation has stayed with you through the Ages.

Communing with your own deeper psyche also allows you to recognise that you are part of the hierarchical, that you are not on the base level. Beneath the consciousness itself there is the subconscious/unconscious as they interact, and beneath that, in itself, there is the psyche which is connected to the psyche of Humanity. Coupled with the psyche and the unconscious are the patterns brought forward through generations, cultural patterns as well as blood patterns.

These hierarchical forces can link you also into your multidimensional self, in through the astral, to those fields of endeavour that you create within the mind. It can open you to the spiritual wealth of knowledge, awareness and recognition that you carry with you through life-times.

Put in the structure of a pyramid, one can see how these various vibrations move, using a graph. As you move into the new dimensional fields that are opening at this time, you will find that this will become spiral in tone. The pyramid will be used as a basis for the spiral vibration and gradually will tone itself completely into the double helix. This will allow you to move freely and more consciously. It will open you more to your inner spiritual dimensions, as well as the psyche that you carry within you. It will allow you to examine yourself constantly and consciously. You will find this force will create more bodies of light. These bodies of light are already forming.

You cannot see them with the naked eye but you are already beginning to sense them around you. These vibrational bodies will be held through sound, through the monadic thought level. You will therefore be able, gradually through time; to travel at will, using sound computation. The sound frequencies themselves will be adjusted through figurations, what is called "symbology". These will be leveled to the awareness of your lower consciousness as the frequency of that consciousness determines the frequency of your own desire and inhibitions. As this grows and opens, so too, the frequency attunes itself and gradually changes. You will find that the spiral forms will begin to take a more dimensional shape within the physical. You will find this occurring gradually through time.

You will notice the change of effect within the physical structure also within the tone levels. As to travel, it is to be recognised, that in the immediate future there will be already changes. There cannot be a continuation of the modes of travel being used at this time. It is not practical, nor ethical for the planet's needs. You will find motor control itself changing into more usage of the atmosphere and the atmospheric vibrations.

Gravitational pull and anti-gravity will become more common-place. Thought, dimensions, and the pattern of exchange within this, must become paramount in your understanding. Recognition of the ability to bring about creativity and need through your thoughts, through your awareness must be recognised. This is not something for a later date but something that needs to be used now, needs to be made aware of now. You need to know that your thoughts carry patterns.

The patterns within this time are still held in abeyance, conjunct to your relative patterns brought through the genetics and sub-conscious. You are not aware of all your thoughts nor the patterns behind the thoughts. To change the thoughts patterning, one must be able to release all of the yesterdays. One must be able to live primarily in the Now and bring one's thoughts into that balance of Now.

You must recognise that thought itself can be counterpart of that which you go towards. Thought must be used primarily, for form creation. It must be recognised as a means of distilling information, as a means of programming that which is necessary, a usage, a tool. When you deal with others, send the quality of the tone of your intent before you use words. Begin to become comfortable with this type of communication.

Awaken those cells that are used primarily through your sleep state at this time. They were not meant to die nor linger and this will gravitate toward a life force in your body which will open you to a much quicker change as well as longer life. Longevity will become common place within your future races and you yourselves can lengthen this considerably. Work upon your own spectrum.

Questions.

Q: At the beginning you spoke of a double helix coming from the pyramids. Are you speaking of the pyramid or is this a figure of speech?

A: This is a visual to the levels of your own hierarchical lines. The pyramid is how the unconscious pictures the hierarchical structure within yourselves. The spiral tone lifts this and begins the consciousness' growth through the lives, not lives on a lateral level. Opening to this now, bringing within yourself the consciousness of your own dimensions, this force becomes a double helix gradually. Your children's children will be born with the natural capabilities already in consciousness, although you do the work for this problem. This will change the structure, likened to the pyramid, fully into the helix through generations. It cannot happen automatically, but merges and moves on.

Q: Is this related in any way to two spirals which are spiraling in opposite directions as if to balance each other?

A: Yes.

Q: I'm particularly thankful that you have answered questions which I wished to ask earlier and actually written down, and you have taken it even further than I have contemplated, in discussing symbolism and sound and patterns of the mind and form and creativity. Thank you for that. You have answered many of my questions. It is so difficult for us to take this one step further and imagine the reality of creating form from our thoughts. That is a very difficult step, and in the construction of new materials, as well as, perhaps, new forms of transportation, it is that last step that we find very difficult to envisage. Can you help us with this at all?

A: It is not so much a difficulty as a fear, and this fear lies primarily within the arms of responsibility. You, all of you, have not been educated into "responsibility".

In the old patternings of your cultures, it was part of the growth of the community to bring the young ones through what became known as "initiations" during the teens and early teens. This was bringing them into the roles of responsibility. This has been denied you, quite consciously, so you would not take what is rightfully yours.

Through time, over periods, it has become a fear within the psyche. This fear is being fought at the very basic levels across your planet, in civil wars and such like. It is also being fought within the individuals as each determines the quality of their outflow into life itself and their inter- action with it.

This responsibility, this fear that we speak of now, with you, is accepting fully who you are and what you are here to serve, to work for. Knowledge of this is not power, as in ego, but it is power of One Self – self empowerment, non-reliance on an outer force, Self- reliance.

You can look through your lives, each of you and you can see more than the fingers and the toes that you have. How many times you have caused form to be, through your need, through your creativity. They were not times of fear, nor harm, and more often than not they became, through thoughtlessness. Control closes you to the eternal flow. It must come from a space of ease and wholeness.

See yourselves, each of you, not just as an individual, not just as a planet, but as a galaxy, the Universe, the planets revolving within you, the Sun, the Moon, and the Earth. Feel the movement of the vibrational patterns that you carry and through that movement you will be able to explore that which you can do.

Now that it is in your full conscious awareness, the capabilities themselves can seem daunting, to the point where they become doubtful. But this, too, is a step one must overcome. Ignorance itself must be swept away. Knowledge must be given and those with the capabilities will draw from it like the sacred breath and will breath out that which is not needed.

Q: You speak of the short time scale. Will these things happen generally across the planet as we awaken in general or as individuals across the planet?

A: This awakening is an occurrence and it is a vibrationary pattern that colours the atmosphere of the planet. Those who draw upon it are many, many, many. How it works through them is how light becomes the rainbow – according to the awareness, the awakening. According to the ability to respond, will each, show itself. The dimensions of righteousness and wrong will become stronger. Gradually the light will penetrate even into your darkest areas. It is a time of transition. The transition will occur.

There will be the march of many feet. After, the light will continue to grow. Chaos will give way to order. Not the order of alignment of the mass for the needs of the few, but the order of natural harmony, the order of the needs, not just for the peoples of the planet, but the needs of the animals, the plant world, the planet Herself.

The scale of the work you do may seem like a drop in the ocean, but the ocean is made of drops and this ocean can be cultivated through your drops. The technological advances must be on-par with the consciousness in humanity. You need not just to awaken the spirit level, but the creative level. It is through creating that there is growth. Stagnation comes through lack of growth. Watch a plant. Look at your fellow people.
Creativity can be brought out through life enhancing technologies. We speak of Spirit and matter, combined. To us it is one. This is part of the separation. There is no well defined line. It is a merging of force that this can occur.

Q: Can I ask a general question about things which you are telling us which we accept here in this small group. Are these things for general publication? Is it permissible that we should talk of these things because they are all good things? Is it permissible at this time?

A: Yes. This is permissible. You will find many can choose. Few will hear. Those that do not, the seeds are laid. Those seeds are there for them and all those they come in contact with and they will lie within their own patterning for their children's' children.

Q: I was asked today if the information we were receiving was anything to do with Galactic Federation.
Could you answer that please?

A: It is direct. This which you speak of, it seems you have not understood, is a Federation of Light Force from various planets already attuned to a high harmonic frequency. Life forces similar to yourselves but varying in degree according to their own planetary needs. None are as far back as you in technological ventures, nor consciousness, but we must say here that there are worse! Not many! A few! Those that are, are not of human form.

This federation has chosen to step into the awareness of the planet's needs. When I speak to you of the Council I am speaking direct. Of those within the Federation, there are three that no longer contain form as you know it.

One holds within liquid and another is able to change through the Will. Others are of form that could be recognised, varying in degrees. These visuals you are given of creatures from other planets are very much there, embedded in your psyche, as keys to fear which can be used if needed. There were also times in the history of the Universe when there were fearful components to this force and this lies also within the vibrational fields of the psyche.

What we speak of and what concerns us is now, and now, onwards to tomorrow. It is relevant to move back in your time scale, your history, to understand the passage of this time in its growth through your unconscious and through the mass psyche; learning, adjusting, releasing and revealing.

There are no more questions? We will leave you, in Peace.

# Energy Levels

(24th March 1993)

Greetings my friends. I come forward here from the Council of Beings and we wish to continue our discourse this evening, talking here primarily upon energy levels.

We wish to talk here firstly upon the sub-atomic particles of energy and 'L' fields, which are affecting you regularly and also positively and retrospect of the negative levels of your atomic bodies. These particles, these vibrationary fields, are in operation not just upon humanity, they are upon all living on and within your planet. The planet is part of the process of the sub-atomic levels. These sub-atomic levels of energy are brought forward through the reactive effect upon the causal level, causal level being one of the principles of Universal Law. This law brings about energy, it brings about magnetic fields of vibration.

The sub-atomic particles, the energy fields that vibrate through this, have their own causal bodies, dependent upon the various rates of density within that.

You will find that is what brings forth the perfection of matter, the variation of matter in its prime operative, through humans - yes - and also through all the living force fields themselves. You will see that in this way, the sub- atomic energy rates, can also be affected and are affected by the levels of exchange of energy through the rate of the humans' endeavour to grow, for the consciousness to inspire and to bring forth all that within its own understanding. These fields are also open to levels called 'L'.

These 'L' levels of energy are coming now very much through the rate of exchange that is based primarily through the genetic input, in its connection to the outer principles of the states of planetary source. When we talk about these planetary sources we are going back through the genetics to your own cultural and through the cultural to the vibrationary rate of your planetary origins, the origins of vibration that you have come here with, working through, and brought forward into this life space.

As they come into their own level of balance, these energies will open you to a rate of exchange that is based primarily on your own need to release the density as you grow onto the next plane or level of consciousness, the level of consciousness being one that goes beyond thought, that goes beyond matter. It travels within its own spatial effect.

This carries with it the need or the principle to bring into creativity, light bodies. These light bodies are being created at this time - be it consciously, or unconsciously, by yourselves: through your own need, through your desire for growth, you are creating these light bodies. The more you do this in consciousness, the more profound, the more collected, the more open, the less restricted, these light bodies become. These light bodies themselves will eventually allow you to travel, will bring into your orb all that is needed, within and beyond thought variance.

When we speak of thought variance, we are speaking of the principles of sound; the use of sound to create that of matter which is necessary. You will be able to use this, indeed you can use this now through your own awareness factors, through opening yourselves to a centre force of internal exchange. Allowing the sound variance to become pure harmonic tone within your own selves, you can begin to use this in its variance, to bring that which is necessary into your life stream. You will find the movement from the dense into the light, one more of ease. The organs will begin to attune and atone to that variance thereby creating the harmonic. You will find this in operation. You will find this is something that needs to be worked with and upon, now, to bring into awareness of your consciousness.

Questions.

Q: Yes. What are these sounds? How do we obtain them and how do we use them?

A: Sound is the principle behind matter. All living force comes through sound. Sound is in harmonics through each people, through each animal, through each human. To work upon sound you must first, primarily, find the balance of your own sound and the harmonics of that sound within the body, within the mental apparatus, moving into the astral, etheric and down into the physical and emotional. Allow yourself to become attuned to sound. Listen to tones, follow the variance of tones. You will realise that you cause the variance through your emotional bodies and how they connect. To create a sound yourself, you will in yourself cause variances, even in the physical tone, you will cause variance. It is this variance that has its own effective flow through the body. Take this sound, work upon this sound, using it, sounding it, through meditation, until there is no variance.

When the tone is clear, held, then you will begin to recognise sound through words, attitudes, thoughts, of your own and of others. You can then explore the possibility of sound in all of your living consciousness. When you reach this point in your life, you will be able to use sound. You can use sound not just for purifying, not just for aligning; you can use sound also to bring the principle vibration of the planet into balance.
To begin with, it is often constructive to use a tone from a gong or something of this nature.

Q: When you said about releasing some of the denser energies onto another level, how do we go about this?

A: The vibrationary planet is working on various levels, various degrees of harmony, each one overlapping the other, through its rays of consciousness. As you move in through to your light bodies, you will find the imbalance of your own psycho-emotional bodies becoming more obvious. There is a need to recognise the levels of operation that you are working through as a coherent mental, physical, emotional being, with spiritual and tribal interplay, having levels of life within every second of every moment. These cause effects on the causal level, bringing to you that which you yourself have created through the bodies.

To bring this to a level where you can begin to release the densities, you must first be able to recognise that which you release. You must be able to see yourself, to see the modes of operation occurring within you, as you go through any reactive phase or responsive motion. The probabilities of life hold you within those forces. You can feel the occurrence, you can register the understanding, you can begin to attune with the bodies in their own interplay. Rather than cutting from you that which holds you, it is embracing and moving through, this then allows it to fall away.

Q: On the positive side, what would these new types of energy be causing - on a collective level?

A: Through the causal vibrationary fields, the sub-atomic energy levels in effect at this time, are bringing peoples to points of crisis: collectively, independently. The crisis point is one that needs to be breathed through. Through the breath of vibration one can move from the structured level, which is based primarily in the genetic, to the unstructured, which in itself has loose atomic particles - even the unstructured can be called structured. Through releasing the principle forces that hold you into structure, be it on an independent or on a tribal level, you can begin to bring into effect, through your own life's path and through the lives of those you are in contact with, the ability of working beyond known factors.

What was known to be is no longer. You are bringing into effect new laws of operation to live by, to work upon, to create within. For some, this may sound as an impossible venture, for structure has become a leaning post, a vehicle, but life is not there to cut off the flow of containment for those in need. The changes that are coming and are amongst you now, will allow the shift to occur that is necessary. The planet is shifting vibrationally; the axis will begin to shift. This is all part of the need to bring again the awareness of truth.

Q: I would like to ask a question on a subject not connected. We received correspondence stating that an object was coming towards the Earth on a periodic level and was due any time, which would cause everything to shift and brought back old stories about a 12th planet. Is there any reality in this and how can I deal with this query?

A: We have spoken at an earlier date upon the proton belt and upon the vibrationary fields that occur through this.

Much of that which you speak is fear orientation. The masses constantly need to hold something beyond that they can direct their negative venture into. Therefore you have a God and a Devil. It is for the individual, the family, the group, the community, to take prime responsibility for occurrences, within themselves and around them.

As we work with you, our operational mode is to help truth, to enlighten your ability to see and recognise need, to open to the levels of your own inner attainment. In this way, the work you set forth is of course a primary function; the main function is one of light. As you become more attuned to the light bodies, you will see much of the work you have done has been to bring this into being.

There was and is still, in the psyche of humanity, the Root memory of the difficulties of the outer planetary experiences, and using this such as your myths, it has been taken and enlarged, to contain peoples' fears and needs. When others speak of forces, good or evil, that come to the planet, will come, will save, will harm, you must look to the truth of your own nature, which is one of light, harmony through the use of service. You will find that this brings you always onto the path of enlightenment.

When we spoke earlier of the "L Fields", these fields criss-cross over your planet, and they can be used as alternative fields of energy. This is something that will be tapped into within the next fifteen years and already there is some work on this in Australasia. This is something that you will hear about, and it will come forward to you again. When you are in contact with these persons, it is important to see how these lines of energy operate across the planet and the mid points. For these mid-points are the points of energy drawn through the planet, and it will be there that you will find that there will be scope, not just for the alternative energy, but in many places there will also be purified water.

These places will escape much radiation; it will be a natural counter balance. These "L Fields" can be set up through these structures, to broadcast the vibrationary rate that will cut through the radiation levels; dissipating. You will find that this will also be used with fresh water.

Q: Are they particularly connected with the old ancient ley lines that they used to measure?

A: They were at one time. But no longer. It has shifted. It is important here also when we speak of the fresh salt water, we are speaking of salt water that has had plankton, which in itself is a source of purification.

It will be used, one; as a source alternatively, like a battery. It will be used, two; also as a means of alternative source of energy for the body. There will be a lot more farming using the sea.

Q: As in fisheries or actually using salt water on the land?

A: Both and also growing certain foods in the salt water itself.

Q: Can we use these areas for healing energy? Can we obtain the energy from these concentrated areas for healing?

A: Healing is something that becomes one's own self mode. Each person will become their own self healer. As you move into your light bodies, you will be aware, by the reflective tone, either the variance of sound, colour or movement within matter, of any imbalance within the body. This can be adjusted through your own light energies. You will find that the light force will be something that can be shared very easily with and upon others, if they themselves have not reached it.

During this period, when suffering of the 'sub rosa' illusions that have been given to you as Humanity as a way of keeping you in your own dullness and darkness, when this itself has broken through and you are able to reach within, to the level of light force that you contain, you will find then, healing to be apparent, permanent and almost instantaneous. Remember that you carry still, very much held bound vibrations that cause reaction and reverse within you.

This constant battle which rages on the greater and the lesser in your world is carried within you all, until you reach a point of equilibrium, where all is and you are contained within that. Light is natural, it is fluid, it is movement, it is sound. Follow this course if you may, and you find that the structures that contain are no longer there. It is no longer necessary for the masses to be kept in ignorance. You need, you are ready, and you are open, to preparing yourself for self- harmonising.

It has been a pleasure that we have shared together. Thank you

# Light Bodies

(31st March 1993)

Greetings my friends. I come forward here from the Council of Beings, to continue our discourse with you. Much of that which we have spoken on has been concerning the light bodies, and the need to generate the vibrationary rate within your own sphere, for the accumulation of these light bodies. These light bodies are in fact, the next vibrationary rate you will be moving into. It is necessary for you, as we have spoken of, to begin to use these light bodies, to begin to recognise and to work at this time with and upon and through, these light bodies. By doing so, you are helping yourselves, not just to heighten the vibrationary rate, to grow and accelerate, but also to bring into occurrence the higher levels of vibration that are affecting the planet at this time.

These levels of vibrationary rates that are coming through to the planet, are also bringing an occurrence on a more detrimental level, to those levels that are not in accord with light. Therefore you will find, within your own structures, the need to bring centred awareness within your own emotional, psychosomatic and mental fields and bodies. You will find that through this apparatus, you can indeed help yourselves to move forward.

There is much talk at this time upon your planet concerning negative forces in operation; those coming through the planets' sphere to this planet, namely those "Greymen".

We wish to say here with uttermost truth and love, that this is something that has been put upon you, as a way of causing fear and disalignment upon your planet.

Many of those who are opening to the higher fields and levels of consciousness, are not doing so in a way that is compatible with the lower levels or the lower bodies. They are therefore being able to be manipulated through these beings, these forces that have been sent from your own planet's sphere. There are those few who do not wish the mass of Humanity to grow, to awaken, to take within themselves the knowledge of wholeness, of co-operation, indeed of communion with self and it is in this communion with self that you must allow yourself constantly to work within.

Hold yourself in the position of light. Know the truth of your own heart. Follow that truth and you will find that you will magnetically approach and be brought forward into those spheres within your own working and personal positions. We are being shown here, that there are also workings of sound upon your planet, some to cause disturbance, again on the lower levels, to cause stages of imbalance, allowing again the populace, the inability to come together and to grow.

It is therefore of vital importance to be aware of these frequency waves, to be aware of using as little as possible of these frequency waves in your daily existence. You will find that in this way again you can help to keep yourself attuned.

Questions.

Q: The frequency of these waves, you have just spoken about. You are speaking of television, computers? Is that what you are referring to?

A: These are partly the waves. There are also waves in operation, very similar to the electrical waves that are being used magnetically, upon the planet. You can use similar frequencies for alternative energy. This is something that has been tried and tested, but not in use and it is something that will again come into use through your technological advances. Tesla was one who used this.

Q: So the sounds that are being generated towards us at this time - is there a way to put out an interference signal to negate these sounds, or is it necessary?

A: This occurs on two levels. 1 it causes the input to bring forth the technological advances to negate. 2. it resurrects the vibrationary force within your own character analysis through the genetics, to actually allow yourself the shift to move more fully into your light bodies.

Q: I misunderstood or didn't follow properly, when we were speaking of those beings that were not opening themselves up to the light properly. It is like a misunderstanding. We were talking about the Greys.

A: Many of those who have had experiences with these 'Grey' forces, are those who are open, but not to the level of attunement of the bodies – most especially, manipulated. This happens 1. on a physical, but also 2. on a lower astral projection of this.

These projectory bodies are used to bring force, through fear, to the individual, thereby eclipsing the actual growth and stimulation of their own force, in a direction that is not of clarity.

When there are difficulties, nay complications, that arise, one must be aware that through the force of your own intellect you have a vibrationary rate that can be called complementary. This in itself can often attune to a flow that brings cause and effect.

This can be overcome through the stimulation, through the pituitary, of your own endocrine system, which can allow the purification of your thought levels, the pattern of these thought levels and the purification of your own nature.

Q: How can we detect in oneself the coming of these vibrations and is it possible to welcome these vibrations and let them rest in oneself, so that through letting them be, they can move of their own accord to transform?

A: Yes. This is an important operation.

As one becomes aware of any festering doubt or fear, as one becomes aware of moments of inability to bring forth clarity in situations, one can also become aware of a similar conjunct within the physical. Be aware within your own physical apparatus at that point. Send the thought, not into that which you are trying to work through, but into the body, at that moment.

As you send your patterning through the body, the clarification itself becomes obvious. You will find this way indeed, a period of rest, respite. You will also find the physical itself being moved through this into a heightened state of awareness.

Q: Thank you. Is there a way of activating the pituitary gland so that is can accelerate the vibrations or pick up the finer vibrations?

A: One simple mode of operation which has been used through your times has been very much with sound. You will find that the gong is very indicative of this. The Buddhists use this very much for this process, using the gong to stimulate the gland into movement. You hold a vision, a point of light, the sound itself magnifies that light.

As it magnifies, it becomes larger, opening. This is symbolic of the opening of the pituitary gland. You will find that as it opens, it will be almost astral bodies that you are able to move through. As one moves in, through to the light, one is also moving out into the light. So the occurrence is both inward and outward. The point, the centre point is the essence of the wholeness of life itself.

Q: There is a relationship between the pituitary gland and the solar plexus and also with much higher levels of communication and communion. These laws, are they becoming activated more through the light or through the sound?

A: They are one in essence. The streams of light carry the impulse of sound. Sound itself is a manifestation of light. The moment one reaches the point of the expression of light, within and through oneself, one is sound. As we speak here, our magnetic impulse is of sound. Your own magnetic fields pulsate with this sound. It creates a vortex of energy that allows an acceleration of movement and awareness.

This is something that is not activated by us purely; this is activated by the communion of our light forces. In the direction of this quality, one can use that flow for direct healing, for materialisation if necessary, for movement and growth.

Q: This healing, is it the healing done through healing of the presence or through the magnetic healing, such as laying on of hands?

A: Movement. The healing is the motion of the direction of the force of your thoughts. Self-healing, the healing of oneself, the coming together of self, is healing. As one moves further towards one's light body this will be the presence of work within oneself and one's nature. Another person often accommodates this process, and can help this to occur by the emergence of their coming together. When one works within a group structure this is accelerated. Most bodies need to experience the presence of love within their lives. The presence of this love force you often named Christ. The presence of this love is the presence of Self.

Q: Is it true that the Greys have been supplying governments with advanced technology and is there anything that needs to be done in that direction or will it simply be worked out in the fullness of time?

A: There are certain technological advances not yet known to the populace, held by certain governments and their agencies. These are not so much given to them as something that they themselves have been a part of in implementation. For many of your years, certain peoples upon the planet have been taken, either willingly or not willingly, to certain specific points, to work upon governmental direction.

This is not something, although overt, that should concern you necessarily. Being aware, does not have to put you in a negative or fearful position. It gives you more recognition but also the recognition that once these technological advances are open in this way, they are also filtered into the mass psyche of Humanity and can be filtered again through certain types of individuals with scientific or technological mentalities.

The recognition that you yourselves are walking a path to bring this awareness of light to your own growth, to use it as part of service to your planet, to your brothers and sisters, allows you a greater force than you recognise. It is a force of protection, as the direct quality of your work is in operation, with movement of light.

Q: The pineal gland is the receptacle for the reception of light. Is it possible to do a specific work to link it more directly with the pituitary gland?

A: There is a direct link in itself, between the pituitary and the pineal, open to a gland more within the etheric body itself, just over, (indicating the head) you understand. This can be felt by those with magnetic force and has also been used more in the past through the ancient Egyptians and also in India. The Sikhs at this time too, work very much with this. As the pituitary itself opens through the light, the directive quality of this, can also flow and very much does, through the pineal.

Recognition not so much of thoughts, but the value of your own directive flow through the thoughts, will be stimulated by this and you will find this will become more visual. This visualisation, much of what can be called psychic, is in fact, opening you to the ability to see rather than to recognise. Much of Humanity looks to recognise. This recognition feeds the brain. As you see, you will be able to direct that flow through the vision, thereby telepathy will become more easy, and also the direct quality of the flow of energy, from one to another.

Q: Is it possible to open oneself directly to the energy of the creative vacuum from other dimensions, and use that energy?

A: This is something that will be used very much within the light bodies. The light bodies themselves will be able to move consciously through the dimensions. It is for this you are working within and clearing your own fields of endeavour of the patternings of the past.

We spoke at an earlier stage of all experience and thought being held within the sub-conscious process of your own organic fields. These capture and hold much energy. As you release these processes from your fields, the energy itself becomes clearer, the speed of motion and also the awareness, become more apparent. You are able, through that, to become aware of the dimensional qualities. These fields of vibrationary rate will be able to be used. We spoke earlier of the need to be aware, at that time, of the physical, as there could be a burn out, when one moves more directly into that flow. One is able to take the physical but not be encumbered by it. So the simple answer is "Yes".

In these dimensions the bodies themselves have a light force, a quality and life. These lives are becoming more apparent not just in your meditative state, but most expressively in your dream functions. You will find your need to be aware of your dreams. Begin to be conscious of your dream states. You will find that gradually through time, there will be those trained dream patterners who can help people to overcome many states, not just of mental and psychological anguish and fear blocks, but also physical through the dream states. This is something that can be used much more proficiently and helpfully.

It will be used also for animals. It can be used through radionic broadcasting, but you will find, that the actual connection, through these dream patterners, will be more of a physical connection. They will be able, not just to help the individuals to achieve, through their dream states, but, by touching certain points, will activate memories. This will be very helpful, most especially for children, and for those that have become enclosed.

At this time it can be used with children, through certain functions of painting, the movement of certain colours, shades, into shapes, into lines, and back again, can stimulate certain functions which can help to activate memory to be brought forward for the dream state.

Using the colour yellow, down to indigo, and back again, can help to activate the birth trauma. Once activated, the child will begin, through its dream state, to recognise the operation, to work through it with a state of understanding and wholeness within the physical, which is most important, and this will also activate memory occurrence as well as a more pronounced physical and mental outlook in life.

Q: Would you talk about the connection between our awareness of the light bodies and our functioning in a business and a physical, material reality?

A: As you move towards the light force of your own apparel, you are able to bring this into clarity with every thought, action, decision. Working this into the business worlds, you will find there will be more group working rather than individual focus. We are not speaking here of the individuals but on a more pure sense.

Using this you will find, in a more personal sense, that you will be able to activate you own sense of light, that is, sense of knowing and directive flow into Being. This is not just within, but directed into that operation you are working upon. When this is directed towards the individual you are working with, or the company or groups of people, you will find the directive quality of your intent, through light, with them, upon them, will bring out always, truth. Whether this is always comfortable or not is another matter, yet it will show truth. Your intent, in light, brings forth its own magnetic quality. That quality always resounds. Working in your light body, you will find, gradually, the work you are doing, will be taken by others in a more physical, mental, material way, as those around you begin to adjust, to the level of intent themselves.

As you move into a new level of enquiry so too the work itself changes. It becomes more inward and it becomes more planetary. The flower itself sends forth the seeds.

Q: You spoke about purification. Is there any way that one can encourage that, and how can that be achieved?

A: First you must be aware of the input of chemical activity in your foods, not just in the meats, but all foods. Through the working of your own directive flow it is important - imperative - for you to begin to change this quality. Gradually this will change in a more holistic nature. But within this space now, it is of importance to move the flow of all this irradiation and chemical input through the foods. This can be done in various ways.

Agriculture itself is changing. That which has worked on your planet for generations is no longer working. There is less joy in those people working to fill you with food. There is no harmony between them and the foods.

Many of the foods are not touched by human hands.

As one works more with that to come, one will see that communities most especially, will have their own farming. Much of that grown within the Earth will not grow natural in the earth but will grow alternatively. This will help while the period of adjustment of your own work upon the level of energy within the earth itself is going on.

You will find that this form of farming will be very productive.

You can use a similar type of greenhouse that will be on various levels and mood. Plants themselves, foods grown through this, are very susceptible to the vibrationary rate which you direct towards them. When you have a very large fruit or organic vegetable, it is not so much the fertiliser, as the intent of the individual working with this. This can be used with the rhythm of the moon to help to produce growth. Will this feed the starving? There is more than enough to feed all. As the deserts are reclaimed, the magnetic flow restructured through the waterways, you will find that much will come from these areas to feed the newly parched areas of the planet.

Q: Is there also a need for purification at the moral or emotional level? I am thinking about possessiveness – at that level of operation?

A: Purification of the self is imminent to any who walk the path to light. One cannot continue to grow, to emerge, if one is held by the denser values of force.

To allow oneself to release these, one needs to live in truth; true to one's own nature. This requires the releasing of toxins from the body, as well as the mind, of working through the structure of one's own genetic patterning, with love and compassion, and cleansing the body physically. Exercises, massage, fasting, are all ways of opening and cleansing.

One needs to look at one's resistance to, one's fear of it. To eliminate this, one can work through the process of the breath and movement.

It has been a pleasure that we have spoken together and we will speak again.

Thank you.

# Water

(21st April 1993)

I come forward here from the Council of Beings and I wish to speak with you this evening, concerning the magnetic flow and cause of events through the quality of water in your region, both within the region of humanity and the planet.

Water carries force, form - within that; we have organisms that are in resonance to that force. This bacterial force is in itself multiplying at this time across your planet.
It is multiplying due to the atmospheric conditions.
It is multiplying due to the chemical conditions in your waterways.
This is also the same with humans.

You carry a resonance; your resonance is a harmonic of each other. As the water - this contaminated water that you are taking in at this time - moves through the body, it is affecting the body physically. It is affecting the body psychologically and emotionally. This occurrence is causing an upsurge of emotion in people. The more contamination there is, the more the upsurge.

The resistance finds its own level. To bring this into a state of balance and equilibrium you need to clear the water. The water, the organisms, are multiplying under the force of the sun. You therefore need to reflect the solar rays rather than have direct solar rays. You need to filter the water through magnets. This will help to nullify, this will also help within your own systems. You can do this too on a larger scale, through your own resonance system using your body as a resonance for the harmonic of the planet.

By changing your resonance you are helping to change the occurrence of the planet, you are helping to clear the vibrationary force which is affecting the planet at this time. Your bodies are working constantly to bring balance to release these organisms within you which are captured through the minute cellular activity within the colon.

Emotion itself is movement. This movement captured, brings a release of emotional toxicity. This is held through control, it is held through

genetic passage. It is held through the various vibrations connected through your auric passage of events of life. These are captured within your own cellular system. They are captured through your need to hold reality as you see it, to give substance to form, rather than recognising, directing, releasing the will.

One can allow oneself to open, to absorb, to become part of and to move through. Fluidity is the vibration that is needed at this time.

These atmospheric holes in the planet's aura are affecting certain parts of the planet more violently than others. Upsurges of emotion and energy will be filtered through, more across the Equator, through the Northern part of Europe down beyond Southern Africa and across the Pacific.

It is therefore important for yourselves, to begin the process of inner cleansing, outward releasing, and healing for your planet. The planet's role within this Universe has its own force and brings to it that which is necessary for growth. At this time, yourselves as humanity, and the planet, are working on a similar construction, the releasing of the inner points of resistance and force within your own psyches. The harmonic points of the planet are in balance. The entity of force of the planet is becoming whole within its own source. This swirl of activity is causing a rebound, spiral in nature, to all that within its orb: - Humanity, animals, plants, reptiles.

'Resistance' becomes illness, 'Passiveness' becomes static, 'Receptivity' merges. Each of you carries within you multidimensional factors allowing you the opportunity to move within and beyond your known circuit of event. This will become more in activity, not just through your dream state, not just through meditation, but through the act of opening and receiving, acceptance of the true nature. The true nature is all and one - constant, yet in motion, the force is likened most to light and yet, in movement beyond.

Questions.

Q: You spoke of using magnets in water. Could we use a light weight magnet which might remove all the signals and information from the water? Would this be effective enough?

A: This is effective on a very small scale releasing the impulses, i.e. information is also opening the structure of the organisms themselves. The organisms themselves through this nullification are able to change through the magnetic quality.

It is very important to recognise the attunement of your own bodies to that of the water of the planet. Water itself in its course, is magnetic. It also carries, it can carry force and it can carry electricity. That which is made of it, and that which it becomes.

You have been educated into the likening of form to the planet as a heavy force holding you here through gravity. Gravity has become a master in many fields of consciousness and yet this is just one force. It is important to explore that which you are made of, in the likening to the planet.

Q: Is it possible to put healing information into water?

A: It is more than possible; it is done through magnetics but more through sound. Healing force itself can be brought into a quality of sound, for example taking a homoeopathic remedy that is of constant use and finding the sound to this. This can be done radionically; it can also be done through broadcasting sound. Each plant, each chemical, relates to sound. The body itself is of sound.

Q: Can I ask, how you would find the sound for a specific homoeopathic vibration or something similar?

A: One would take the preparation at its more dense level that is as a flower or root or some such you understand, before preparation, before the changes of harmonics. Taking it at this level - one can begin to broadcast sound upon it, one can watch quite easily the growth of this through different sound qualities. You will see the pitch will vary as the growth itself varies One must be aware in working with this, that one is also working with the variations of vibration of the quality of the moon and the phases of the moon.

For example here, we can have alfalfa growing on a AB tone and the intervals between (AB equating to musical scales) bringing through from sharp down to flat and you will find this is also quite significant for the movement of the fluids in the stomach. By broadcasting this you can begin to see the rate of activity of the growth then when you take it for preparation, the preparation can be done within the orb of that sound. You will find that your remedies will be of more value at a lower component. You will need less, much less.

Q: What about a magnetic or radionic or sound that could negate a quality in water for instance radioactivity or toxicity?

A: Taking radioactivity which is more difficult for you, than the toxicity, it is to be remembered that the planet Herself is at a certain level of radioactivity. Being so, your bodies are already absorbing certain levels of radioactivity which cannot be cleared immediately but must be filtered.

Working on sound for this, you will need to use a great deal of kelp and iodine - the sound within this is very much in the higher tones. This can be expressed through a bombardment of sound and it needs to be worked upon, it can be done, yes radionically, but it must also be filtered, the water must also be filtered through a type of filter that has the components of the salt sea within it. It is something that needs to be worked upon, but is something that can be done and should be done.

Q: Can you comment on how we can attune the resonance of our bodies to that of the water of the World?

Q: At this time it is more important for you to begin the process of cleansing. Unfortunately, if you attuned yourself precisely, with the tones of activity within the water of your planet, you would be very ill. So the need is to cleanse that which is coming in to your body, allowing the cleansing process to occur within the body and to begin the process of cleansing the water within the planet.

Q: Is there a specific amount of water which should be taken in every day?

A: It would be helpful for the body to have at least 2 litres of water to continue the process. The body itself, at this time, is absorbing much of the radiation and toxicity occurring, and this is causing a depletedness within the body - a drying out in areas that need to be kept moist. Most importantly at this time there needs to be the movement of the fluid from the stomach down towards the intestine. This area most precisely is causing a great deal of difficulty in many. There is a need here for massage very gently around the pancreas area and also here the awareness of the fluidity of the food that you eat. You will find the atmosphere becoming drier and drier.

Q: What is the nature of the currents, of the swirls happening from the Equator and does it affect particularly the British Isles?

A: Not particularly, but also. This activity is very much the emotional balance we spoke of. Imbalance of vibration as it comes through the pockets of atmospheric vibration. This is having an effect upon the body, within the body, and also upon the mass psyches. It is a time for realignment, a time for cleansing, a time for opening one's own restrictions on one's self. Use this time not as a time of detriment but as a time of purification. It is a time of inner purification and this will continue for some time to come. It will be a time when each has to release and look within. There will be much submerging into past as each person has to come to terms with their own psyches.

Q: Are there any particular places in Great Britain, in Europe where the water coming from the Earth is charged with this energy of another dimension?

A: Yes. For your continent there is Wales, in the mountain areas, some deep springs which have a very strong force upon them. Also we are being drawn here magnetically to Scotland, the very top and to the left and again into the Midlands to the left. You will find that moving towards all the mountainous regions there are strong magnetic flows which are recapturing, realigning and bringing forth this vibrationary field at this time.

It is important here if possible, to attune yourselves if not physically then psychically to these areas, to allow this mass vibration to help permeate with you in your own growth. The mountain regions are most important, here in Europe. We are taken of course to the main mountain range, but we are also taken up here to Sweden, also to the uppermost brim of Russia, where there is a deep up-welling of water that has not yet been tapped into. The water surrounding it, the lakes surrounding it are very contaminated, but they are not touching this deep water source which will be used within the next period of your time.

Q: Can colour be used in the purification of water?

A: Of course, but you need more. Colour is good but for the organisms growing at this time it is necessary to use also sound or the magnetics.

Q: If you have a good water filter, a mechanical water filter, is it advisable to use also sound or magnets in your home, around it, to improve the water?

A: Yes. These organisms cannot be filtered with the filters that have been produced at this time. They are continuing to reproduce especially under the sun.

Q: What type of organisms are these, are they something that is new to us?

A: They are new, and yet very old, because the Earth is releasing and cleansing this force of emotional uprising. It comes from another age when the emotional traumas were such to cause physical havoc upon the planet and to humanity, the people of the time. As man and woman grew towards their higher egoic bodies and roles, the source of discontentment, the force of separation, was never completed within them, never released, but lay dormant. This power was a power of force that may be likened also to the forming of the Earth. You must remember that one is of the magnetic quality of the other. These organisms have again been activated now and through the work of your own light bodies, through the work of your own need to grow and open, these continue to be released rather than to be lodged within you.

The imbalance otherwise is not just emotional, physical within the individual, it is also, or could also be, distractive within the mass, the group mass, and this can be of uprisings upon the planet. The time of dissension is very near on a mass scale.

Those who work within the light are also strong but awareness comes as awareness does, and knowledge finds its home. Those that work, those that fight, those that grow, and those that pray, are all open to this force. As you centre upon your own force of light and activity, so the knowledge itself becomes a component of that growth - it opens you into new areas of awareness, into new arenas of work and ability.

For those for whom this opportunity is not available, then their own inner nature will take control, and that inner nature is determined not just by their spiritual and genetic background, but by their life and how they have lived that life.

The day of reckoning is coming within you, by you. This cleansing is one that allows you to grow into that light-body for which you have been preparing and as time moves, that light-body will become more and more that which you work within. The physical itself will be that which you use when necessary.

Q: The rise of the emotional world when it is transformed, can lead to deep communicational communion? Is that communication going to happen through the bodies of light or through for example, the way the dolphins use, or other ways?

A: The communion will happen, through the bodies of light. It will also allow you through that to connect with each other on a more dense level. There will be gradually, as your times unfold, a more group communion, which will emerge as you are drawn towards your 'families' and you begin to grow and unfold together, sharing the truth of your natures. First with yourselves and with others, you will find that this communion will also be of one within you all.

Q: You mentioned the effect of the moon. Is there a time during the cycle of the moon that contamination or organisms have different effect on our bodies?

A: At the time of your full moon, the effect is higher than at the time of your new moon. Also when the moon is with the influence of Mars, Neptune, and also when it is moving through the constellations known as your water signs then it is also more pronounced.

We are speaking here not of the signs as you know them but as the times have changed now, the precise movement.

Q: Could you clarify that?

A: The work that many of you do with the influence of the planets for the understanding of the psyche of the individual or even the mass is done according to a routing or mapping, many centuries old. This does not continue to move at the same speed of effect as the Earth with the Sun. Therefore the mass hold themselves within the awareness of a constellation and its vibration, a planetary influence, so then the mass is affected by such influence which is working through the psyche of that mass or individual.

The planet in its movement is actually in operation through another constellation. It has moved on. This can be adjusted and you can find this quite simply and you will find that working with this adjustment will make things much more specific for you.

Q: I should like to ask another question. I am assuming that the magnet we would use would be round and with a hole through the centre. Much like the type they use to treat water so it will not let calcium deposits round a kettle of boiling water. If we used the system that took away the information of the water then used a magnet with a spiral to re-energise the water, would that be an efficient way of treating water?

A: It would. The spiral, of course, is very important energizing. Also if, when you are building larger units, you place in rock, jagged, that has any type of crystalline structure - specific crystals from the structure and also some life in the water growing - as it moves through the spiral, the life and the jagged rocks, then it takes on a fuller life force. This will accelerate the growth used by the water.

Q: By life are you speaking about something like moss?

A: Yes.

We will go now and we will talk again.

# Psych-kinetic Energy

(28th April 1993)

I come forward here from the Council of Beings to continue our discourse together.

The psycho-kinetic energy emanating from your minds through the brain which continue to allow the reality of the materialisations primarily in origin is based within illusion. It is held together by the mass function, the function of the unconscious, the unconscious needs, swamped through fear and necessity. These vibrations are waves of energy, emanating from the psyche of the individual and also from the consciousness of the mass. Thus this can be manipulated consciously and used. It has also been played with by replicating that vibrationary rate through machines both in Russia and Israel and at this time in the Northern States of America. Using the psychic potential of the individual, more on the unconscious than conscious, is very much something that is being worked with at this time in those areas, particularly Israel. Part of the work they have done in their desert regions has been within this focus. Mass hysteria, mass vision, also comes through this psycho-kinetic vibration.

You are a participant in life. You are a participant in the life of the planet, the life of Humanity, but you need not be a blind participant. You can be aware, awakened. You can use your own kinetic impulse to direct the flow of the creative force, the vibrationary rate, within your own bodily structures. As they become more subtle and attuned to their own sound frequency, you will find that you will be able to direct this vibration, this force, into the greater force of Universal essence that is impregnating across the planet. The waves of vibration, the revolution of the energetic flood of these vibrations, is bringing forth impulses of energy within the individual and within the mass, allowing, directing, the need for change, swamping many within that need.

Clarity is the force that is holding. It is allowing yourselves to become the essence of space within. Do not try to negate or fight but allow yourselves the movement and the quality of adjustment. This adjustment allows your own states of vibrational quality both within the conscious and unconscious to begin to resonate at one. This resonance holds you as a tone or a force of vibration that will keep on -key, as the level of vibrations around you begin and continue to change and swamp the mass unconscious. Your own kinetic output is to bring peace and a quality of life to the individual, to the peoples and to humanity.

Questions.

Q: Could you define 'mind' as you use it?

A: Over the centuries the imbalance between the functional works of the brain and the emotional interplay of the psyche have grown, and separated. Through the lack of education, through the necessity of the few to keep the many within shadow, this has grown to its own entity, an entity that is captured within the emotional and psychic interplay of the individual. It is coloured by that interplay, it is also coloured by the chemical balance or imbalance of the individual. It is also coloured by the mass psyche.

The essence of receiving and transmitting primarily works through the heart. The mind became a region which was used, to begin with, as a play-toy for inter-visualisation and script. As this became more pronounced outwardly, so it took on its own force, this resulted in the separation we have spoken of. As you begin again to unify within, to have your own inner communion, the mind itself will begin to dissipate - dissipate through lack of use. It does not need to be held. It is not a sign of intellect, but it is impressed constantly by the emotional and the egoic.

Q: What is the function of the brain - as opposed to the function of the heart?

A: The brain is similar to your computers. It is there for receiving memory and for using this – storing. It can be used very productively as a means of opening the intellect to the intuitive, not through the restriction of the mind, but through the enlightenment of consciousness.

Q: What is the origin of the creative impulse?

A: The creative impulse is the spark ignited by original thought. This came through the vibration quality of movement of the Divine force - Source.

Q: It is apparent that we need to achieve 'Divine Breath', in order to achieve this oneness that we spoke about this evening.
I know this question has probably been asked before - but can you give us a short lesson on what 'Divine Breath' is and how to do it?

A: This question has been answered before but we will tackle it from another angle. The breath is the essence. Your body in essence breathes. To inhale is to draw in the essence within you, not just through the mouth, nose, but through the fibre of your body. The skin itself breathes and the organs are affected by the breath. As you know, the nervous system and the muscular system are affected by breath. When you open and inhale, you are breathing in the essence of the life force within every fibre of your Being. The inner breath brings inspiration. When you exhale - expire, the body releases. As it releases, it is able also to release the toxins in the body, through the breath, through the naturalness of the breath.

If you could become aware, first for an hour, then for a few hours, then for several hours, then for a day and several days, of breathing consciously, constantly, you will see how the breath, not just moves within the body and thought, but how it can begin to dictate movement and thought. For you are breathing in life flow, life force. To continue to do this will restrict ageing. The body need not age; it can slow down the process as you move in harmony with this. Is this answer acceptable?

Q: Yes. So essentially it is not the pattern of breathing that's important just the awareness of breathing?

A: If you can be aware of the body itself opening to breath then you will find that the whole of the body will open and not just the top functions or the lungs.

Q: Can we move from this to the art and practice of directing our own reality?

A: First you must become aware of fear. Fear is a large component in directing reality. Fear has been fed like a household pet and now you are beginning to submerge this within your own realisations. Submerging is not necessarily the answer. One must always open fear through love, through expressive understanding.

When we speak of expressive we speak of this in the way that you can open fear through:
1.     A type of therapy that is comfortable for the individual.
2.     To be aware of why one constantly draws to oneself certain necessities, certain life - plays.

When one is able to embrace one's fear and through that, love and growth, then one indeed can use one's kinetic impulse for full creative functions. Knowing as you do that all thought creates, you will also find materialisation occurring very quickly. The kinetic impulse is to materialise. You can use this for adjustment both in technological and humane fields. It can be accelerated with certain types of energy fields, knowing the force of your creative function is always a doorway into your interstellar self. As one works in this field one begins to open those doorways and you will begin to attune and integrate your interstellar selves.

Q: Can you say more about how some are using technology for nature/agriculture.

A: They have a type of Orgone generator which five to seven of them are linked with. It is in the centre and there are coils from this to each of the seven, or it can be as little as the five. Holding this, they create first visually then aurically that which is needed; water, greening, wind, slowing down some local opposition and this is built up within the generator. The peoples working with this, as we said, are very aware individuals and are not doing this in any type of harmful conditions. This has been used for a number of years for the techno- agriculture areas. Five to seven people is the energy needed for this.

Q: Would it be recommended for us to attempt something like this or are we not ready to do that?

A: We do not feel that this is necessary at this time.
And it is important not to play with such things, but to use it in full consciousness. One has to be clear, both chemically, physically, mentally, organically within one' self to be able to work with this. You would all therefore need to go on a very drastic course of cleansing. They have no personal gratification, no need through this. It is primarily a function of service they give. They are beginning to look a little further afield but very warily. They have their own consciousness and acceptance of responsibility within this.

Q: We spoke before about a lot of the problems we have about mind development, its execution. Can you give us some hints on how we can educate children, so that they won't have such a difficult time adjusting to this as we had?

A: As we spoke before it starts not at school level but before conception. It will take two to three generations to see very clear results, but you are already seeing results within the children today from the changing patterns of their parents; attitudes carried within the parents' own vibrationary fields. The most stimulating function that is positive for the oncoming child is music, sound and quality of life within the individual. When we speak of quality of life, we do not mean material riches. We mean the quality of life; the individual is able to experience, to taste and to find joy in.

It is important with the new born, as we have stated before, the awareness of their needs, placing no restriction firstly to eye level six to eight feet and then from five days, eighteen to twenty feet, also around the body. This begins to lift any restriction of value, restrictions through peoples' needs not on the sense of clothes, but pressure of essence of energies around. It is primal and important that the child stays within the orb of the mother's sphere and now as the father becomes unified with that, the father's sphere also for those first days and gradually the family also become a part of that.

Q: We come back to the energy generators. At the moment because of pollution, we take in lots of pollution, is it possible to think in terms of building houses that would absorb, transform and diffuse the energy so that is free of pollution?

A: This is a very important point you have made here and we will bring this forward for you. We will now begin to stimulate that so that it can begin to be produced. It is also important when you breathe to be aware of the essence of light within the breath. Visualise it as a means of producing this for yourselves. Regular high intake of kelp, iodine, will also help to break down those unwanted in the body.

Q: We have a solution of atomidine which is a solution of atomic iodine from the Edgar Casey foundation. Will a drop of that in a pint glass of water be a possible solution to pollution?

A: Partially, not fully. It is more conducive to an inner cleansing of the bodily functions, especially that of the liver and kidneys.

Any last questions?
Q: Are we more at risk to the negative vibrations during our sleep state and do we need to protect ourselves or can our consciousness do this?

A: This is a good question. Again one must look at one's own mental/ emotional interplay. One must look at one's chemical balance or imbalance. One must look at the foods that one has taken in those last twelve hours. These play roles during your sleep state through the physical/mental. You absorb the energies around you, many of these you cannot contain or deal with through your daily function, so they are set aside by the psyche to be worked through in your night sleep.

This is often the basis for many dreams.

Those you have dealings with, also come into this category and if this is also not cleared and/or released within that day and space, then this too is carried into the night space and this has a very strong vibration for emotional reaction within the bodies. The chemical input within your body - you know your body or you should do, you should be able to feel and sense the body, see the needs, look at your thoughts and movements, are they conducive? Is there a chemical balance/imbalance at play here?

This can bring up a whole stream of events from your night space. Looking at these and also at the food you eat, the energy of that which you have taken into you, the energy as it works within the body, the interplay of energies producing enzymes, directing the flow of proteins, carbohydrates, fats, pushing through that not of necessity- all this is also worked within the night space.

Before you sleep if you have not been able to be aware through the day, then it is good to take a little time, and it will need only be little, to let yourself drift into the day again and see what is being held by you.
Release that in the aura of light.
Connect with your essence as you lie to sleep.
Do not go to sleep if you can help it with thoughts of mundaneness but with thoughts of light and joy and awareness.
This would keep you open to your more subtle vibration and can allow that subtle force to be more prominent through your night space. You will find more visions occurring, more healing and more rapid learning.

Thank you my friends.

# Proton Belt

(5th May 1993)

Greetings my friends. I come forward here from the Council of Beings and I wish to continue our discourse this evening.

As you are probably aware, you are moving through a proton belt at this time. This vibrationary field occurs infrequently in your Earth's history. At times of this vibrationary rate, you will find that it denotes great change. It also allows, through the atmosphere, levels of vibration that bring forth teachers into your Earth's realms. These teachers are enlightened beings who are able to manifest through the physical. Occasionally they come through the realm of the normal channels of your life i.e. birth and growth, but in most cases they are enlightened brings who are able to attune to a physical entity who has grown and opened themselves to a certain level of enlightenment and awareness. At this time as you move through this vibrationary factor you will find that the rate of acceleration is causing a breaking down of structures.

The structures are the structures within your own innate vibrationary field; they are the structures also within the vibrationary fields of humanity, the psyche of humanity, the physical material structures set forth by humanity to hold you in, like a zoo, to keep you enclosed and encased within your own fields of endeavour. As they affect you on the more personal, psychological levels they are also opening you to your own Soul vibration, they are allowing you to progress beyond the innate ability of the physical, material and mental density. They are allowing you to bring forth the consciousness of light bodies within the realms of the physical, allowing you to move towards and within these light bodies, bringing forth awareness factors that help to inhibit the density of fear and negativity.

You will find on the greater scale that the breaking down of structures can come through the communal, through the country, through the planetary realm of the psyche. This you will find will help to bring together gradually the idea of unity, of community and unity. The unity that grows within the individual has to be the mirror of that which grows within the planet.

The structure of the psyche of the planet, brought about through the needs of humanity, have to now be cleared from the debris of your own unconscious and from the materialisation that it builds up within the realms of your physical domains. Therefore it is necessary to look within oneself, as well as the planet, to see what is needed for recovery and growth.

As we move to the growth of the planet, you will find that the proton vibration helps the alignment of your own psychic abilities in the endeavour of bringing in to materialisation, that which is necessary for growth and enlightenment. This can be done on a mass scale; it can be done on an individual scale. It should be done on a conscious level and it can also be brought forward through the use of specific electrical equipment.

It is necessary with this proton vibration, to be aware of the cleansing that also occurs with this.

As one materialises, one brings forth the vibrationary rate of creating one's own seed bank. Of necessity, one can, through that, begin to vibrate from those seed banks that which is necessary for continual growth, not just that growth of the self nature, but growth of the egoic nature, the larger nature, which can bring about the emergence of the light bodies within your own time spheres.

You will find that these proton vibrations can be brought through the cleansing of your own physical, mental, apparatus. It can be brought through the realisation of the attunement of your dense bodies with the light bodies in the materialisation of growth and the working of service. These seed banks can be used not just for self enlightenment but it can be used also as a way of nurturing the planet. They can be used by you, by group endeavours consciously, to bring forth the balance in nature and in planetary awareness of the mass unconscious realms.

The changes occurring at this time both on the individual and planetary level are necessary for the breaking down of the structures that have been contained. These structures are held both within the physical, psychological and within the mental. It is necessary for growth to evolve beyond the need of structure. The planet is going through an evolutionary change. The change in the weather denotes this, not just through the ozone levels, not just through your own incapacity to digest that which is no longer necessary to the needs of the planet, but in the breaking down of that structure.

As a whole, humanity bases its need and its growth on a rhythm that has been given to it rather than drawing from the natural rhythm of its own light force. The rhythm humanity draws upon is one of structure and containment, to grow within safety and yet within that also, is lack of expression and freedom.

To move beyond this, one must break down within one's own unconscious ideology - that which one envisages as the norm, as regular structure - equating to structure. The changes in your weather variances, the changes in the tone of nature, the vibrationary forces affecting you all now, are here to help to break forth and to break through that structure.

Expect nothing, never look to tomorrow for what is needed now, live within the moment and see that moment as the whole, in your expression, in your desire, in your force. See the outer plane as the manifestation aligning one to the other. Beginning to align yourself, you will begin to align the outer to you. You, as a people, can bring balance again to your home by working first on yourselves. Your own atomic structures are not there to inhibit, but to enlighten and to bring growth. The alchemical process is a process that occurs not just on a daily scale within your own physical bodies, but occurs within seconds, constantly.

The process of change is within you all. You have but to recognise this to live with this and this will progress along to all and all that you work and are part of. You will find that this will help to bring forth the light bodies, shifting your awareness into awareness of light and unity. Movement in the future will come within thought, within intention, this is yet to be. You begin the steps of this progression, this transitionary movement, and allow this to be the operative tool that you can use for awareness of self and the awareness through the necessity of the needs of those around you. It is important during this transitory stage and for the next 10 - 15 years this will be most prominent, to be aware also of others in your domain, not just of the human family, but of the animal, the reptiles.

All go through change. When it affects one, it affects the whole, and the more you can bring the paths into awareness, the greater the step of the whole. Your responsibility is to self, is to your whole human family and to those of the animal, plant kingdoms. Recognise the needs, do not work against those who oppress and suppress. Work instead towards that of enlightenment and joy. These are the factors that will carry you through the changes of occurrence, for changes there will be, not just within your own innate forces, but on a planetary scale.

Questions.

Q: Yes, you spoke of access to seed banks to be used for growth and enlightenment; can you explain more – what seed banks consist of?

A: Originally, in the shift of awareness upon the planet, when those who came to live here, there was also put within the monadic levels, seed banks - a collection of vibrationary factors brought through the thought level as memory, as vibrationary rates of energy that can be used for that which is necessary. These seed banks are also within your own innate structures. You each carry seed banks of energy.

To relate to your own personal seed banks, you need clarification of self; self clarification - you need to be able to relate to yourselves as light force. 'How many relate to yourselves as light forces? Constantly. No, not many, if at all.'

The more you are able to relate to yourself in this way, the more you are opening up a factor of your own vibrationary rate connected to the lineage of memory that can then use the seed bank vibrations to bring into awareness that which is necessary. This is all done and can be done consciously.

The greater seed banks are being used to a lesser degree through your technological advances. This is why when the necessity dictates, through the instruction of the need, certain individuals or small groups connect with such seed banks and use them. As you grow in awareness and even now, you can begin to use these seed banks more fully. If you could see it as a collection of vibrationary rates similar in design to your brain, encapsulating fields of operation that can be manifested through the intuitive and mental levels to facilitate needs. To do this, you need, as I said, clarification, and you need, through clarification, instruction. First clarification, second instruction. You can then open to the collection of this, through your own connection with the seed banks via your brain access.

Many people use this in dream state, be it unconsciously. Try doing this and see how it works for you. Once you become attuned to it you can begin to shift, from one level of seed bank to another according to the need and purpose. There are then also seed banks, each connected to a certain level of understanding and working for the planet i.e. education, healing, and technology.

Q: Do the changes within ourselves and the planet involve moving from the third dimension to the fifth dimension and how would that happen?

A: Good point. It is through the fifth dimension that the light bodies are in their growth stage; 'growth' as in their connection to your physical. Light bodies themselves are already whole. You move into that through your own awareness factors.

To bring this into being, first you need to see beyond self. This sounds very simple, but can be quite difficult to do because you have been educated into complications. Things become complicated. It is simplistic. You move beyond yourself as the physical material structure. As you move, the motion of movement itself is going through the dimensions. This passage is a passage of time and from that passage of time are you restricted. To move beyond the passage of time, you move through yourself into those dimensions. You are able to create a pattern of movement beyond time. Thought itself is restricted to time - limitation, therefore you move beyond thought.

To give you an instruction here. Sit very quietly. First be in full awareness of the physical body - in comfort of the physical, in enjoyment of the physical, in love of the physical. Then be in full recognition of the mental, the movement of the mental, the acceptance of the need of the mental for movement through its own addictions that has been fed to it, through the types of education. As you become comfortable within that, be aware also of that around you: noise, movement, and people travelling. Move beyond that, step forth beyond that; see, do, feel beyond that, leave the comfort, the love, the addiction, move into the space of your own forces. Let it take you on a journey, the movement might be small to begin with or it might be sudden, and vibrant. Try not to think of where or what or how, but just go.

Thought can take you through the dimensional fields of the astral, holding and bringing forth the fourth dimension, but not to the fifth. The experience through this will begin to become more pronounced. You will find that it will become quite whole and lengthening, while, as you move back into your physical, little of time as you know it will have passed. You move beyond the necessity of time. You can hold time while you do this. This helps to begin that growth. First the body itself must be in comfort. We say comfort, not just in the way you sit or feel, but the comfort of clarity within, of relaxation of the organs, the growth and the movement, the balance, the oxygen within the body. This is most important, the balance of the oxygen, the balance of the blood - most important.

Q: How long will we be affected by the proton belt?

A: Approximately 25 to 100 years. It denotes change and it has always held in movement. It brings forth velocity of vibration that can help the acceleration of this movement, within the personal and within the whole. The usage of this was known many of your Ages past and this time was used as a time of heralding that which was necessary for change.

Q: Does the proton belt affect the outer planets as well as the Earth or even the whole Solar system?

A: It affects the whole solar system. You will find in the next coming years a build-up, mass-wise, around the Sun from this. This will be effective not just on the rays, but also there will be some bursts of energy vibration that will be felt upon the planet. It will cause some 'black spots' to occur.

Q: You mentioned the balance of blood and oxygen. Can you explain a little bit more about it - what they represent?

A: It is of vital importance to oxygenate the body fully at this time. With the accelerated vibrations affecting the planet, it has brought with it the planet's own imbalance and imbalance of factors, through the air element. You will notice this not just in your weather, but it will begin to show within the reproductions of the birds, fish and reptiles. You move towards your light bodies, that of density within the physical must be transmuted or die. The way to bring transmutation is primarily through cleansing and oxidization. You need more oxygen in your bodies, all of you. You are all suffering from oxygen starvation. Very slowly but gradually en-mass, it is becoming depleted. It is causing a greater number of diabetes; it is causing a greater number of heart problems. It is also causing a greater number of cancers in the bodies. When you breathe, imagine yourself like a living tree.

Your subconscious minds are able to reproduce almost exactly that which you feed it on a 'pictorial' manner. Breathe like trees; this opens the whole of the upper self for that which is necessary, drawing in that which is necessary for the bodily needs. Releasing the poisons. The poisons are encapsulated within the blood. Oxygenisation can unclog this, can move this, also fluids which are more pure, or as pure as possible. Water is also very beneficial for this. Chalk can also be used to help this in the body.

This oxygenation starvation which is slowly occurring will continue to disable people. It will affect the mental bodies and it will not allow for clarity. It is therefore of vital importance to open yourselves up. When possible, go to where it is not so smog-full and breathe. Yes, it does make a difference.

You have these little things. We are shown pyramid shaped ionizers. No, they are not so good. They help a little not so much. There will be a technology that will help to clear much of the dirt and poisons in your air on small levels, but not on the greater, for a time yet, so it is important that as self-responsible human beings you take care of your needs.

The blood carries your impulses of energy. It contains all that is necessary for your growth and instruction is in the blood. The messages it gives you, the impulses it carries and sends forth, are those not just of your own genetic ilk but factors of responsibility that have been carried from the beginning of time. Clouded through dirt and decay, there is also a lack of instruction, lack of originality. As this begins to be cleansed, you will see originality emerging again not just in your own personal fields but in the arts, where it can be seen very prominently and quickly how society is moving and growing.

Q: I'd like to ask a question about oxygen. There are therapies that are arising, using atmospheric chambers. There are experimentations using hydrogen peroxide and also using germanium.

A: The chamber you speak, of can be used very productively but we would imply that it is used alongside therapy, not immediate you understand, but over a period. This second one you speak of, you will have to explain. We do not see this.

Q: We are injecting hydrogen peroxide into the body. Care has to be taken with the liver.

A: Okay. Yes. This is something that is not so very beneficial, on the long term. It can help but it must be done with a very trained physician and very small doses and one has to be aware of the build-up of the individual that it is given to, not just of their physical build up, but of their chemical and alchemical build up. We therefore support this being used on a level with Chinese medicine, so the five pulses are taken and it is in balance with the pulses. The third one you spoke of is beneficial organically and this again is a slow steady stream which can help to alleviate many of the metals/toxins in the blood stream.

Q: You mentioned a new technology, a purifying technology. Is there some distinguishing feature of this new technology that we would be able to recognise when it appear

A: You will know it. You will know it.

Q: You spoke about watching the animals in the next period of time and the reptiles and fish. You also mentioned something about the babies that they have. Could you comment more on this please?
Response: We do not understand the "babies".

Q: I was just going to find the word for reproduction.

A: Not in the same vein. When we speak of the animals, the changes of awareness that are occurring with yourselves are also occurring on a lesser scale within the animal kingdoms. The animal kingdoms themselves are reaching a level of consciousness.

This is affecting both positively and adversely. There is a greater degree of resilience, stamina, almost into anger. There is a greater degree of fear within them. Part of the role of the human on the planet has been a kinship with the animal domain and a caring for. This has become very lukewarm, as the need to fulfill your own material terms has taken over.

Animals have become a design, be it unconsciously, of food, the motivation of need, one of the prime forces that move you. The reality is quite different as you know intellectually. Animals, themselves, have their own life. They have their own force of energy. They have their own psyche of which they live through. They have more group awareness and memory. This is more prevalent to those in the wild than those domesticated, but the domesticated still hold true to this, to a lesser degree. It is important not to step back and care only for the planet; you must also care for the animals living upon it.

When you look to build, to nurture, do not just do it for humans, but do it for the love of the populace, which is human, animal and mineral. The eco-structure of the humans includes animals. They are not there purely for food or to magnetize you as mirrors for your lower, dense selves, but as a harmonic vibration of the whole. It is important.

Q: You seem to imply that to increase our oxygen ingestion, we should use our subconscious to train ourselves to also breathe through the epidermis?

A: This is a simple answer. One day we will give you a new technology for this. The need is to inhale, to draw in, to open up to take that which is necessary. Not just for living, breathing and opening of your lungs, but for that which is necessary for every atom of your Being. Drawing in life force through the breath is not just the oxygenation, but is of light and life itself.

As you become of light you become of breath. You are the living breath of the Divine.
It has been with pleasure we have talked.   Good evening.

# Dimensional Alignment

(23rd of June 1993)

Greetings my friends. I come forward here from the Council of Beings, to share a discourse with you.

We have spoken of the changes within the physical structure of humanity. It is important also to relate this to the changes biologically that will occur and spread forth through the etheric realms.

Each dimension itself will go through a shift. This level of awareness, this movement of occurrence will allow the variation of vibrations to come into forms of alignment, as the alignment itself occurs, from discord and accord. In this way the shift or level of your own consciousness will begin to vibrate in essence with the level of force from your own Soul rate.

It is important for you all to be aware constantly and consciously of the essence of your own breath. Use this as your motion and force. Allow this to divine for you and direct that you keep in harmony with the inner and the outer breath of existence. Let not the trains of thought direct you into fear, negativity and restriction, for this delays your ability of being able to attune to the essence of your own force, the force of alignment that is at-one with the whole essence of creativity. It allows growth and productivity. It brings into manifestation, that which is necessary for your evolvement. The manner of that evolvement is dictated by the level of your emotional interplay, with your own subtle bodies. As you move into new levels of awareness, fear, anger, restriction cannot be carried forward. They would begin to age the body prematurely. They would begin to cause disturbances, eruptions in the body, in the blood.

It is for yourselves to use the breath, to begin to open your own channels of vibrationary rate and allow yourselves to live in light, to feed on light, to breathe light, to allow each thought to be one of light, each word a representation of the supremeness of light. Hold back nothing from yourselves. Learn to honour and grow through that which restricts you from the wholeness of your own divinities. As the bodies themselves incorporate the dimensional qualities, the shift of occurrence allows you freedom of movement. The body itself becomes your home, not your prison.

You must care for this home. You will be able to travel in the new dimensional fields at will, carrying the force of light within you; you will be able to use this in all of your manifestations. Of all the aspects of the outer changes of occurrence, there must be the inner force of vibration that aligns with the higher. There is still choice within the individual of humanity and in this you must design for yourselves your own level of growth and awareness.

Q: In the beginning you spoke of alignment within the dimensions, in the ethers. Would there be the shift in the consciousness in the elemental kingdoms as well?

A: There will be a shift on all levels, the elemental, the plant, all animal life. Many within animal form have given of themselves for the growth of humanity. Within your own structures, you carry the lowest and the highest dimensional levels that hold you through the shift of awareness. The hold will be loosened, you will be able to grasp and align those various aspects multi-dimensionally of yourselves as the lower animal, plus the recognition of as supreme beings.

This shift allows freedom; it also brings the opportunity for growth and awareness. It is not a step to be taken by all. It is not a freedom imposed upon you, but a choice taken by those who have used their lives and awareness to bring themselves to that point of transmutation. You hold within you, spirit, you hold within you, the animal. Matter need not bind you through the levels of sound; consciousness will become equipped with realisation. This changes the structure of your growth as a unit upon the planet, it affects the whole, and it moves the level of consciousness of the whole.

Q: Does this also mean that gradually in the future that sound will have more effect on our consciousness, that we will become aware of ourselves and around us?

A: Sounds bombard you constantly, even in your sleep states you are surrounded by frequencies – lower frequencies – alternative frequencies. The electrical currents themselves give out certain sound qualities.

These all cause disturbances through the bodies and the bodies' functions. It is important to note; it also causes disturbances in the bodies' functions, it can cause disease and disharmony in the body itself. It can cause cancer, tuberculosis; it can bring up the main functions of disease that was shared in Humanity.

As one becomes more attuned to one's own level of consciousness - opening oneself for the moment when one is drawn into the higher dimensions - you will find sound on the denser levels, rather than bombarding you, by- passing you, for you yourself will be a creative sound. Rather than being affected by, you will be affective of, you will cause sound to change by your own occurrence. It is important to note your own awareness in sound and how you have closed down on certain levels to cope with the level of reality you live within.

You live in city borders; it causes some mental occurrences and inhibitions. Gradually as you move from these city boundaries, your capacity to embrace and release your own inner sound vibrations will continue to change the force within you. Sound is the key to the manifestation on this planet.

Q: Can you suggest a sound to balance the children in the city?

A: Working in small group activities it is important to bring sounds, first of the vowels, through the body. Sound a vowel and ask the child to relate it to an aspect of their body, AAA, EEE, you will find that OOO comes through the solar plexus. As the child relates to the vowels, place a hand – they place their hand to where the sound comes from. Doing this quite simple exercise will help to create awareness on the subliminal level of their own sound frequencies, will also cause an adjustment into the levels of light that are working constantly in operation across the planet, and will also too bring the vibration of the mother force within them.

Q: You said some time ago, that the sense of touch and the sense of taste were linked and somebody should be working on that, made aware of that. Is the sense of sound and the sense of touch, not necessarily the fingertips, but throughout the whole body, is there something we don't understand about that? Can we use the dolphins to help us with that, because they work with sound such a lot and it's a whole body reaction from them, isn't it? They take in sound throughout the whole body.

A: All living bodies respond to sound, all bodies in the animal, finned and plant life respond to sound. As you touch another, this is translated into your own system, rather like the frequencies translated onto a television screen to give you a picture. It is translated in a dense way to touch, to feel, this is skin, this is bone, this is muscle, because this is the only level of education you have been given. Children, very young children, move out and touch and before they touch, you will notice that they nearly always stop and touch and move back and often touch again – very young ones, for they feel the vibrationary rate before the physical.

This vibrationary rate is related to sound, it has a frequency that is a harmonic vibration of your own note. These changes over the body and this can be shown now through certain equipment, one in the States and one in Canada. This sound frequency once related to, can be used;
1. as a mode of communication and you will find that this is very helpful into those areas of maladjustment.
2. it can also be used as forms of healing and bringing again, harmony. It can be used to show significant areas of disharmony, before they become diseased. It can show immediately how thought transforms itself into the body and this is a golden opportunity for the use of this as a level of awareness or as a growth product.

When you yourself or others choose to touch another in love, in healing, become aware first of yourself. Hold yourself in your own force of breath and create a sound for you. It could be an I, or an R, or hum. As you reach the other person you will find your own sound has changed. It has become lighter, lower, heavier, whatever. Then you can move this over the body and you will find again there will be changes, as you are reading the vibrationary field of the individual. This can also be done on animals.

You will find where there are tumours, cancerous growths; the hum or the sound will be almost nil. At first you will think, "Ah, it is because I have had to take a breath," but you do it again and you will see that this is the working of sound. So you can use this to understand, play with this to grow, and to recognise.

Dolphins of course are legendary in their quality of sounds and the vibrationary fields they create with those sounds. It is through that, that the Earth is being held now, while you humans get yourselves together. They work and cooperate as a living unit and that unit is also Unity. They have chosen to make themselves more known to you, to help to bring this onto the land mass, because the Karma that you as humanity have created on the land mass is over- spilling into the seas, distressing those living in their own environments.

There has to be balance. Much of the environment has been stretched to the point of almost non existence yet there are ways and means of fulfilling the needs of creating balance. Not by looking at the past and bringing it again into balance, but by stepping into the future, determining needs, fulfilling light and this will bring the new planet through its own conception into birth and reality.

Q: You spoke of sound being an instrument of manifestation and when we have a thought or concept, when we speak a word, it is also sound coming into manifestation. If we conceive of anything to help the planet, is there a sound that we could use while we were thinking it, to bring it into manifestation?

A: First let us explain the occurrence of when you speak. When you Humanity speak, you speak words. Those words are carried on a sea of vibrations, which is sound. That sea of vibration carries all of your emotions and interplays. Not just of the day but of all that is still held within you, all that you have not released or forgiven.

Therefore this denseness which pours forth is also pulled down through the levels of this vibration. If you could step back and look at some others speaking, you would see these various forces all pulling and pushing.

When you come together in a group consciousness and harmony, when you share in light, in openness, in speech, you clear these vibrations for a small level of time. That which you speak, lifts up in light, is transported into the forces of manifestation, which is why it is always important when you come together, to come with peace and goodwill in your hearts.

As individuals, you must allow yourselves to go through the process of change, releasing the bonds that hold you to any thoughts/vibrations that do not allow full creative growth and capability. To open yourselves in light, to breath the essence of eternal force through you, to speak the Word; and the word is One.
Life then is whole.

On that note we will leave you and we will come again to share.

# The Future

(14th July 1993)

Greetings my friends. I come forward here from the Council of Beings to share with you the future as we see it within this time and space.

Your future, as you envisage it, is one of change. During all times of change, concepts themselves begin to dysfunction, allowing the scope of creative venture, allowing you to express from your own innate natures that which is possible, that which can come into being through your own realisation of your divine forces, these forces of divinity that you are and carry within you. What you see and will see are aspects of one level of creation according to the alignment of your own consciousness.

As there are many bodies, there are many worlds and these worlds move in alignment with each other and one can live and perceive within these worlds of reality and illusion, and these worlds come about through one's own needs and desires, through one's fears and levels of personal attainment and group commitment. And as one grows in consciousness, one is able to move through these various levels, these lives, these growths and one is able to manipulate in a positive function, the awareness of one level into another. One is able to bring these lives into one living force, one force, one act of commitment. That act can only be the act of one's supreme self – the self that is at-ease with one's own sense of divinity and growth.

The various realities and interplays on these levels then begin to dissipate; the worlds themselves gradually drift into their own organic structure which becomes part of the atmosphere of the living force of one, bringing this into the essence of one world.

One must live fully within the supreme moment; one must be able to be fully present in all things, even in one's sleep. The presence of one's consciousness must be attuned to the force of awareness of one's own inner realisation and outer commitment. One's creative functions must be able to grow in alignment with that awareness. As a people there is a strong move towards peace, a commitment towards working into co-operative ventures, and yet within that there is also dysfunction, tribal warfare.

The living earth holds the atoms of your subconscious as a people; it holds the memories, as do you all. That archetypal force is being broken down, the atoms themselves are awakening. They are causing within the individual the need for inner realisation and alignment. They are causing within the individual, the need to bring the body both physically, mentally, emotionally, into a pattern of alignment and working order. It is opening up to the very levels of one's own basic fear functions, realising the need on a cellular scale, of one's own sense of security and fear of, within that.

This is being played out and will become more solid within the tribes. It will show itself that, as the world in general moves slowly but very gradually towards world peace, there will be these "fractions" growing of more tribal disharmony. To understand this you must understand that the unconscious itself works in fear. It propagates through fear, it feeds upon fear. It holds within it the need to express one's own basic functions for the realisation of "I am", little understanding that the true essence and presence of "I am" is one of attunement in light. The force and presence of one's own divinity, not one's density.

This dense interplay within the individual shows itself very well within the tribe, bringing together the mass unconscious, the need to clear one's own present negativity and fear projected onto an outward force, a representation of that fear, which of course plays itself out within the game.

It is therefore important as this warfare on a tribal level plays itself through, that you keep yourself clear of any misunderstanding within your own nature. Recognise the need for alignment, for precision in your work, in your thoughts and in your actions. Keep things clear and simple, relate only to that of truth, love and harmlessness. This imbalance we speak of will continue for some years to come, before it too, is able to be penetrated and worked through. The key is mass awareness through education, mass awareness through the alignment of the planet.

At this time in the Earth's growth, industry has a major hold as does technology, but the future will be more within agriculture and growth. There will be many re-forestation projects. There will be a need to cultivate the desert and to find new forms of food. You will find that industry itself is beginning to determine this flow. Their own top analysts have recognised this and there is a shift toward this. Take advantage of this. Direct your quality thoughts into this. See this growth and this awareness as part of the light of the oncoming ray into the planet. The future is not to move back again to Duchies, but to bring forth the tools necessary on all levels to create a living, growing productive community of planet, humans, animal, plants.

Q: On this last subject you got new forms of food. Can you be more specific about what types of food this means?

A: There are several already coming in. You will find that there will be seed banks, different to the seed banks we spoke of at an earlier time, where they will cultivate these seeds. There will be new forms of wheat. Specific types of grasses grown for animal fodder. There will also be a great deal more used from oceans-food. The light bodies as they grow will gradually have no need for animal food, and will gradually move from some other foods too, but there is the mass to take care of, and for that, one has to have understanding and awareness. One has to cater for the needs of the moment, propagating
– propagating the growth of and for tomorrow.

Q: The industry seems to control most of the seed banks. Do you see a movement towards individual seed banks?

A: Oh yes. There are seed banks. There is one in America. One in the South of America, and also one small group working on this in Germany – again in Israel. You will find that these will connect. There will be seed banks connected to each other, feeding and filtering information.

Q: With the sea is that the 'double protease form of algae' that you are speaking of?

A: That is one form, yes.

Q: Does the tribal disharmony have to take its course? Is there any way you can influence it to prevent it getting out of hand or is it something that must go through its own course.

A: We are not allowed to influence more than this. We can share information that will be beneficial within your own growth. You yourselves can use your probability factors to bring more awareness on your planet. In this we speak of visualising and creating an orb of energy of a vibrationary rate that can help the mass unconscious to gradually take shape, in a level of awareness where it can function without fear. It can begin to open into the individual's thought patterns that are of self-propagation and communal harmony rather than collective fear. This is important.

As to whether it has to occur, there is a great deal of what you call history that has been accumulated, a great deal of 'drudge' that needs cleansing, held by the psyche of the mass. This has to play itself through in any cleansing process. Again you can use your energies to help this; you can also see how this could be addressed through education.

What you have is not education, it is dogmatism. To educate will bring both to children and adults an awareness of the process of life and an understanding of the growth of nature. This will be far more productive and it will allow for individual thought and interaction which will bring about mass co- operation.

Q: I would like to address the illusion you spoke of and I may be stating the obvious, but I would like to address the scenario as I see it. You spoke tonight about the fact that fears drives us to create illusions, to make decisions, to create our boundaries. It occurred to me that the left brain receives impulses in the subconscious and if the sub- conscious is motivated by fear, then fear is emotional, so the left brain could only make emotional responses based on which is going to cause less pain, less damage, less destruction. If that in fact is true, then we cannot be emotional and breathe at the same time i.e. in the control of it. The way forward is for the mass to learn how to breathe properly and therefore the trigger from not being emotional to not being fearful, then shutting down the left brain would come as an automatic response and we would have a lot less illusion?

A: Yes and no. No and yes. We have spoken at great length about the breath and the need for you all to become aware of this living force of vibrationary light that you take into yourselves. Remember that this is a conscious function; it is a conscious function that you breathe. This is very important – it encapsules much. The left brain is not pre-determined purely by the emotional body, but can also be used as a function of memory, that does not necessarily relate to emotion. It therefore has no creativity. This is why you can get many scientists who seem to be devoid of emotion, but whom are what you would call very left brain.

The breath brings alignment this is true – it brings alignment. It is also important to note that it can be done too, with the eyes. Using the eyes in various exercises, (which of course we expect to be the next question) can also help to bring an alignment here.

Now as one breathes in and infuses oneself with light, one can also open one's eyes and lift them to the highest. As one breathes out the eyes go down to the lowest, one begins a process in this gradual movement of slightly separating and bringing back into focus the eyes themselves, so that they separate and come back, separate and come back; up, centre, separate, come back, down, centre. This has an effect of scrambling the unconscious programming. It throws it into disarray, which allows then a point of light to enter that one holds within one's own mind's eye, it begins to grow within one's mind, within one's brain. One very quickly throws oneself into more disarray by suddenly focusing on completely various parts of the body, the left nail of one's little toe, one's right eyebrow, a spot on one's back, a touch on one's ankle, again breaking up functions that are static, relaxing again to a point of one light; opening again into the mind/brain function.

You will find that after such an exercise one can become very creative. One also has the need often to move about, because one has filled oneself with a specific energy force that needs to be used and directed. This can be used physically or it can be used mentally and in the building up of the magnetic body.

Q: Can we go from there to the comment you made about being conscious in sleep? How would one do that?

A: First one becomes comfortable in becoming conscious through one's waking hours. When we speak of 'comfortable' we speak of doing it in a state of ease, rather than tension. As this grows through days, weeks and months, one would become aware that this has also reflected itself in sleep. You must have become aware of this already to a lesser degree.

Q: During this sleep state, unconscious sleep state, can we then alter the outcome of our dreams?

A: It is important to register within the dream what lesson it is teaching one. What specifically is the dream telling you? Many times it can be a subconscious function of your own need not played out. It can also be something you have not understood nor heeded. If there are still vestiges of fear it can also be this. As one is able to determine and understand, the dream itself changes without one having to change it. One's understanding changes one's concepts immediately. One's understanding, one's embracing of knowledge, changes immediately the concepts one uses in one's life.

This is why it is important to understand, to use, to embrace and to direct, not just values that change, but one's own physical world and make up; the material world you yourselves are part of through your creative functions that you hold and change. You are not dogs held on leads, you hold yourselves, but you are not aware even yet of the potential of your true essence.

And while you are not fully prepared on all levels it is quite good that it is so, to bring into alignment while you grow, change, become aware that it is more productive and harm free for both yourselves and the environment. The sudden destructive forces created through this century have come from great swings of consciousness and in the mass the un-receptivity of being able to be aware of those forces and therefore the use and abuse of the destructive energy.

Q: Does the breathing pattern change at sleep time and is it a better breathing pattern, more relaxed – and can we use it in a healing way?

A: Yes the breathing pattern changes and it is aligned to what you would consider R.E.M., aligned to the eye movement. The key here is quite important. You can use this to enhance healing for both yourselves and for the planet.

Q: Is the immediate change of attitude, the important or healing phase of someone who undergoes regressive hypnosis. Is it their understanding of the problem or the old information which effects the change in this time space?

A: Is it their understanding of old information? Old information somehow does not compute, old memory yes, but information and being old, cannot come together. Old memory.
For many, regressive hypnosis can become in itself like a drug. It becomes something that one can use and abuse as a means of giving labels to certain situations or conditions.

It is productive to look now within one's own present situation and to see what is not working within that situation. To meditate into that situation that is not productive to the whole. If that takes one into a regressive state then this also can be very productive. This cannot necessarily give one the mental apparatus of recognition, but the emotional experience. Giving oneself the emotional experience through the breath, using the breath, at this point, can allow one to release in love and light, using the element of Air and move on. It is important to be able to release and move on, but it is not so important to know, necessarily, what one releases. Just to be able to live fully in that force of light, love and productive activity.

Do you see? This way you can use this. You can become what is known as a programmer. A programmer is one who uses their psychic capabilities to help others to re-programme their own psychic nature that has been pre-determined by past influences and experiences. It is becoming increasingly popular to use subliminal tapes and hypnosis to re-programme the subconscious and as an aid to give a person courage to change.

Q. Can you comment on this?

A: If the person chooses this, then it is within their choice.

Q: Is it a constructive thing to programme the subconscious to make a difference?"

A: We are not here to judge.

Q: Let me try this again.

A: We understand the form you speak of, and if the individual chooses to use this then that is their need to re-programme, to substitute one thing for another, and if that is their need then that is their need. It can only be within their choice. We leave you now. We thank you for your continuing attendance and sharing together.
Thank you.

# Variation of Vibrations

(14th July 1993)

Greetings my friends. I come forward here from the Council of Beings to share with you the future as we see it within this time and space.

Your future, as you envisage it, is one of change. During all times of change, concepts themselves begin to dysfunction, allowing the scope of creative venture, allowing you to express from your own innate natures that which is possible, that which can come into being through your own realisation of your divine forces, these forces of divinity that you are and carry within you. What you see and will see are aspects of one level of creation according to the alignment of your own consciousness.

As there are many bodies, there are many worlds and these worlds move in alignment with each other and one can live and perceive within these worlds of reality and illusion, and these worlds come about through one's own needs and desires, through one's fears and levels of personal attainment and group commitment. And as one grows in consciousness, one is able to move through these various levels, these lives, these growths and one is able to manipulate in a positive function, the awareness of one level into another. One is able to bring these lives into one living force, one force, one act of commitment. That act can only be the act of one's supreme self – the self that is at-ease with one's own sense of divinity and growth.

The various realities and interplays on these levels then begin to dissipate; the worlds themselves gradually drift into their own organic structure which becomes part of the atmosphere of the living force of one, bringing this into the essence of one world.

One must live fully within the supreme moment; one must be able to be fully present in all things, even in one's sleep. The presence of one's consciousness must be attuned to the force of awareness of one's own inner realisation and outer commitment. One's creative functions must be able to grow in alignment with that awareness. As a people there is a strong move towards peace, a commitment towards working into co-operative ventures, and yet within that there is also dysfunction, tribal warfare.

The living earth holds the atoms of your subconscious as a people; it holds the memories, as do you all. That archetypal force is being broken down, the atoms themselves are awakening. They are causing within the individual the need for inner realisation and alignment. They are causing within the individual, the need to bring the body both physically, mentally, emotionally, into a pattern of alignment and working order. It is opening up to the very levels of one's own basic fear functions, realising the need on a cellular scale, of one's own sense of security and fear of, within that.

This is being played out and will become more solid within the tribes. It will show itself that, as the world in general moves slowly but very gradually towards world peace, there will be these "fractions" growing of more tribal disharmony. To understand this you must understand that the unconscious itself works in fear. It propagates through fear, it feeds upon fear. It holds within it the need to express one's own basic functions for the realisation of "I am", little understanding that the true essence and presence of "I am" is one of attunement in light. The force and presence of one's own divinity, not one's density.

This dense interplay within the individual shows itself very well within the tribe, bringing together the mass unconscious, the need to clear one's own present negativity and fear projected onto an outward force, a representation of that fear, which of course plays itself out within the game.

It is therefore important as this warfare on a tribal level plays itself through, that you keep yourself clear of any misunderstanding within your own nature. Recognise the need for alignment, for precision in your work, in your thoughts and in your actions. Keep things clear and simple, relate only to that of truth, love and harmlessness. This imbalance we speak of will continue for some years to come, before it too, is able to be penetrated and worked through. The key is mass awareness through education, mass awareness through the alignment of the planet.

At this time in the Earth's growth, industry has a major hold as does technology, but the future will be more within agriculture and growth. There will be many re-forestation projects. There will be a need to cultivate the desert and to find new forms of food. You will find that industry itself is beginning to determine this flow. Their own top analysts have recognised this and there is a shift toward this. Take advantage of this. Direct your quality thoughts into this. See this growth and this awareness as part of the light of the oncoming ray into the planet. The future is not to move back again to Duchies, but to bring forth the tools necessary on all levels to create a living, growing productive community of planet, humans, animal, plants.

Q: On this last subject you got new forms of food. Can you be more specific about what types of food this means?

A: There are several already coming in. You will find that there will be seed banks, different to the seed banks we spoke of at an earlier time, where they will cultivate these seeds. There will be new forms of wheat. Specific types of grasses grown for animal fodder. There will also be a great deal more used from oceans-food. The light bodies as they grow will gradually have no need for animal food, and will gradually move from some other foods too, but there is the mass to take care of, and for that, one has to have understanding and awareness. One has to cater for the needs of the moment, propagating – propagating the growth of and for tomorrow.

Q: The industry seems to control most of the seed banks. Do you see a movement towards individual seed banks?

A: Oh yes. There are seed banks. There is one in America. One in the South of America, and also one small group working on this in Germany – again in Israel. You will find that these will connect. There will be seed banks connected to each other, feeding and filtering information.

Q: With the sea is that the 'double protease form of algae' that you are speaking of?

A: That is one form, yes.

Q: Does the tribal disharmony have to take its course? Is there any way you can influence it to prevent it getting out of hand or is it something that must go through its own course.

A: We are not allowed to influence more than this. We can share information that will be beneficial within your own growth. You yourselves can use your probability factors to bring more awareness on your planet. In this we speak of visualising and creating an orb of energy of a vibrationary rate that can help the mass unconscious to gradually take shape, in a level of awareness where it can function without fear. It can begin to open into the individual's thought patterns that are of self-propagation and communal harmony rather than collective fear. This is important.

As to whether it has to occur, there is a great deal of what you call history that has been accumulated, a great deal of 'drudge' that needs cleansing, held by the psyche of the mass. This has to play itself through in any cleansing process. Again you can use your energies to help this; you can also see how this could be addressed through education.

What you have is not education, it is dogmatism. To educate will bring both to children and adults an awareness of the process of life and an understanding of the growth of nature. This will be far more productive and it will allow for individual thought and interaction which will bring about mass co- operation.

Q: I would like to address the illusion you spoke of and I may be stating the obvious, but I would like to address the scenario as I see it. You spoke tonight about the fact that fears drives us to create illusions, to make decisions, to create our boundaries. It occurred to me that the left brain receives impulses in the subconscious and if the sub- conscious is motivated by fear, then fear is emotional, so the left brain could only make emotional responses based on which is going to cause less pain, less damage, less destruction. If that in fact is true, then we cannot be emotional and breathe at the same time i.e. in the control of it. The way forward is for the mass to learn how to breathe properly and therefore the trigger from not being emotional to not being fearful, then shutting down the left brain would come as an automatic response and we would have a lot less illusion?

A: Yes and no. No and yes. We have spoken at great length about the breath and the need for you all to become aware of this living force of vibrationary light that you take into yourselves. Remember that this is a conscious function; it is a conscious function that you breathe. This is very important – it encapsules much. The left brain is not pre-determined purely by the emotional body, but can also be used as a function of memory, that does not necessarily relate to emotion. It therefore has no creativity. This is why you can get many scientists who seem to be devoid of emotion, but whom are what you would call very left brain.

The breath brings alignment this is true – it brings alignment. It is also important to note that it can be done too, with the eyes. Using the eyes in various exercises, (which of course we expect to be the next question) can also help to bring an alignment here.

Now as one breathes in and infuses oneself with light, one can also open one's eyes and lift them to the highest. As one breathes out the eyes go down to the lowest, one begins a process in this gradual movement of slightly separating and bringing back into focus the eyes themselves, so that they separate and come back, separate and come back; up, centre, separate, come back, down, centre. This has an effect of scrambling the unconscious programming. It throws it into disarray, which allows then a point of light to enter that one holds within one's own mind's eye, it begins to grow within one's mind, within one's brain. One very quickly throws oneself into more disarray by suddenly focusing on completely various parts of the body, the left nail of one's little toe, one's right eyebrow, a spot on one's back, a touch on one's ankle, again breaking up functions that are static, relaxing again to a point of one light; opening again into the mind/brain function.

You will find that after such an exercise one can become very creative. One also has the need often to move about, because one has filled oneself with a specific energy force that needs to be used and directed. This can be used physically or it can be used mentally and in the building up of the magnetic body.

Q: Can we go from there to the comment you made about being conscious in sleep? How would one do that?

A: First one becomes comfortable in becoming conscious through one's waking hours. When we speak of 'comfortable' we speak of doing it in a state of ease, rather than tension. As this grows through days, weeks and months, one would become aware that this has also reflected itself in sleep. You must have become aware of this already to a lesser degree.

Q: During this sleep state, unconscious sleep state, can we then alter the outcome of our dreams?

A: It is important to register within the dream what lesson it is teaching one. What specifically is the dream telling you? Many times it can be a subconscious function of your own need not played out. It can also be something you have not understood nor heeded. If there are still vestiges of fear it can also be this. As one is able to determine and understand, the dream itself changes without one having to change it. One's understanding changes one's concepts immediately. One's understanding, one's embracing of knowledge, changes immediately the concepts one uses in one's life.

This is why it is important to understand, to use, to embrace and to direct, not just values that change, but one's own physical world and make up; the material world you yourselves are part of through your creative functions that you hold and change. You are not dogs held on leads, you hold yourselves, but you are not aware even yet of the potential of your true essence.

And while you are not fully prepared on all levels it is quite good that it is so, to bring into alignment while you grow, change, become aware that it is more productive and harm free for both yourselves and the environment. The sudden destructive forces created through this century have come from great swings of consciousness and in the mass the un-receptivity of being able to be aware of those forces and therefore the use and abuse of the destructive energy.

Q: Does the breathing pattern change at sleep time and is it a better breathing pattern, more relaxed – and can we use it in a healing way?

A: Yes the breathing pattern changes and it is aligned to what you would consider R.E.M., aligned to the eye movement. The key here is quite important. You can use this to enhance healing for both yourselves and for the planet.

Q: Is the immediate change of attitude, the important or healing phase of someone who undergoes regressive hypnosis. Is it their understanding of the problem or the old information which effects the change in this time space?

A: Is it their understanding of old information? Old information somehow does not compute, old memory yes, but information and being old, cannot come together. Old memory.
For many, regressive hypnosis can become in itself like a drug. It becomes something that one can use and abuse as a means of giving labels to certain situations or conditions.

It is productive to look now within one's own present situation and to see what is not working within that situation. To meditate into that situation that is not productive to the whole. If that takes one into a regressive state then this also can be very productive. This cannot necessarily give one the mental apparatus of recognition, but the emotional experience. Giving oneself the emotional experience through the breath, using the breath, at this point, can allow one to release in love and light, using the element of Air and move on. It is important to be able to release and move on, but it is not so important to know, necessarily, what one releases. Just to be able to live fully in that force of light, love and productive activity.

Do you see? This way you can use this. You can become what is known as a programmer. A programmer is one who uses their psychic capabilities to help others to re-programme their own psychic nature that has been pre-determined by past influences and experiences. It is becoming increasingly popular to use subliminal tapes and hypnosis to re-programme the subconscious and as an aid to give a person courage to change.

Q. Can you comment on this?

A: If the person chooses this, then it is within their choice.

Q: Is it a constructive thing to programme the subconscious to make a difference?"

A: We are not here to judge.

Q: Let me try this again.

A: We understand the form you speak of, and if the individual chooses to use this then that is their need to re-programme, to substitute one thing for another, and if that is their need then that is their need. It can only be within their choice. We leave you now. We thank you for your continuing attendance and sharing together.
Thank you.

# Magnetic Impulses

(22nd September 1993)

Greetings my friends. I come forward here from the Council of Beings and I wish to share our discourse with you this evening upon magnetic impulses. The magnetic impulses penetrating through the planet at this time are affecting your physical, material make up. They are affecting, of course as you know, the psychological and the psycho-history itself, of the planet. The change in velocity, which is having an effect on a planetary level, is occurring also within the psyche of the individual.

You will find the magnetic impulses themselves growing in strength and velocity through your own systems. It is through this that the changes are occurring, on the most cellular regions and structures, within the DNA itself. The magnetic impulse is beginning to draw forth from you the cellular memory - that which we have spoken of before - this cellular memory, holds, contains within it, the aspect of the whole. As it re-emerges through you, it allows you the impulse of the movement towards your light body at an accelerated speed. It brings forth into production, all that which is necessary for the continuation of growth across the planet.

The changes occurring at this time on a planetary scale are all within the force of the magnetic impulses. These impulses move through the planet. They come from the outer planetary regions. They come also from that which we have spoken of. The movement of certain planets across the proton belt, as this is moving now through your own system and beyond these, is causing an extreme variance of change in the magnetic impulses.

It is bringing forth a variance of this in people's own psyches and also within their physical make up. It is allowing changes within your own circuitry. You will find that the circuitry itself will begin to move; it will move from the lobal areas down towards the heart level. This is meant and was how it began. It was not meant to be used from the level of the mental realm. It was used only primarily in that realm as one of production for future memory.

You will find that the usage from the heart brings forth the impulse not just of, as you see it, in love and compassion, but also the ability to empower yourselves with your own knowledge of strength and change. It allows you to accept the commitment of change within your own system, within your own recognition of One in light and to use this to bring forth the creativity and the value of light in all work and space.

The magnetic impulses on the planetary level are of course, part of the changes of occurrence of the vibrationary rate of the planet herself. The variance of this vibrationary rate moves across the planet as it does within the individual. It changes not just on thought occurrence, but also on the psyche of groups, the cultures, Humanity, as you move across the planet. According to the consciousness of such, it will bring forth the changes of occurrence. You will see the changes but you can also see the interconnectedness through this according to their ability to merge with the consciousness that is forcing its way through.

Q: If the magnetic impulses are linked with planetary activity, we can then expect an increase at the time of particular effects of the moon. How is it linked in with the moon?

A: The magnetic impulses we speak of are not of your own system, but from beyond this. These impulses come from the outer levels of the system rather than your own inner. Those planetary influences that you are aware of and work with, work very much on the levels of the lower three bodies and also on the dimensions. You will find that as you become more attuned to the subtle bodies, the magnetic impulses themselves will be felt more clearly and will be able to be directed.

Q: Will this magnetic impulse affect the sub atomic particles of matter, or energy systems?

A: Yes. Yes. And you have seen the effects of this already. This will continue. It will accelerate and it will affect these parts. You will see that there will be more of a breaking down of the structure within the sub-atomic levels in such things as your nuclear. This nuclear power is also connected very much generically here to some of your more ancient cultures on a psyche level, an unconscious level, rather than a conscious. The drawing away of these cultures, the moving into their own form again of ritualistic endeavour, and the uses consciously of these rituals, to bring forth again their own empowerment and planetary alignment and use of planetary energy, earth energy, the transmutation of earth energy, is also breaking up on this nuclear level. We are talking here of the indigenous peoples.

Q: Is there a relationship between a human Being, being affected by these magnetic impulses and specific areas of the Earth, and can you comment on that, and is it possible to find out ourselves where on earth the right place is for one?

A: The magnetic impulse works, as you know, very much through subtle bodies. The vibrationary note of the accord of this has its affect upon the psyche of those on the planet. Cultures, groupings, communities of people carry the harmonic chord.

You must be aware first that as you move into your light body, you can attune to various parts of the planet and not just to one, for as you move into the flow of the light body itself, you are also moving into the field of light of the planet. The magnetic impulse in the light body of the planet is different to that which affects the physical magnetic body. This force allows you to move yourself at will. It also brings into effect your ability to be within the space, the centre force of your own field. So although at this time you may feel, and rightly so, the need to centre yourself within a certain magnetic vibration on the planet, in the future this will not be necessary.

Q:  It just happens spontaneously?

A: It will be that. As you are able to express through the light body, the needs of the physical, emotional, material, falling away and becoming one with light force, you will be able to carry your own source with you wherever you are.

Q: Does that mean that for us, there is a distancing from the physical aspect, does that include procreation, and can we envisage it happening at another level, especially the bodies of light?
A: Yes. As it moves more into the forces of breath and movement.

Q: So it is all the centres of the Being that will be involved in procreation?
A: Yes, within the light bodies. Even at this time now, those working consciously upon their own development and growth to bring forth a new sense of Being, a new light force upon the planet to actually physically bring forth a child, there is the awareness first of bringing this forth within the light body.
Gradually, as people move from the third dimension into the fifth, this will become the norm, and it will be through this that procreation will occur. By attaining the sense of the inner balance, they can use their creative flow not just in the genital area, but can be directed into various parts of the body and can be used gradually for procreation, through the conscious attunement of living breath.

Q: So it will be through the breath that what we could imagine as thought forms could come into being? In the light dimensions?
A: Yes, the living breath. The living breath carries a wholeness of sound through breath.

Q: Would we then see any physical changes occurring? You mentioned the change of location of circuitry. How then would it affect the human body as we know it?

A: We have spoken before of the changes in human structures. It is important to note that as you move into your light bodies, that the physical itself is still a vehicle for it. It is a vehicle that you can move into and out of, gradually with much swiftness, but the physical itself must always be cared for, until there is no longer a need. The physical will stay with you until, there has been complete clearness within, of one's own senses of limitation and restriction, not just on a mental, physical and psychosomatic level, but also on the level of the psyche of humanity, which is why the movement of the cellular memory is so important.

It will bring about an adjustment and a releasing. For many, this can cause fear. To suddenly be released from restriction, allows one to participate fully in life. This participation is strength, growth, power, and commitment. It is the merging of all that one has ever envisaged, with all that one has ever contained. To open oneself from the outer to the inner, and release every vestige of restriction in the recognition of its honour, will bring forth balance and allow you to care for the physical as well as move through it when necessary. What we speak of in the light bodies for many will take more than one generation, for a few the numbers of years can be counted. We counter this against the scope of humanity, not against the scope of a hundred or a thousand.

We will leave now and speak again. Thank you.

# Planetary Crisis

(20th October 1993)

Greetings my friends, I come forward here from the Council of Beings and I wish to converse with you this evening upon the point of crisis. Crisis.

The planet at large is going through a point of crisis. This crisis is having an effect upon all the levels of being. It is having an effect upon the molecular structure. It is having an effect upon the atomic structure. It is having an effect within you all physically, emotionally and psychologically. It is bringing an uprising of vibrationary factor. This uprising of vibrationary factor is based within your own innate system, the systems of your genetic code and make-up. It is bringing forward through memory banks, all inputs of information that has been gained through your own lives.

When we speak of your lives, we are speaking here in a genetic term, a family term, rather than what you would envisage as spiritual. This input of information that is coming through, does not come with labels. It cannot be analysed and looked into; it is expressed through you as different varying levels of emotion and expression; expression in attitude, expression in your lives.

These expressions are ones that you need to be able to receive, to accept and to work through. It is no longer enough, to be able to step from yourself and try to pinpoint these levels of activity, in a way of bringing forward that which is necessary for growth. You are part of the involvement. You are the whole of the involvement. It is for you all to be aware that every psyche, every atom of your energy levels, are at this point in a moment of crisis.

This moment of crisis moves from one to another moment of crisis. This continuing movement of moments of crisis allows you the opportunity to grow. Not through the delving of the mental, not through the expression of the spiritual, but through the alliance of your own heart factor - the recognition of yourselves as souls, as omnipotent beings and the recognition of yourselves as part of the

growth and the involvement, evolve-ment, of the planet, the planets and the solar system moving through the Galaxy. The recognition of this crisis you can see around you. You can see it economically, you can see it politically, and you can see it in the religious structures. Structure itself is breaking down.

It is being eaten. It has its own cancer; it has its own AIDS, from within. This can be fear induction. Part of this fear induction is self-fear induction. Part of this fear induction is a fear that is constantly being fed to you, to Humanity, as a way of keeping the mass in fear, unable to hold and take full responsibility and evolvement, and part of it is the fear of the growth itself held on a planetary level.

Now as you express this, as you work through this and as you taste and witness this within yourself, you can allow yourselves the presence of creativity. See crisis, not of fear induction but of change and growth. See it as a movement towards the new, as a movement towards allowing your own life centres to become in complete operation. Allowing yourselves to merge, not holding nor carrying, not fearing nor resenting, but being present in the moment. Allowing yourselves the opportunity to grow in harmony with the growth of the alliance with the planet. The planet Herself is moving through her own changes and part of these changes will be seen physically.

The psyche of these changes will be felt emotionally and it is important to recognise that you are part of that psyche, that the expression of your feelings are not just personal, individual, but part of a mass unconscious. This is also part of a structure; it is part of a structure that has fed Humanity from near the beginning of its time. This structure itself is breaking, dissipating. In its own dissipation it is causing changes on a planetary level, it is part of the changes that are happening to your planet.

You will find yourselves that as the psyche begins to dissipate, this will allow you the freedom to express yourselves fully and in so doing, you can no longer point a finger in any direction, for any pain or restriction in your lives, in your feelings, in your make-up, to any situation or person. You can only recognise it fully as yours, own it as yours, work through it as yours, lifting yourself within it.

You cannot work with this in a mental capacity. You cannot deal with this in a logical sequence. You can only operate through the heart, relying on your own self-nature to see you through.

Questions

Q: As the increase in this energy brings up our past lives genetically, I take it, it will come forth in terms of emotion and thought forms. Now these thought forms will attract events themselves will they not?

A: They are not so much thought forms as expressions of vibration. As an expression of vibration it has to move through you and the word itself; expression, it has to 'find expression'. If the expression itself is not moving through you, then through your own will, be it unconscious, it is then reflected back to you in your own life.

Q: Has this anything to do with changing of the DNA structure?

A: Yes.

Q: As the DNA spiral strengthens will it become less kinky?

A: When humans first walked, worked and lived on this planet, they carried within them only the expression of Divine, of 'good'. Memory was one of wholeness. It was not subjected to the casual observation of wants/needs personified through lifetimes. This, what you carry now, not just marks you in your physical make-up and mental abilities, but also marks you in your recognition to completeness.

Completeness is there, also, but has a lot of baggage tied to it. The releasing of this is part of the movement towards the light bodies. You will not then be giving your children specific codes of memory. This will all change and even more, children may be born and grow with children of their own as you release that from yourselves and from them.

You also allow the process to take occurrence within them.

You are moving away from this three dimensional belief. You are allowing yourselves to release that which is no longer necessary. One does not need to wear a heavy coat in your Summer.


Q: What changed from when people first lived on Earth?

A: This we have spoken of and a copy can be provided to you of the explanation of the separation that occurred. To abbreviate, partly it was the movement away from their own planets' alignment. You are human Beings and you are Earth Beings but you were not once, and partly it was the taking on of the psyche of the movements of the planet, light and dark, day and night; but this information can be provided to you.

Q: Can you give a time span when you mentioned as you grow, so you affect the children. Do you mean within fifty years?

A: It is occurring now. The changes you are experiencing, you are aware of. The crisis we speak of, you are aware of. Your DNA is changing and in doing so, it is becoming more available to the understanding by the scientific body. Of course in doing so, they will hold to the theory they find and not to the continuous movement or change. They capture a point and hold it, but this continuous movement does have its cycle.

This will be seen by the scientific body and it will be recognised as such, but the full understanding and implication will not be felt. There are now two bodies - scientific bodies, working on the actual DNA structure itself, to bring changes before embryonic form, and this is something that is a very difficult transition and one that as a people you should be very aware of. The implications of this are very far reaching on many levels.

It is something that as a human Being, you must be conscious of, what is going on in your name.

Therefore the children are changing and will continue to do so at a far accelerated rate than the older children. When you label an adult that is for you an age physically attained, for in some cultures it is when certain applications of the body change. The reality is that it is the movement into Self-response consciously.

Q: Is this enfoldment the process by which we recognise and work with our animal natures?

A: It is.

Q: The scientific research you are speaking about are genetics, the manipulation of DNA. Is that to create a superhuman being?

A: That is a term. Yes. It is not a term being used, but, yes that is a term. It is for, at this time, to bring forth one without certain diseases, most especially structural, but it is fed with this – we mean financially – by certain bodies that see other far-reaching effects.

Q: This will create humans with ability to have a consciousness that wouldn't be earned as we earn it, I should think?

A: It would create very good servants, very little creativity and expansion of life force. The spark of creativity brings change.
Change is good.

Change is always good. It cannot be seen as such, often within the moment when one's bodies are expressing fear, concern and environmental decay on a personal level.

Change can be fearsome, but your planet is dying. It is dying for need of creativity. Look at the arts; this is the first expression of a living or dying race. Creativity must be stimulated. Your gifts must be stimulated. The wondrous gift of humans is the spark of creativity.

Q: Is this change in the DNA that scientist are working on, leading to humans without diseases that they suffered before? What is the analogy for the planet? What then would the planet not display or go through that they have gone through before, with the changes that She is then going through?

A: It causes more of separation between the expression of the planet and the expression of humanity rather than more of a holistic movement.

Though the planets changes, the cleansing is from within, ridding Herself of what is necessary, bringing forth children without disease is something that one must always attain to, but one must do this

holistically, otherwise the disease itself that eats away at the individual is more emotional and psychosomatic. It is weakening your people, not strengthening them. The physical structure has its counterpart astrally. That will not change, if you change the physical on that level. Therefore imbalance will continue through the individual. There will be pain felt.

There will be pain felt.

Q: If scientists are working on changing the DNA structure, can they be prevented from causing serious damage?

A: Yes and no. Through your own awareness you can change this by standing and taking responsibility. You can change this also through your own broadcasts of light. Be conscious of broadcasting light for truth and evolvement across your planet, affecting those working on the various levels. This is a very powerful tool that you have and this can be used very objectively in this way.

We will finish now and talk again. Thank you.

# PART SEVEN:

'Hawk'
The Lady of Shamballa:
        'Shamballa'
        'Memory and vision'
        'Love'

'When the world was young – 2'

# Hawk

(10th September 1987)

I bring forth my greetings to you, in the name of light and our blessed Mother and by the Great Spirit and stars that give us life.
The name I give to you is Hawk.

In my tradition we are given three names, the first my given name, was Spotted Elk, the second was the name that the youth takes upon themselves from their Vision Quest and the third is the name that comes to them continuously in their dreams and visions, the name that is held sacred, and only given to those of their blood brothers and sisters and this name I give to you, I give you this that is me and mine which we share together, for I am a part of this Being that comes to work and to live among you.

And it has been in my joy and memory, this life that I come forward with now, that of my native tradition, where I worked and traveled and walked many miles to teach the way that was given to me by the Grandfathers and the Grandmothers.

It was an ancient tradition that was passed through from the grandparents not just on the physical plane, but those that travelled with us that filled our dreams and our visions, that opened us to our quests and allowed us to see our brothers and our sisters in the animal and plant kingdoms, for these worlds are worlds to the Native that are one. That we walk together, we eat together, we live, we breathe, we die and we are reborn again upon this sacred planet, and so the circle continues and so the cycle lives on through us and ours.

And I was one who travelled, living with each tribe, nine moons to thirteen, sharing with them my 'visions' and my understanding and they shared with me of their women, though I bedded them not and they shared with me their joy and they shared with me their worries and concerns for their children and for the children of the planet.

And I brought with me no instrument, no sound, but the sound of the voice of the Grandfathers and the Grandmothers who talked through me and at night we would sit together and the Grandparents would come forward and share with them and they would have understanding. And slowly they began to learn.

They began to learn to use the land to propagate. They began to learn to see beyond their own circle.
They began to understand the circle of life and the spiral that continues forever onwards. And so I come again, in a new guise, in a new form and I come again to teach and to learn and I come again to bring forward the words of the Grandparents that we may share together and we may have understanding again of the sacred planet and that She may live through us, through our eyes, through our hearts.

That She may live through our voices, through our actions. That She may live through our children, through our wisdom and through our care.

And I come forward now as one, but in this one we are many, for we join together in the holy, holy act of becoming.

## The Lady of Shamballa - Shamballa

(1st August 1985)

Blessings my friends.

Blessings of Shamballa be with you. Love is like an ever-budding tree. True love in full giving, brings fruit continuously.

True love is giving without thought of oneself or one's needs.

True love is being in harmony with Nature and the Whole; with Oneself, where there is no need to project with others but to be within one's centre point.

True giving is Love, is the heart of all foundation.

Give and you will receive; you will bear fruit and grow in the everlasting
light.

Give and be giving. Love and be loving.
Know in each other the fulfilment of Love.

Love always finds its way home, always finds its space. Blessings. Blessings.

# The Lady of Shamballa - Memory and Vision

(2nd October 1988)

When one remembers the oneness, one truly creates the wholeness of the divine.

The creativity of the planet and Her planetary needs must come from this essence.

To bring forth your memories you must return to the source of all things - the nuclear cell carried as the hidden child within you all. Protected and surrounded by its cellular companions deep within the essence lies, captured, the vibrationary tone that brings forth the memory.

By returning, you allow the essence of change to manifest into form. Decay, die, transform anew.
Within the change, there is the stillness that encaptures the picture of the memory.

The vision of this stays with you, carried forth through its tone to be reminded and returned constantly within your thoughts and activity.

Search within for your fire. Unite the fire of passion with the flame of compassion within the heart.

Carry forth the flame and you see anew.

# The Lady of Shamballa - Love

(23rd November 1988)

Greetings my friends. Greetings.
Love is like the ever eternal flower.

There are loves that grow and flower and wilt but true love grows continually.

It gives forth life, it gives forth light, colour and sense and its seeds fall forever to continue anew.

Let yourselves be like the flower that gives forth love and beauty, continually.

Let yourselves grow and blossom and know yourselves that in each of you, you carry the seeds of tomorrow, and in tomorrow there is the possibility for everything, anew, afresh.

All is contained within. Each of you carries seeds.
Let yourselves grow them forth, sharing and loving, loving and sharing.

When the World Was Young - 2

When the World was young And Humanity was but a dream Held in the mists of possibilities WE were there

When the Cosmic Egg broke And the seeds were thrown Across the Universe
WE were there, WE were there

When Light and Darkness Emerged from the Void
Who was there to see, but US

For
WE are the breath within the wind WE are the flame within the fire WE are Life's longing for Its self

# About the Author

Amantha Murphy is a Medium, Shamanic Healer & Teacher who follows the path of the Goddess.

Amantha started her work professionally in 1970 as a clairvoyant and moved into trance-mediumship and healing within three years. Since then she has worked with, and continues to work with, groups and individuals here in Eire, in the UK and the USA.

Her passion is the Land and returning to HER story – working through the Grandmothers, the "Shining Ones": the Tuatha de Danann and the Ancient Ones.

She has been running Sacred Journeys successfully in Ireland since 1995 and returned full time to her roots in County Kerry, Ireland in 1997.

Amantha facilitates workshops on a variety of subjects including: "Pre-Celtic Shamanism", "The Way of the Seabhean"; "Astro Drama", "Rites of Passage", "Faces of the Goddess" & "The Arcane teaching of the Tarot" for women; Sacred Ceremony, Meditation groups and Women's groups.

Amantha also works with the sacred ceremonies relating to the Celtic Wheel and is available as a Dula. Amantha sees her children – and grandchildren – as her greatest gift of Beauty.

Amantha's teachings come from her Spirit and ancestral teachers.

---

Amantha Murphy lived in a conscious community from 1984 to 1993, and in a series of trance-medium sessions, channeled a number of energies – including:

'The Council of Beings'; 'Te-Khan'; 'Tutulla'; 'Red Bear'; 'Red Cloud'; 'Hawk'; 'Makara'; 'Nieda'; 'Kima'; 'St. Germaine'; and, 'The Lady of Shamballa' plus her own spirit teacher "The Lady".

Some of these sessions have been transcribed and assembled into this one volume.

Printed in Great Britain
by Amazon